What Was I thinking?

A MEMOIR

CAROL FLEMMING

authorHOUSE®

AuthorHouse™
1663 Liberty Drive
Bloomington, IN 47403
www.authorhouse.com
Phone: 833-262-8899

Published by AuthorHouse 07/22/2022

ISBN: 978-1-6655-6495-3 (sc)
ISBN: 978-1-6655-6494-6 (hc)
ISBN: 978-1-6655-6496-0 (e)

Contents

SECTION 3: FRESNO

SECTION 4: THE HIPPIE YEARS

SECTION 5: SANTA CRUZ

Dedication

This book is dedicated to my inspiration my bestest friend who has never said an unkind word about anyone. My partner in crime Marti Ochs.

Thank you to the many women who have encouraged and helped me along the way, including Ruby, Marjorie, Lynne, and Julie. A special thanks to Catherine Lenox for her patience while editing my first draft. And a very special thanks to my granddaughter Aimee who told me not to edit out the parts that would embarrass Lisa.

That Woman Is A Success . . .

Who loves life
And lives it to the fullest,
Who has discovered and shared
The strengths and talents
That are uniquely her own;
Who puts her best into each task
And leaves each situation
Better than she found it;
Who seeks and finds
That which is beautiful
In all people ... and all thing.
Whose heart if full of love
And warm with compassion;
Who has found joy in living
And peace within herself.

Poem by Barbara J Burrow

Foreword

It is an honor to be chosen to write this foreword. After reading this book at least a dozen times, I feel like I know Carol like the back of my hand. I am the granddaughter of Carol, as well as one of the editors of this book. It was about eight years ago that she gave me a chapter called "Cop Karma," and two things occurred to me: Great Carol has a zest for life, and I had a craving to know more about it. What experiences did she have that brought her to be so unapologetically herself? That's when our relationship truly began.

After pulling many weeds together and washing dishes from several of her wonderfully cooked meals, I realized that who I was standing next to can not only be an inspiration to me, but to everyone. From being the first woman to become a booking agent in San Francisco, to obliviously becoming one of the leaders of the hippy movement during the late '60s, to owning a costume business for fifty years and counting, it was never a question in my mind that Carol is a legend of her time. Born in the early '40s, this resilient woman openly shares of moments that are so embarrassing it will make you turn pink, traumas that will tug at your heart strings, and blessings that make you wonder if you ate enough dirt as a child. A cat of nine lives, Carol will humor you with stories of her first six husbands and the lifestyle that followed with each—one of which is a love story we all dream of having. In the midst of the organized chaos, she also unexpectedly had five children along the way.

As you read her book, you will quickly realize that she repeatedly asks herself the question: what was I thinking? I think it's safe to say we all have those glorious memories that cause us to shudder at the very thought, but she reminds us that no matter what life throws our way, it is all part of the adventure, and everything happens for a reason. Her eccentric way of being is within all of us, however, only some are brave enough to expose it to the world.

Proofreader
plaimeethis@gmail.com
Plaimeethis.com
June 6, 2022

SECTION 1

In the Beginning

CHAPTER 1

Growing up

(if my childhood memories bore, you start at Chapter 2)

It was 1941. My first memory is being rocked in my mother's arms in the farm's kitchen during a blackout. We were at war with the Japanese. Fade to black.

Second memory: Riding in the back of a 1936 Ford with my brother and a Shetland pony to visit my grandmother in Oakland. Yes, a pony in a car. My dad made extra money by taking kids' photos on her.

My father came through the Great Depression. He left school and sold vegetables, which my grandmother sold from a truck. I have a black and white photo of my dad standing in front of the truck loaded with vegetables. My grandparents' home was a wonderful place that we would visit on weekends, and I spent my summers there. My grandfather was a carpenter and built their house, and my grandmother helped design it. I saw an early picture of it when there were rolling hills and fields of waving grass all around. The house was set in what became the middle of the block many years later.

By the time I arrived, they had neighbors, but the house was so beautifully located between tall cedar trees, hedges of roses, and bushes that bore berries that made the birds drunk. I loved the two giant crab apple trees on either side of the front porch. The house was a brown shingle with windows that opened into the garden. My grandmother used to pick apples upstairs out the window, and she'd pickle the crab apples with cinnamon sticks and cloves. They were beautiful in their glass mason jars.

On the side of the house was a lathe house where my grandmother prepared her seedlings for the garden. It smelled of earth, and I loved it. Her garden was full of fragrance. The best was a leggy lemon verbena that grew in the partial shade next to the fireplace. That smell still reminds me of my grandmother, and when I was young. I would crush the leaves in water and make a perfume-water. There was a stone patio with green mossy stuff that grew between the stones and many flowering shade plants in the back. Past the patio was the main garden where the vegetables were grown: potatoes, chard, lettuce, tomatoes, pole beans, eggplant, broccoli, beets, and carrots. Off to the side was the garage/workshop—my grandfather's hideaway. It smelled of wood shavings, tobacco, and him. As kids, we snuck in there once in a while and found his stash of alcohol and told my grandmother, who immediately marched out there and took it away.

On the side of the garage, in full sun, was the place my grandfather grew his sweet peas. They grew eight feet tall, climbing on the twine he'd strung—a profusion of color and the sweetest fragrance. We would gather bunches of them and put them in fruit jars, which filled the house with their sweet smell. Across from the sweet peas were the raspberries. I would spend time standing in the patch of sweet berries daydreaming in the sun, eating berries until my heart's content. Mom, who we called our paternal grandmother, made fabulous jam with those berries.

This is where I developed my green thumb and found that what my grandmother used to say was true for me: "You are never closer to God than when you are in the garden." Later, when my parents split up, I returned to live with my grandmother. I felt like I was the lucky one. Back to the house tour from the tile covered porch.

The key was hung under the thermometer on the wall to the left, through a glass door. I have since come to love glass. I don't understand people who live in dark spaces like caves with the drapes drawn. Let the light in! The living room had a library table in the entry, always with flowers and something beautifully arranged. To the right was the staircase landing where my cousins and I used to perform plays and skits on holidays to amuse ourselves and anyone else we could get to watch us.

To the left was a little room with windows on four sides, the kind with small squares. This well-lit, filled-with-sunshine room, was my grandmother's sewing room. A large cabinet stood filled with all the makings of beautiful things and a trundle sewing machine, the kind operated by your feet. My grandmother would hum softly while she sewed doll clothes for me, telling me that she could be making something for me to wear in the time that she took to making doll clothes. It was a magical place.

To the right through two glass doors was the dining room. In the center of the room was the large, oak, claw-footed dining table in front of the fireplace. I remember once the roof caught on fire on a chilling night, but the fireman arrived in time and put it out, and all was saved. To the left were more windows looking into the side garden. My grandmother planted sweet-smelling carnations there, and when they were open in the summer, they perfumed the house.

On the opposite wall was the couch where my grandfather spent his time when he wasn't in the garage. His pipe was there along with a box of wooden matches and a ceramic figurine of a miniature Chinese man sitting under a cypress tree. We called my grandfather Frank because that was his name, but my cousins called him "Grampa." For some reason, he was always Frank to my side of the family. The couch was covered with an old quilt because my grandfather dropped ashes on it and sometimes burned holes in it—a bone of contention between my grandparents.

Now into the kitchen through the dining room: To the right was the breakfast nook. It was another sunny place with windows that looked onto the front garden where a birdbath was always filled with birds bathing cheerfully, feeding on the bread my grandfather put out—a very pleasant experience. I watched them while my grandmother made breakfast. Across from the table was a sideboard with glass china cabinets filled with beautiful china. My grandmother had her good china and her everyday china. Thankfully, I now have her good china, and it's amazing how small the dinner plates are. I guess people didn't eat so much back then. My grandfather's chair was larger than the rest of the chairs and had arms on it. No one dared to sit in his chair—never, ever.

The kitchen had a wood stove that kept us warm and cooked our food. There was a cooler built into the wall next to the stove. A cooler is a cabinet with a screen on the outside wall letting air from outside the house. That's where the milk and other perishables were kept for up to two days. Shade plants surrounded the outside, keeping that area cool. Later, an icebox was added in the outer kitchen and a gas stove, but there was only the wood stove and the cooler in the beginning. Under the cooler was the bread drawer where loaves of sweet bread were stored. Mom used to make a snack at night by cutting the bread into cubes in a bowl and sprinkling them with sugar and milk. Delicious! The sink was set parallel to a window. My grandparents did the dishes together, quibbling all the time. He washed, and she dried, but he never got them clean enough, and she returned them to him as he insisted they were clean enough—it developed into a nightly row. He was English, and she Irish, and English and Irish don't mix, at least that was my first impression. They constantly argued throughout their fifty years of marriage.

A small white door set halfway up the wall with a glass handle to the left of the kitchen sink. This was the door my grandmother would open and call up the stairs to announce breakfast. She had used it for years to call my father and aunt, and now she used it to call her grandchildren when they stayed over. What an ingenious idea—hers, of course. The finely polished stairs lead to a large central room with a handmade braided carpet and a chest of drawers with lovely little glass knobs on it. A door on the left opened into my grandfather's room, the next left to my grandmother's room, and the third was the room overlooking the crab apple trees and was to become mine later. After that, there was a small alcove with a tiny door again with a glass handle. It felt very "Alice in Wonderland" to me.

When my grandfather built the house, he used all the space, so in the corners where the roof slanted, there were tiny rooms four feet high, completely finished with pink floral wallpaper on a white background and little windows that opened out. My cousins and I stayed in these little rooms when we visited in the summer. The bathroom was the next door on the left, which held a clawfoot bathtub and a standing washbasin, always smelled good, except when my grandfather had just used it!

So, that completes the tour of the most wonderful, magical house I have ever been in. To this day, when I cannot sleep, I mentally take a walk through that house. To my great disappointment, my father sold the house when my grandparents passed. I never understood how he could part with a piece of history—he had grown up there. But maybe his boyhood wasn't as joyous as my visits there were.

My grandfather was the meanest man I've ever known. I was told that at one time, he had abandoned my grandmother and stayed in Hawaii for several years. I'd bet she didn't miss him at all. The man drank and was not a happy drunk. He would walk the six or so blocks to Frazier's pub, where he was well known and liked. Sometimes he took me with him and bought me ice cream. I remember dropping the ice cream once and crying. He returned and bought me another one, so I guess he wasn't all that bad. However, after a few beers, he would return home, and the nice friendly guy at the pub disappeared and the man who showed up at the house was a mean drunk. He was verbally abusive to my grandmother and later to me. Nasty, snarling beast, accusing my grandmother of being a whore, hating and belittling her. If not a daily occurrence, it certainly was weekly. I wonder now if my father was subjected to it. I'd never thought of that before.

My grandmother didn't drink, except at Christmas she would sip at a little wine, never finishing the glass. I think Frank was at Frazier's every day after he retired. He also drank in his garage. Once he was so ugly, my grandmother went after him with the washing stick. That's a long stick used to push the clothes down in the bluing, a product used to whiten clothes before bleach. I remember him raising his hands to protect himself as she swung wildly at him and chased him back to the garage. I'd watch wide-eyed. They were both strong, passionate people (English and Irish, remember), but whether out of love or duty, she stayed with him until he died. That is, except for the times when she would come and stay with us on the farm after a particularly nasty fight. She would call my father, who would pick her up and bring her to the farm. She would swear she was never going back. After a few days though, she would start to worry about him and wonder out loud if he was eating right. She would pick up his favorite food, poi, and go home until the next incident. But while she was there, she baked, made jam, and cooked fabulous meals.

My grandmother was a great cook at one time. She had her own restaurant in downtown Oakland called the Country Kitchen. She never spoke of it, but she did tell great stories about her girlhood and the great earthquake in San Francisco. It was after that when they left San Francisco and moved to Oakland. She and Frank had two children. My father was the oldest, named Winston Irwin Northup, after Winston Churchill. His sister, my aunt Pattie, was born on Saint Patty's Day. My father married my mother and moved in with his parents.

MY MOTHER

Little is known about my mother's father. There was a black and white photo on the piano of a stern-looking man with a mustache, dressed in black. Well, maybe it wasn't a black suit. Everything was black and white in black and white photos, and didn't all the old photographs of ancestors look grim? That was definitely before the term "say cheese" came into effect. Mother had a Dickens childhood, as in Oliver Twist. Her mother worked as a companion for rich old ladies. She was raised in boarding homes where she was fed porridge and dry bread and slept on a hard bed. She was not loved, encouraged, or nourished, living with uncaring strangers whose job it was only to provide a place to live, not necessarily thrive.

Her mother visited her on weekends and sometimes would take her out to lunch and buy her something—a doll, hair berets, socks, things like that. I never got to know my maternal grandmother as I did my father's mother, although she was around and did come to visit at the farm. We called her "Money Mom" because she always had a coin purse that she slept with under her pillow and would dole out change to her grandchildren. She always had favorites, and they would get quarters and sit on her lap. Whoever was not in favor got nickels and was largely ignored. This grandmother was a strange one. In her youth, she had been beautiful with violet eyes and auburn hair. When I knew her, she used too much powder on her face, and her nose was always wet. As kids, we hated to kiss her, as we were required to do because her nose always touched your cheek and left a wet spot. We just giggled and wiped our faces. I think my grandmother was never married and that my mother was born out of wedlock. That's what I think because there was never any mention of my grandfather, and my mother certainly never met him. Mother was a painfully shy child and told me stories. She would hide in the cellar at school behind the heating units at recess and sometimes not return to class at all. I doubt that she had any friends. I know that she had low self-esteem, but she was pretty with dark hair and hazel eyes, with a slender, almost delicate build. But she never thought that she was pretty, probably because no one ever told her.

Mother managed to make it to college and somewhere along the way learned to play the piano. When I would come in from school in the afternoons, she would be sitting and playing beautifully. She gave me my love of music, but she sure didn't teach me to cook. She was the worst cook I have ever known, really! Mother married my father because he fought for her. She had another boyfriend, and my father actually fought him with fists. My mother was so impressed that he wanted her that much that she married him. I don't think she ever loved him, although I'm certain she loved all of us children. Her having been a neglected only child, her dream was to have a large family, which came true as she became pregnant again and again. Later she would tell me that when my father came home from work as a machinist on the swing shift job he held for twenty-five years, she would hide from him so as not to have sex with him. Not that she didn't like sex, judging from her numerous affairs. She liked it just fine, just not necessarily with my father.

THE FARM

My cousins called the farm a ranch. They lived in San Francisco in a row house. With his parents' help, my father bought thirty acres in the foothills of Hayward, about thirty miles from their home in Oakland. He moved us in, my mother, brother, and I, and started remodeling while living in one room without heat. Both me and my brother, Tim and I, had been conceived and born in Oakland. Every couple of years, another child was added to the work crew after us. First, Molly, a towhead blonde, then Willy, a strawberry blonde. My brother Dale was known forever after by the name Robin, which mother had given him in the hospital when she saw the first robin of spring on her windowsill. Robin was also a strawberry blonde with hazel eyes. Then Martha was born, her hair a mousey brown, followed by Jeannie, another towhead, who completed the first batch of children. Another child came later, John, who died at birth. Mother said he circled her asking, "What's my name? What's my name?" until she gave him his name, and then he departed.

The old farmhouse sat alone on a hill, and the road we lived on was called Hill Road. There were only two houses on the road, ours and the one at the end of the road inhabited by an old German couple who had a crazy son they kept locked up. Sometimes he would escape and run naked down the road, ass over teakettles, and sometimes my father would give chase. He was always caught and returned home and would not be seen until his next escape, usually several months later. Our house, a run-down two-story farmhouse, was remodeled slowly, my father doing most of the work himself. The room we originally lived in became the backroom or washroom. Today they'd call it a mudroom. The kitchen was very large and where we spent most of our time. It had a woodstove that smoked, and my mother cursed it. It was also our heat source. She did cook on it, although she never mastered the oven. The only baked goods I remember was when Mom, my grandmother, came to visit. I remember once there was a litter of baby pigs under the stove to keep them warm and we were feeding them with a baby bottle. It turned out that the mother pig was eating her young. We rescued the last two. Ah, farm life.

The dining table was positioned in front of two long windows that overlooked the yard and the valley below. From the upstairs bedroom that I shared with my sisters, we could see the lights of San Francisco at night. I would lie watching the far away lights and think about many things.

Back to the kitchen. The kitchen floor was green tile and very hard to keep clean. Mother mopped it several times a day and would put newspapers on it until it was dry—a strange custom, I think. The sink set among many cabinets along the wall and was not a pleasant place to spend so much time, doing dishes and cleaning chickens—ugh! My mother cursed a lot while cleaning chickens.

Actually, neither of my parents cursed, it was more like, "I hate these darn chickens, I hate cleaning them, ugh, ick! Darn," all said with a wrinkling of the nose and a grimace.

The opposite wall had a blackboard and a large map of the world. A lot of my education took place in this room. My mother taught us to dance here, where there was also an old Victrola with records thick as pie plates, and, of course, a radio. Many evenings after dinner, she played records and we learned to waltz, jitterbug, do the Charleston, and the black bottom. My brother Tim and I did an Apache dance that was perfect for us since he loved throwing me around. The kitchen's only furniture was the table and chairs and an old raggedy couch in the corner by the woodstove. So, we had plenty of room to dance and play games. On the fourth wall was a door exiting onto a porch enclosed on three sides where the dogs slept and ate, and an outside bathroom. Not an outhouse, there was one of those up by the barn, but a very cold little room holding a toilet where I spent a lot of time, especially after eating green apricots.

In the summers, we also put on plays, directed and written by yours truly. Off the porch was an expanse of concrete walkway stretching the length of the house where we played, rode tricycles, and did hopscotch. During long summer nights, we counted while one of us was on the pogo stick. One, two, three, up to fifty, and Tim could do a hundred and fifty before he got tired and fell off.

The living room was added later and took years to finish. It was through the door of the kitchen, with a red brick fireplace on one wall and the outside wall lined with the same kind of windows found at my grandmother's house. The windows overlooked a front porch with a view of the sloping lawn, the driveway that circled the house, and a view of rolling fields and Hill Road dropping down the hill at a slow twist with the valley below. No homes were in sight. The door opening onto the porch was a Dutch door—you could open the top or bottom. The living room walls were covered with a floral print, light green with white and pink apple blossoms. My father picked out the wallpaper. I remember my mother sulking about it. He paid for it. Therefore, he made all the decisions.

The hallway leading to the downstairs bedroom, which my parents shared, and the stairs leading to our bedrooms were also wallpapered in a pheasant pattern my father had chosen. My mother hated that wallpaper. Their bedroom, off to the right, was never finished. The walls were prepped for wallpaper that never happened. Their room was small, with two windows looking out onto the cement walkway and the driveway. Later this room was rented to a man who worked with Father, probably to help pay the mortgage, although money was never discussed in front of us children. I was never aware that you had to pay for anything except for movies and candy. I was in my teens before I knew anything about household bills. I was shocked by what you had to pay for water!

A long flight of steep stairs led to two large bedrooms and one bath. The girls' room overlooked the valley, and the boys' windows opened over a roof. We used to climb out onto it and climb down the weeping willow tree that grew at the house's end. The windows had a view of the fields and a path leading to the barn and the hills beyond.

I lead an idyllic life as a child. I imagined I was the star of a musical show, and God was a giant camera in the sky recording me. I sang most of the time and danced all day. I would rise at the crack of dawn and slip outside where I roamed the hills—exploring, I called it—usually alone, but sometimes with my sister Molly. We explored the surrounding hills, wooded areas, canyons, and a nearby rock quarry, ravines dark and dank, hills covered with wildflowers in spring. Apricot orchard was one of my favorite places. I climbed trees, caught frogs, and brought home small animals. For the first ten years of my life, I was a wild child. Mother never asked me where I went, she had too many other children to think about, so I was free to roam, unruly, wild, and unhampered.

I used to ride my horse atop the bald hill with a eucalyptus grove on the side and gaze at the world. The horizon was the whole world to me. To the west was San Francisco, twinkling with lights at night. In between, to the southwest, was San Jose, still farm country with miles of orchards and the college that my grandmother Mom had gone to. Santa Clara, I think. To the north across the ravine were miles of mountains and a valley that led to the Sierras. For me, this was my whole world, as far as I could see.

Back to the eucalyptus grove: tall trees blowing in the wind with their silvery leaves and magic little button acorns. They were not, of course, acorns, but similar. I didn't know what they were called, but I cupped them in my hands and breathed in their scent before filling my pockets with them. Someone had built a small one-room log cabin there, and it was a great place to hike or ride to later when I had a horse. I'd pretend that I lived there, in the old days. There were animal trails all over the hills. In the early morning, I followed them to the quarry in the ravine. I would cross paths with all kinds of animals—deer, raccoons, possums, jackrabbits, and a hill full of ground squirrels. I would sit uphill from them and watch the colony, including lots of pheasant and quail. I stepped into a nest of quail once, and it seemed like a hundred little birds scurried to get out of my way. I tried to catch one, but there were so many, darting all over the place, I couldn't catch one. Probably a good thing because I would have taken it home, and eventually, it would have died. Like the pigeons, I would steal them from their nest high in the barn and put them in cages, but most of them died.

The barn was up the path from the house about five hundred yards, with two lights on poles between and the vegetable garden on either side. We had tall corn, squash, tomatoes, cucumbers, peppers, and potatoes. We sold the veggies at the fruit stand at the bottom of Hill Road. Back to the barn. It was a huge barn with two stories. It was cool in the summer and very dark at night—black you could not see your hand in front of your face. You'd step into the barn, turn right, and reach back into the corner to flip on the light, hoping that someone wasn't there to grab your hand and scare the bejesus out of you. We loved to do this to mother; she was a scaredy-cat. When frightened, she would drop to her knees and wet her pants. We children found great pleasure in watching this! On the occasions when she had to go to the barn at night, four or five of us would gather at the back door. The light was controlled from both the house and the barn. One of us, usually Tim, would sneak out the back door and run up the road paralleling the path to the barn, and when mother would get halfway there, I would flip off the light, and Tim would jump out and grab her. When we flipped the light back on, she was on her knees, wetting her pants, and we would fall all over ourselves laughing! Another variation of the game was to get to the barn before her and hide in the corner and grab her hand when she reached for the light. This wasn't quite as much fun because all of us couldn't see her and had to rely on Tim's retelling of it.

My father tried his hand at everything and failed at most. We had milk cows and sold milk for a while, then it dwindled to one cow, Bossy. Mother had to milk the cow in the evening, and father milked her in the morning. We raised chickens for a while and sold eggs. I actually had an egg route like other kids had paper routes. Well, I'd had a paper route at one time too. Track houses sprung up by the hundreds on the neighboring hill across the ravine, creating customers for whatever product we were growing at the time. Mostly vegetables or eggs. When the chickens quit laying eggs, we butchered them and sold them.

The barn was so big, there was also a place to play basketball. My brother and his friends spent many hours shooting hoops and playing

Round the World. When there were not enough people to play a real game, I was sometimes allowed to play as a fill-in. I was pretty good for being a short person and could dribble with the best of them. I usually played guard—no, I always played guard.

Being that the barn was so tall, there was another dimension above us, pigeons. Hundreds of pigeons nested in boxes nailed to walls. Along with pigeons comes pigeon shit. I remember once coming into the barn singing with my head tilted to the sky for the great God camera and a pigeon shit in my mouth. My mouth was so wide open, and my head tilted so far back that I swallowed the damn stuff before I knew what had happened! Certainly an embarrassing moment for me, and the camera in the sky.

The barn's front had an apartment built-in with two large rooms: a kitchen-living area, and a bedroom. This was rented to a couple with two small boys. Since there was no bathroom, they used the outhouse and our upstairs bathroom to bathe on Saturday nights. I remember them well, Barbara and Al Freitas, with sons Danny and Larry. Barbara was a skinny blonde with bad teeth and big boobs. She was my mother's best friend until she found my father feeling her up. After that, the Freitas' moved.

Although my mother loved kids, she also loved to scare kids. Where do you think we got it from? I remember my mother at sunset, just as it was beginning to get dark. She would lie on her stomach and crawl up the sloping lawn wearing a plastic Halloween mask, toward where Danny and Larry were playing. They were maybe two and three years old. Coming out of the darkness, just at eye level, came this scary creature, my mother. When they saw her, they screamed in terror and did the terror dance little kids do, feet moving up and down but unable to run. My mother found it so funny; she rolled in the grass laughing her ass off—the most fun she had had in a week of Sundays!

Back to the property description. To the side of the barn was the outhouse, a place we all used sometimes. It was a double-seater. Can you imagine anyone sharing a toilet? Well, maybe Larry and Danny. It smelled awful, and I learned to hold my breath while using it.

Past the outhouse was a fenced-in area for the horses. In the beginning, it held only one, a large draft horse named Hazel. She was as gentle as she was big, and the first horse I learned to ride. The Shetland was a mean little pony, a general characteristic of small ponies. They would bite you when mounting or any other chance they could. They also kicked and bucked. Big horses, like big men, are gentle and sweet. That's my story, and I'm sticking to it! Once in a while, my father would hook Hazel up to a buckboard, although it took hours with all the harnessing. Then she would pull us around the house while my mother fed her carrots while riding in the buckboard. Mother never sat astride any horse as she was afraid of horses; feeding them carrots was as close as she would get.

There was an ancient almond tree in the horse pasture with a rope swing. That was a place I liked to go alone and contemplate my world. Did you know that almonds are good eaten green? They're a little hard to open but tasty.

The property behind the barn was the hill and took up twenty acres of the thirty we owned. This is where the cattle and later the horses grazed. Off to the right out the back door of the barn were the rabbit cages. My brother Tim took great delight in locking me in the rabbit cages. I would only fit scrunched over on my hands and knees. I learned to hide a stick in there so I could unlock the cage after he went off whistling. Otherwise, he might leave me in there for hours. Beyond the rabbit cages, there was a small corral where I broke my first horse. Up a small hill were the pig pens, and beyond there another pasture for horses or cattle, also where we picked mushrooms in brown paper bags in the spring. After that was an expanse of the pasture where we grew alfalfa hay, which spread off into the distance, running parallel with Hill Road.

On the other side of the pigpen was an old bathtub used as a watering trough for the horses and cattle. My father kept a couple of very large catfish in it as they kept the water free of algae and mosquitoes. Sometimes the ducks would flap their wings, jump up in and take a swim. Once I saw a little yellow duck jump down on the wrong side into the pigpen, and a fat old sow snatched her up and ate her in a second, right before my eyes. There was just a lone feather flowing in the breeze.

Oh, and the geese—did I tell you about the geese? In front of the barn under the apartment, there was a large cage that housed the geese.

In case you didn't know, geese are mean! I used to have to go under there to gather their eggs, even though I was short, I still couldn't stand up in the cage. So, in a stooped position, I would brave the cage. The geese would attack me, flapping their wings, honking and pecking at me. They would surround me and then come flying at me, pecking and flapping their wings, jumping on my back and pulling my hair. I battled with these fierce fowl birds regularly. I think I was pretty fearless.

I don't know how my brothers and sisters spent their time except when we were all together in the house. Most of the time I wandered alone in the hills and fields, sometimes with the pack of dogs that slept on the porch. Spot was a black and white Dalmatian mixed with something much larger than a Dalmatian. Then there was Smokie, a large black curly-haired mutt, and my brother Tim's Shepard, Rin Tin Tin. My dog was a small terrier-mix named Candy. I wrote a poem about her. My mother said it was too good and accused me of plagiarism. Yep, that's the kind of support I got from my mother! Here's the poem:

"I have a dog. Her name is Candy and I think she's quite a dandy.

Her chest is black. Her face is white.

Otherwise she's brown, except for her back."

There was more, but I've since forgotten. I wrote another for my mother. It began:

"A mother is like an angel's song.

I love her at night and all day long."

It went on and on. Actually, I think this was the one my mother accused me of copying.

MY FIRST HORSE

I remember that I was eight or ten in the fifth grade, when I first saw her. I named her Trickle because of the Indian way of naming, which was the first thing you saw when you came out of the hut. That's pretty much like how my mother named my brother Robin. I closed my eyes and turned around three times, and the first thing I saw was a faucet with running water, so I named her Running Water and called her Trickle for short. My brother called her Drip. She was paint, meaning she had three colors: black, white, and brown.

Photo 1 - Trickle

Pintos have only two colors. She was a yearling when I first met her. She belonged to the neighbors up the hill in the little brown shingle house that Mrs. Jones lived in until she died.

I had forgotten about Mrs. Jones. I used to visit her when I was very young. She would give me cookies and tell me about the Seminole Indians from where she was raised in Florida and showed me baskets they had made and arrowheads she had collected. She was very old, tiny with white hair tied on a bun. Her table was covered with a crocheted cloth and there were always fresh flowers and a flowered teapot. I liked visiting Mrs. Jones. After she died a family moved in, a mother and father with two boys. Lenny was the same age as me; porky was a few years younger. They were in the pony business. They took ponies to fairs and gave pony rides. They had this one horse, the paint, tied out to keep the grass down around the house—she was not kept with the other ponies in the corral. I fell in love, and they agreed to sell her to me. The price was for me to feed the animals while they were away for the summer. So, each day I would fill the water trough and throw each pony a flake of hay and open a can of dog food for the mutt. That's what he was and that's what they called him, Mutt!

Of course, I gave extra care to Trickle, brushing her and talking to her, and gave her a carrot when I had one. By the end of the summer, I was the proud owner of my first horse. I led her down the road with a rope about her neck. Happy, very happy, and dreaming of the time I would ride her. I needed to break Trickle; they called it breaking back then, breaking a horse to saddle. Now it's considered "breaking their spirit." I brushed her, handled her, lifted her feet. Okay, hooves. I crawled under her, walked around her, touching her until she was comfortable with me being all over her. Then I filled two gunny sacks with straw and tied them together and slipped them over her back and walked her around. When she was comfortable with that, I started leaning on her. From a fence post I would put one leg over her, never putting on my full weight, but slowly I was mounting her. She took the bridle alright, rolling it around in her mouth, so I led her around by the bridle. Next came the saddle and finally the cinch—loose at first, then firm. All this took several weeks of after-school working with her out behind the barn.

Finally, on a warm Saturday afternoon, I climbed on board and rode her down to the house, on the ledge just under the apricot tree. I hollered for my family to come and see as my father came to the screen door with my mother behind him. Just as he stepped outside, Trickle bucked! I went flying over her head and landed on the ground face down. Ah well, back to the barn. Trickle had had her way with me. It was her joke. Within weeks I was riding all over the property, and she never bucked again.

Unfortunately, our time together didn't last that long. Yellow star thistle grew all over the property. It causes an illness in horses that they never recover from, and Trickle ate it. Most die from yellow star fever. It makes their throats swell so they can't eat, and most starve to death. I would not let her die, so for the next several months, all through the freezing winter, I would make a mixture of ground alfalfa and water, forming it into fist size balls. I'd put my arm into her mouth and just shove it down her throat. Then I would take a garden hose and shove that into her mouth and turn it on until she had the equivalent of a bucket of water. This procedure took hours, and my hands were painfully cold. She made it through the winter, although she never returned to her spirited self again. She walked about with her head down and never galloped again either. The fever had left her partially paralyzed at the young age of four. She was reduced to a pet that children could climb on while she wandered in her lethargic state, but I loved her just the same.

One day I came home from school to find my mother washing dishes and crying. It was not a sad crying. It was anger. Her mouth twisted. I put my arms around her. I asked her what was wrong. Between sobs, she told me that my dad sold Trickle.

I protested, saying, "No, but he can't, she's mine," not understanding. She was my horse; I bought her with my work. I took care of her! Mother said some people with small children came looking for a gentle horse for their children, and father sold them my Trickle. That afternoon I couldn't go to the barn, that day nor the next. Instead, I turned to books; I started to read voraciously.

I would stop at the library every day after school. It was a long walk, but I would carry home five books, which was the limit you could take out. I'd read them at night under the sheets with a flashlight. I read everything I could get my hands on. I went through shelf after shelf in the children's library. I read all the dog and horse books, books on airplanes, books on plants, books on bees, and all the classics. Tom and Huck became my best friends, plus the Five Little Peppers, Nancy Drew, and The Boxcar Children. Once I'd read everything in the children's department, I requested a special pass, since I was under twelve, to the adult library where I discovered Anthony Adverse. One passage I marked and read again and again. I didn't have any real friends for a couple of years, just books, and that was all I needed. I traveled the world and broadened my horizons through books. Then I discovered movies on Saturdays. For twenty cents, you could watch movies all day long, starting at ten in the morning until four in the afternoon. I'd spend hours watching Tom and Jerry cartoons, serials of Tarzan, and two double features. I fell in love with musicals.

There were two theaters in Hayward, The Hayward in the center of town and the Ritz, a newer theater at the end of town. I saw every movie that played at both of them for the next couple of years. I'd work for the twenty-five cents I needed, twenty cents for the movie, and a nickel for the phone call home to be picked up. Work consisted of pulling weeds, washing windows, or scraping bricks. My father had a large pile of used bricks. We were paid one penny a brick to scrape the cement off using a metal tool that looked like a pancake turner. Tim and I would sit on the ground and scrape bricks till we earned enough money to go to the movies. Tim would scrape more so he could have candy. I didn't care about candy, I just wanted to get there in time to see the first feature.

So, off we would go, walking the five miles into town. Brother Tim with his friend and me walking behind them. I wasn't allowed to walk with his friends—he only took me because mother insisted. I was supposed to pretend that I wasn't with him, or he would beat me up, which consisted of him pummeling me with his fists while I dropped to my knees and covered my face. This happened often; Tim turned mean and took his frustrations out on me. Since Mother turned a deaf ear to my complaints, I finally learned to fight back.

By the time I was eleven, I was a real tomboy. My uniform was a pair of baggy jeans and t-shirt. My hair was uncombed most of the time. I could run like the wind, which helped me to escape my tormenters. I learned to punch—slapping was out of the question. Wrestling became part of my life, too. With my brother Tim, the younger children were never his targets.

I really didn't know my younger siblings very well. Molly, Willy, Martha, and Jeannie played as children did around the house. They didn't spend much time in the barn. Although Molly and I played dolls together and she was usually involved in my plays that I put on: writing, costuming, and acting in my one-act plays. I also practiced ballet, something I learned out of a book. I could stretch my legs on the Dutch door I mentioned with the top open and do ballet exercises using it as a bar. I could do a perfect plié. Later, I took dance lessons in Castro Valley. I earned the money by hoeing weeds for the neighbors, which gave me calluses on my hands, which I still have to this day. I would walk the twelve miles to my dance lesson reading a book while I walked. I've since learned to read a book and drive a car! I would dance for one hour and walk twelve miles back.

To make money, I would also sell stuff like seed packets that I bought from the back of magazines or cupcakes that I would bake myself. Looking back, I realize I was an independent, energetic spirit. I was always looking for a way to make more money, planning adventures, and exploring—a blossoming entrepreneur. I sometimes wonder what I could have done if I had the support of my mother. I think that because of her lack of self-confidence and low self-esteem, she carried that over onto me. It wasn't until I was twenty-five that I really came into my own and knew who I was.

When my mother asked me what I wanted to be when I grew up, I said a singer, since I sang and danced all the time. I tried out for choir in school, and when I finished my solo, everyone in the class said, "Oh, she will get it!" And I did. But my mother did not share the same confidence. She laughed and said, "I don't think so."

I certainly wasn't the brightest kid in class, more of the class clown. In sixth grade, I spent most of my time writing, "I will not talk in class" or "I will not chew gum in class" hundreds of times. I learned to write, holding three pencils. Sometimes I would write the required 500 times in advance to have them ready to hand in. Pretty ingenious, right? I always had bubble gum in my desk, although I don't remember where I got it—probably from my many enterprises.

I remember selling Girl Scout cookies and was surprised when I did not get to keep the money. What fun is that, working for someone else and getting nothing in return? I still think it's a scam, sending little girls out to sell cookies when the people that run the scouts get big fat salaries and everything for scouting costs money. The uniforms are very expensive, and you have to pay for every merit badge you're awarded. I decided I wasn't a joiner at an early age.

In sixth grade when I was playing outfield, a place they put me because no one ever hit a ball out there, I picked up a rock and threw it at George, the real class clown. He had a crush on me. Although I didn't mean to hurt him, I made direct contact to his head and blood spurted. The expression on his face was one of amazement as they took him to the nurse's office and me to the principal's office. Later I was to spend so much time at the principal's office that she would take me to lunch. That was great!

Sixth grade, my first boyfriend and my second horse: His name was Michael, a dark-skinned boy smaller than me, with a dazzling smile. My first kiss, my first dance but I lost him because I could outrun him. Really! During recess, we had races and I was a very, very fast runner from years of running through the fields with the dogs and staying away from my brother. Michael was my first taste of Latin ego; he broke up with me after I outran him in a race.

GEORGIA

Walking home up the hill on the dirt road, to the right up a steep incline, two horses stood in the tall green grass with their heads over the fence biding for attention. It didn't take long before I scaled the incline and started pulling grass from my side of the fence and feeding it to them. Even though there was plenty of grass on their side, they seemed to prefer the grass I was feeding them. They were the most beautiful horses I had ever seen! One was a sorrel, the other a bay: copper colored with a black mane. They were big horses with shining coats and big brown eyes that said, *I trust you.* Every day they would be in the same place at the same time. I would always stop and feed them and talk to them. The bay stole my heart.

After a few weeks, one day, there was a truck parked nearby, and the horses were on the outside of the fence on the road with saddles. On their backs were a very handsome man and beautiful lady, and by the looks of them, they'd just come in from a ride. I stopped and told them how much I admired their horses, and they asked me how old I was, where I lived, and asked if I had a horse. I told them about Trickle, and the man gave his wife a knowing look as silent communication passed between them. He then turned to me and asked if I would like to take a ride.

"Boy, would I!" I replied.

"Which one?" he asked.

"That one," I said, pointing at the bay.

It turned out her name was Georgia. He cautioned me to keep a tight rein on her as she loved to run. My wildest dream had come true! The hours of daydreaming while I pulled grass and fed her had arrived. It took some doing to mount this huge horse, hiking up my skirt. Girls didn't wear pants to school back then. I was on her in a moment, and she did need a tight rein. It was all I could do to hold her back, but when I got my seating, I let her out, and she ran like the wind in a smooth gallop. I became one with her. We went up the road a short way when I reluctantly turned her around and brought her back, grinning from ear to ear as I approached the beautiful people.

The man called out, "You look good on her. How would you like to keep her?"

The excitement in me burst out, "Yes, oh yes!" No, he must be joking, I thought.

"Let's talk," he replied seriously as I dismounted.

Still holding the reins, I began to shake. This tall, handsome man with a beautiful smile was talking to me like an adult. He said they had decided to give up their horses because they were too busy for them, and in that, I needed a horse and could ride Georgia, they felt that she should belong to me. I couldn't believe what I was hearing. He then said she would cost eighty-five dollars, and my heart sank. Where would I get eighty-five dollars, I thought. They were prepared for this, and asked if I could pay three dollars a week. Oh, boy, could I! I would find work and work hard. Yes, I could. So, the arrangements were made.

The man was a realtor and had an office on the main street several miles out of town. I was to ride there once a week and make my payment. The deal was sealed with a handshake, and I rode her home. I don't know if I have ever been that happy since. The beautiful people also insisted that I keep the saddle. After all, they wouldn't need it.

Georgia and I went over to the other hill.

THE OTHER HILL

On the right side of Hill Road, there was a deep gully crowded with trees and bushes. Through the ravine wound a path frequented by animals and us children, wide enough for a single file. At the bottom of the gully was a small creek, dark and slippery. You had to kind of slip down the hill, catching onto small trees as you went, then jump the creek and climb up the hill at an angle so as not to fall off. At the top of the other hill was a small settlement of houses, six in all. This was my territory; I sold seeds, cupcakes, and my services as a laborer. I would hoe weeds, clean houses, or baby sit.

The first house I came to was through their back garden. It was a white, wood framed two-story with a beautiful garden and owned by George and Betty. He was a gruff old codger, slightly balding with a twinkle in his eye. She was a typical 1950s TV wife who always wore a dress with a bib apron. He was always in the garden; she in the kitchen baking cookies. She would pay me fifty cents for drying dishes. He paid fifty cents for pulling weeds and they always bought whatever I was selling. Their kitchen window looked out on our farm, across the ravine. They could see our large white farmhouse, the expanse of green lawn, the apricot orchard, and the sandy hill where the swing set stood and we children played. Betty could stand at her window and watch us. So, I thought that maybe she was the camera in the sky I always performed for.

Once a burglar climbed into my mother's window in the middle of the night while my father was at work. She ran up to the boys' room and screamed bloody murder. George came crushing through the ravine to save us. I think my mother's screaming scared away the intruder. After that she slept with a small hand pistol under her pillow.

Further up the hill on the right were two houses that sat right next to each other. One was a perfect white cottage with a white picket fence and a well-cared for lawn with a rose bed. The Baxters lived there with their two children, Buddy and Sarah. Buddy was a weird little guy, skinny with a big head and glasses that made his eyes look gigantic. He was famous for flushing little duckies down the toilet. I mostly avoided them.

Next to Baxter's house, there was a house that needed a paint job, and the yard was just dirt with bicycles, tricycles, and toys in the yard. The Cardenas family lived there, and the mother's name was Connie. She was short and round, had dimples with a ready smile, and she always had a baby in her arms. Her husband, Joe, was a train engineer and was gone most of the time. They had four children: Charlie was the oldest; Ritchie was the same age as me and had his mother's dimples; Irene was called "Irene-e"; and the baby probably had a name, I just don't remember it. These were my friends. The house was barren with only a few furniture pieces in the living room—a couple of chairs on a bare wood floor and a television. No one on the hill had a TV, and I spent many Saturday afternoons there watching Western's hour after hour with the Cardenas family. One of their chairs was a rocking chair, and Irene-e rocked the baby for hours on end. Although their furniture was sparse, this was a very loving, happy family. I tasted my first Mexican food at a birthday fiesta there: a simple tostada with beans, lettuce, and salsa. It was delicious!

Did I mention that my mother was a lousy cook? I mean bad! She boiled all vegetables, fried eggs in burnt bacon fat, and she never baked a cookie. Breakfast was cold cereal. My father got bacon and eggs or ham and eggs; we kids were second class citizens when it came to food. Lunch, I don't remember lunch except at school, probably because I was never around during the daytime. Dinner was canned tomato soup, sometimes fried meat, greasy potatoes, and always vegetables with the life cooked out of them. Canned apricots were a staple because my grandmother canned them when she visited. Saturday morning, we had stale donuts brought home by my father on Friday night. On Sunday, my father cooked, and he could really cook. We had roast beef or roast chicken, uninspired salads, and boiled vegetables. Sometimes he would get Chinese take-out, which was a real treat with pan-fried noodles and chow mien. Sometimes he went to the bait shop and bought little silver smelt that he floured and fried. Other times we might have pheasant or rabbit, and once I remember squirrel stew.

Pheasants were fun at two o'clock in the morning. When my father got home from work, he would wake us, and we would drive in the fields standing on the running boards of the '36 Ford with shotguns and shoot the pheasants when they flew in front of the headlights.

Back to the hill and the Cardenas' family. As I mentioned, these kids were my best friends. Growing up together, we formed Club 6 with my sister, a group that I organized that met in our house's basement. The basement smelled of wet cement and could be entered by jumping down a couple of feet and crawling through a window frame, then jumping another six feet again. There was only an old trunk in the basement that held old clothes, ancient clothes—now they would be antiques—white lace dresses from the 1800s and bloomers and corsets. We often dressed up and paraded about. The boys were the funniest, Charlie in bloomers and a corset. We laughed and laughed as he'd bat his eyelashes and giggle like a girl. I was always dreaming up things for Club 6 to do. Once I decided to dig a hole to China and put everyone to work digging by the swing set. After a week of digging, the hole was so deep that we needed a ladder to get to the bottom and a bucket with a rope to empty the dirt. Before we got to China, the fire department came and filled our hole in.

The last house on the other hill was occupied by a family of four: Mary, Robert, and their two children. I babysat, cleaned their home, and hoed weeds. This is where I made most of the money to pay for Georgia. The ground outside their house was red clay and rock hard. I hoed for hours after school until I had blisters on my hands. Why they had me hoe I will never know since they never planted anything; they just liked the red dirt without weeds. Maybe it was to avoid a fire hazard, or perhaps they were just giving me a job. After school, I spent many long hours crossing the ravine and climbing up to the road to their house, passing the Cardenas' house, and wishing I could play. But I was on a mission to make the three dollars a week, and it was well worth it.

After school, I rode Georgia down to the real estate office on Main Street every week and paid my three dollars to Fred Cox, one of the most handsome men I had ever met. He invited me to visit him and his wife at their home, where he helped me shoe Georgia. Their home wasn't actually a house, but a water tower they lived in until they built their house. It was warm and cozy with Persian rugs, lots of leather-bound books and beautiful wildflowers in pitchers, comfy couches, and lots of incredible clutter. They gave me lemonade, and Fred proceeded to show me how to shoe my horse. Georgia was patient and lifted each hoof for me. Fred did two, and I did two. "Now!" he said, "You really know how to take care of your own horse."

And I did. I cleaned her hooves daily, curried her, and brushed her until her coat shown coppery red. She was the most beautiful horse I had ever seen, and she was mine. She was so tall that I had to find a stump or rock to mount her. A fence would do, too, and I took to riding her bareback. She got into the habit of coming down to the lower pasture by the school at three o'clock, and I would hike up my skirt and climb aboard without bridle or saddle, and she would give me a ride back to our house. There I was, with my books under one arm, holding onto her mane with the other. After a few weeks, she got bored with the routine and gave me a surprise ride. She took off at a gallop that made me clench my knees to her as she made a mad dash up the hill, headed for a bale of hay. She jumped that bale of hay, sailing through the air with a very surprised little girl on her back. She then came to an abrupt stop at the fence, throwing me over her head and tumbling me onto the ground, books all helter-skelter. When I sat up and turned to look at her, she showed me her teeth—she was laughing at me! What a horse. Instead of being mad, I laughed with her. The next day I was prepared for her antics, and I was not disappointed; this time I was ready for the jump and the quick stop and hung on. We were both pleased with this game and repeated it many times.

Georgia was fast and loved to run. I was light and used no saddle. Therefore, I could beat any rider around. I would go looking for other horses to race and would bet anything. If they didn't have any money, I would literally take their shirt off their back or their riding crop. I had a collection of things I won from innocent victims that I had challenged. Some of them came back thinking they could beat me a second time, but the stakes were now higher. It would take a dollar if you wanted to race me again. We would go up to a reasonably flat place on Hill Road past my house and out of sight of my mother and race from telephone pole to a telephone pole. I never lost, and I soon collected my three dollars weekly payment by racing Georgia.

Another way I raised money was by giving horseback rides. I would take Georgia, Tim would take his horse Nugget, and my sister Molly would ride Linda, a black thoroughbred we boarded, and ride down Orchard Street to the new track homes that housed many families with young children. We would charge whatever they wanted to pay, letting them ride behind us on the saddle or in front of us if they were very young. Of course, it would cost more to gallop. After an hour, we would come back with our pockets stuffed with change.

Photo 2 - Horses and friends

Then I got a bright idea! I painted a sign and nailed it to the telephone pole at the bottom of Hill Road: "Horseback Rides $2.00," and they came, families with children. I would saddle up and take all six horses. By that time, we had acquired a tall, lanky buckskin named Buck and a dapple gray named Lady. A lady she was not. No one could ride her but me, so I would put a child on my precious Georgia and ride Lady to lead the pack. Before I could take Lady anywhere, we had to do a series of circles, turning her this way and that until I had established who the boss was, then she would settle down, and we could go. I took the kids up the hill through the eucalyptus grove past the place where my brother burned my tepee.

Oh, did I tell you about the tepee? One weekend we had Club 6 and collected the dry eucalyptus branches from the grove to a sheltered place on the side of the hill where we built a tepee. It took two days and lots of slave labor. The central pole was put in a hole several feet deep, and then the supporting poles were lashed to it, then it was covered with branches and leaves. It looked great and had enough room for all of us to be comfortable. Outside we built a fire pit surrounded by stones, and mother allowed us to camp there Saturday night. We had our dinner of hot dogs and marshmallows and were settling down for the night around the fire, when over the hill rode my brother Tim and his friends with torches. They burnt down our teepee. I told you he was mean.

Back to the horseback rides. I took my paying customers on a ride around the perimeter of the property, which took about an hour, and made twelve dollars an hour, sometimes with three or four trips a day. When my father saw what I was doing, he made a bigger, more professional sign and took over the business, and I was allowed to keep half of the money. The ride around the hill became so boring that I took a pair of hedge clippers and a hacksaw and began clearing a path on the backside of the hill. What was once a deer trail became a horse trail. I rode Georgia down it a little bit at a time, cutting my way through until I had an interesting trail to ride through brush and pine. There was always some wildlife to be seen: raccoons, deer, quail, and pheasant. The trail was steep in parts, and in some places, you could see clear down to the bottom of the ravine to the babbling brook.

On the other side of the ravine was another group of houses where my friend Sandy lived. She had a horse and was a real cowgirl, meaning she competed in rodeos and won ribbons and had pictures of her on horseback all over her house. In school, she was more of a tomboy than I was. She fought with the boys, actual fistfights, no hair pulling here. Most of the boys were afraid of her. She always wore jeans and a handkerchief around her neck. She had frizzy blonde hair, dirty fingernails, and a gruff voice. She laughed with a hardy ha-ha that bubbled up out of her throat. Sandy would cut through the steep, dark, and dangerous ravine to come meet me on the other side of the hill and helped me with the clearing of the riding path; then we found something strange.

On the west side of the ravine were perfectly round deep holes, a lot of them, maybe eighteen or twenty. They were about eight feet wide and six feet deep on the side of the ravine in granite with little poke marks in them. Some held a couple of feet of water, and ferns grew around then. We climbed among them, examining them with wonder, looking at each other with questioning eyes, an expression I would now call, *What the fuck?* We backed off, climbing up the hill to a sunny spot to sit and ponder. Nothing we knew about could explain these holes in the side of the mountain. We decided it was scary and we should stay away from there. Secretly, I thought that those holes were made by meteorites falling from the sky and striking the earth so hard it left holes. But the granite was strange with all the ground around it black and loamy. To this day, I have wanted to go back and have another look. The property is now part of the University of California, and someone must have discovered what we found, but I've never heard anything about it. We cut the trails around, avoiding that place, and never told anyone what we had seen.

Once while riding the trail alone, I was on a stumble-footed pinto who stepped off the trail and tumbled. I jumped off him and watched as he tumbled over and over, rolling down the steep ravine crashing through the underbrush. He fell to the bottom of the canyon, some fifty feet, and then dropped off the edge another ten feet to the stony creek below with a sickening thud, thus beginning a nightmare that I would never forget. When I climbed down to him, he was very still lying on his side with his eyes open. I worked quickly to get the saddle off him and tried to get him to his feet, pushing, prodding, pulling, pleading, and crying, all to no avail. He refused to get up. Then I sat down and talked to him, begging him to make an effort. I was praying, plea bargaining with God, promising anything if only this horse would get up. It turned out to be the longest night. I spent it at the bottom of a dark ravine where no moonlight shown, listening to the babbling brook and the noises of the animals around us while talking to the horse that would not get up. At daybreak, he closed his eyes and died.

I climbed up the hill dragging the saddle and bridle, ready to explain what I had done to my father. As I stood at his bedside, I told him the story between sobs that the horse I had been riding was dead at the bottom of the ravine. Then I ate my cold cereal and went to school. Nothing was ever said by my mother or father about the horse. Sandy comforted me and told me it was not my fault, that pintos were stumblebums and just clumsy, and how brave I was to spend the night alone with a dying horse. She offered me an orange from her lunch and put her arms around me, and cried with me. This was at recess while we sat on a bench in the sun away from the rest of the kids. She was a compassionate person, and later I would call on her strength once again.

School wasn't important to me. I was never popular and certainly didn't have the clothes to keep up. One girl, Wanda, I called my friend. She was one of the most popular girls and had the most beautiful clothes, every day a different outfit, always new. I envied her something fierce, and I would wait to see what she was wearing each day. Admiring her, I never put two and two together. She was an only child with a doting mother who spent all her time dressing her daughter. She sat next to me and was as kind as she was beautiful and never seemed to notice that I wore the same shoes every day until they wore out, and then they got replaced by another cheap pair. Sometimes she invited me to stop at her house on the way home, where she would open the fridge and pull out all kinds of snacks. She made the best tuna sandwiches I've ever had, using a whole can of tuna. There were always chocolate chip cookies as well.

Sometimes I longed to be her, but once I was on my horse, I forgot about school, and clothes, and Wanda as I roamed the hills as far as I could go and still get back by nightfall. Sometimes I'd ride at night, but mostly on Saturday mornings. I would get up before dawn and slip downstairs, grab a piece of fruit if there was any or make a sandwich and put it in my jacket pocket. It was a black-and-red plaid jacket with frayed cuffs. I'd then slip out the door, pick up my bridle from the barn and go in search of the horses.

Now I wonder if my mother was ever concerned. At the time I was just one with my horse, living in my own fantasy world. I'd decided that I'd been an American Indian in my previous life, wandering in the woods and trapping animals. I would prop up a box with a stick and tie a string to the stick, spreading corn under the box. Then I'd back off and lie in the grass waiting for the pigeons to go for the grain. When they did, I would pull the string and the box would fall, trapping the pigeon. I didn't kill or eat them, just trap them for fun.

I also dug holes and covered them with light sticks and straw and waited for small animals to fall in. I spent hours sitting upwind from the squirrel colony, watching the pattern of their lives. I'd brought home wild animals regularly. Once I found a baby possum and kept him as a pet. His name was Herman. One night I awoke to my mother screaming. Herman had climbed in bed under her pillow. She refused to touch him and called for me to get him—the same thing when she found him in the kitchen cupboard. In the summer, I built a brick oven making the bricks of adobe and straw. I dug up plants with bulbs that acted like soap, and you could wash your hands with this. Where did I learn these things? Yes, I read a lot, but my feeling is that I had actually lived another life as a native Indian. Later in life, I had more reason to believe this was true.

One night I was wakened at one in the morning. The horses had gotten out and went down the road. My Brother and I were summoned to round them up. Pulling on jeans and my jacket sleepy-eyed, we began our walk down the road. I was not prepared for what I saw. Georgia, my beloved horse, was lying dead on the road. She had been hit by a car. The man who hit her was laughing with a police officer. I froze in place. It was a bad dream while I watched them put chains around my Georgia and drug her to the side of the road. I will remember that sound for the rest of my life. I called Sandy, my loyal horse friend, and she came through that deep dark canyon once again to hold me while I sobbed my heart out. Wherever you are Sandy, thank you from the bottom of my heart. It was years before I had another horse.

CHAPTER 2

Married at fifteen

At fifteen, besides having sex for the first time in a trailer, I had my first liquor. One day Lee's friend, Glen, picked me up because Lee had to do something for his parents. Glen bought a bottle of vodka and some orange juice, mixed it in a paper cup, and gave it to me. Well, it was a hot day in July, and we cruised the main drag while I sipped the orange drink. It did not taste like anything but orange juice, so I drank more than a few before my world turned upside down. I was suddenly cross-eyed drunk; everything was a blur. By the time Glen turned me over to Lee, I was a knee-crawling, toilet-hugging drunk. Coincidentally, I was meeting his mother for the first time that day. I spent most of the introduction in the bathroom on my knees, throwing up. Oh boy! What a first impression.

Lee's mom, Nancy, or as her friends called her, "Great Nancy," was a Southern lady and carried herself like one. Tall and stately with snow-white hair that framed an angular face with the same piercing blue eyes as Lee, she had square shoulders and a broad, ample chest. She always wore a dress or two-piece suit at home, even in the kitchen. While sitting, she crossed her ankles, not her legs. She was straitlaced and stoic, passionless, and indifferent to pain or distress. Upon seeing my distressed situation in the bathroom, she brought me a towel and a cup of tea and then drove me home, staring straight ahead, not saying a word, while I tried not to throw up in her car. She dropped me at my mother's house, sniffed, and left without a word. I am sure Lee got a strong tongue lashing after that first encounter.

For three days, my mother stood over me while I clung to the toilet and threw up little white puffs of foam. She said nothing, but nervously tapped her toe. After that, Lee decided it was time to officially introduce me to his parents. It was clear that they already disapproved of me, but they had decided it was better to keep an eye on our relationship than ignore me. Therefore, I was invited to Sunday dinner.

Each Sunday after that first meeting, we would sit around the large table in the dining room with Lee's father, mother, and grandfather, affectionately known as "Pa." A landowner and farmer, Pa was retired now. His only son, Al, had taken over the family farm. Al had been Pleasanton's Mayor and was now its postmaster. The family was second generation and well known and respected in town.

At almost ninety-two years old, Pa was tall, slightly bent, with pale skin and a knobby nose. He wore overalls and had a set routine. Each day, Great Nancy would fix him a soft-boiled egg with toast. Then he would rise from the table and walk out the door and down the street two blocks to the Pleasanton Hotel. There, he would stand at the end of the bar with his foot on the rail and the bartender would place a glass and a bottle of Four Roses bourbon in front of him. Pa would stand there until quarter to twelve, sipping and watching the world go by. By noon he was seated in his usual place at the dining room table where Great Nancy would serve him lunch. Then he would return to the bar and drink until dinner time. He was a fixture at the hotel bar for years.

One time Pa came to dinner at Christmas so drunk, he sat down at the table and ate the whole serving bowl of mashed potatoes.

Nancy said disapproving, "Grandpa, you're drunk."

Pa retorted in his German accent, "Veil, someone's gotta celebrate the little baby Jesus' birthday by God."

Most dinner conversations were kept light with comments like, "Looks like no rain in sight," and "Please pass the potatoes."

Great Nancy was a good cook, and, like most Southern ladies, cooked the exact same meal each day of the week. Sunday was leg of lamb with baked potatoes and a tossed green salad, with little, round, pickled beets. One Sunday, I stabbed a beet with my fork, and it went flying across the table into a vacant chair. I giggled and flushed with embarrassment. But Great Nancy just reached over and picked it up and carried it into the kitchen without saying a word and returned, showing no emotion. Proper etiquette ordained that it had not happened. No one at the table said anything, either. I was learning what was expected of me.

Spending a lot of time with Lee and his friends in his knotty-pine room upstairs, we were surrounded by sports pendants and jazz. With rapt attention, we listened to Mose Allison, John Coltrane, Quincy Jones, and Dave Brubeck. Brubeck's "Take Five" would later become a classic. Jazz was new to me, and I loved it!

Lee and I never touched each other around his friends or in his home as he was not affectionate in any way; no hand holding or kissing. But we continued our secret rendezvous in the trailer covered with overgrown ivy in Glen's back yard. Then I missed my period, lost weight, and slept little. I told Lee, he told his mother, they had a family conference, and it was decided that there would be a wedding. I do not think Lee ever loved me, or if he was even capable of love. Lust, yes! Love, no. Our five years of marriage would prove it.

Lee's father wanted to have a big, white wedding and pay for it, but Lee's mom thought that was shameful to have a white wedding when I clearly was no longer a virgin, and that the wedding should take place out of town. It was decided that it should take place in the Presbyterian Church where I was baptized in Oakland. I asked my father to give me away, but he refused, saying that he would have had to take a night off work.

The wedding was on Friday, the seventh of March. From what happened later, it should have been on the fifteenth: the Ides of March.

Great Nancy's friends insisted on giving me wedding showers. Nancy was pleased that I knew the protocol about sending thank you notes. Though my mother found a reason not to attend any of the three showers, she was amazed at the gifts. Nancy's friends were very generous. My mother's mother paid for my wedding gown.

Photo 3 - Wedding with Lee

The day of my wedding, only Lee's parents, my mother, grandmothers, cousins, and my father's friends attended. It poured rain all day, and even heavier that night. Uncle Elwood, my godfather and not my true uncle, who was an old letch and had tried to grope me on several occasions, gave me away. With a sweep of snowy-white hair, he was handsome for an older man. He and Aunt Fern lived in the Oakland hills in a lovely house that was decidedly different from ours. A beautiful lady with auburn hair and blue eyes, Aunt Fern had been confined to a wheelchair after an accident. She always remembered my birthdays and sent me gifts at Christmas. She gave me my first lipstick; a brassy, bright-red one. I was twelve years old. My cousin Marilyn was my maid-of-honor, and my Aunt Pattie and Uncle Harry also attended. After my wedding, I would never see any of them again.

Glen was Lee's best man, and I am sure he supplied Lee with plenty of booze fortification to get him through the wedding. Backing up, I need to say that I was not pregnant after all; I got my period before the wedding. But Lee's mom decided we needed to go ahead with the wedding. After all, we could not return all the shower gifts, and what would her friends think? And then, of course, there was "the talk" that would happen if the wedding did not take place.

Shortly before the wedding, Great Nancy invited me over and instructed Lee to leave the house. Sitting at her lace-covered dining room table in the middle of the afternoon, she cleared her throat. *Ah ha.* Twice then, she looked at me for a long time in silence. I stared back.

Finally, she spoke and said, "What do you intend to do about birth control?" Startled, I blinked. Birth control. It never entered my mind. "Ah," I said.

Stalling for time and looking at my hand, the one with the small gold diamond that Lee had presented to me without ceremony, she brazenly went on.

"Apparently, your mother has not provided you with the information you need. Therefore, I will." She took a deep breath, sniffed, and then reached under the table, withdrew a bag, and emptied its contents on the table.

A yellow rubber douche bag flopped out. I was flabbergasted. I had never seen one before and did not have the slightest idea what to do with it. Noting my expression, she continued with her instructions: "Use this each time with vinegar and water after having intercourse," she said firmly. "Or these," she added, pushing a few packets of powder toward me. Then, straightening herself even stiffer in her chair, she said curtly, "I have also provided Lee with protection." Having finished her speech, she then put the bag back in the wrapping and handed it to me. We were done.

After the wedding, Lee planted a long, comic kiss on me, bending me over backward. Glen was the only one who thought it was funny. Leaving for our honeymoon in the 1942 Plymouth that Lee hated driving, we pushed through the pouring rain to Santa Cruz, where we stayed at a hotel overlooking the beach boardwalk. For years, just the sight of passing by it would make me shudder.

On our way there, Lee reached into the back seat and pulled out a six-pack that Glen had provided for the occasion, popped one and finished all six before we reached our destination. We had sex, and I dutifully went into the bathroom, hooked the douche bag to the hook on the back of the door, filled it with water and the packet provided by Great Nancy, and inserted it. Well, not thinking that what goes in must come out—that was stupid! The next thing I knew, there was water splashing all over the tile floor. Da! I was so embarrassed that I did not come out of the bathroom until Lee was asleep. Our two-day honeymoon was a miserable experience. The next day, Lee caught a cold and lay in bed reading *Car Life*, wishing out loud that Glen was there to get him beer. I walked on the beach in the fog and rain, wishing for happiness.

Photo 4 - Honeymoon

Back home in Pleasanton, Lee went to work at the Vallecitos nuclear reactor site as a nuclear reactor technician. He had given up going back to school, much to his mother's disappointment, after being expelled for non-attendance. We got an apartment in town next to the railroad tracks a few blocks from his parents and settled into domestic life. Lee went to work while I kept house. We entertained his friends on the weekends, had dinner with his parents on Sunday, and since we did not have a television, we watched TV with them.

Our first piece of furniture, other than our bed, was a bar; Lee's proudest possession, other than me. He treated me like a chattel. I had learned to cook and made his meals to his specifications. Meat, medium rare. Ham, thick. Potatoes mashed or baked and a green salad with vegetables, and Girard's dressing. I tried other recipes, but that only angered him. He wanted only a green salad with Girard's, and no desserts. He got enough sugar in his liquor. His friends were regular guests, and for them, I made beef stroganoff and baked pies. Appreciative, they thanked me, which is something Lee never did. He expected me to have meals on the table when he sat down and for his clothes to be ironed. I ironed everything, including his t-shirts, shorts, white work shirts, pillowcases, sheets, and even dish towels. If it got washed, it got ironed.

In the morning, Lee would read the *San Francisco Chronicle* with his coffee. I made his breakfast and served it; two eggs over-easy, ham or bacon, and white toast. I hovered quietly. If he needed anything, I did not sit or eat with him. There was no morning conversation. Meals were eaten in silence, the same as at his parent's house unless we had friends for dinner. Only then was there was lively conversation and a lot of kidding, in which his friends included me. They liked me, but Lee did not like them liking me. He would let me know that our conversations were childish and embarrassed him. I quickly learned to stay in my place.

Lee's friend, TJ and I had a secret bond. His eyes would twinkle, and he would wink at me behind Lee's back. One day he met me on Main Street and walked with me for a while. We stopped to look in a dress store window. There was the cutest little summer dress hanging there on a mannequin.

TJ said, "That would look good on you. Let's go in, and I'll buy it for you."

"Oh, no, I couldn't," I replied.

Gently insisting and holding the door open for me, he said, "Come on." The dress fit me to a T, and I proudly walked out on TJ's arm feeling wonderful. Great Nancy would have been scandalized if she had known.

Another one of Lee's friends became my favorite. He lived in Seattle but often came to visit. His name was Paul Aerosmith. Lee called him by his last name. Aerosmith was tall, dark, and handsome with a laugh that shook the house. He would throw his head back and roar at anything he found amusing—and he found a lot amusing. He was mischievous, and his eyes sparkled with impish delight. Lee was working the night shift at Vallecitos, and Paul and I would stay up late into the night waiting for him to get home. I did housework, and Paul helped me with the laundry. We chatted and laughed, played tricks on each other, and plotted and schemed. One night Paul brought home a bagpiper he had found on the street. He paid the guy twenty dollars to play for me and brought him into our tiny apartment. I was in the kitchen when I heard him. Do you know how loud a bagpiper is? Paul stood there and laughed and laughed while I covered my ears with both hands and shook with silent mirth. Paul was a bright spot in my married life with Lee. He always brought out the best in Lee and kept everyone laughing. It was Paul that brought home Hamlet.

Hamlet was a twelve-year-old Great Dane huge as a lion and gentle as a lamb. He had been a mascot at Paul's fraternity. Hamlet was getting on in years, and they gave him to Paul to look after in his retirement. So, Paul brought him to us—a huge dog in a tiny apartment. Being a frat dog, Hamlet drank lots of beer. Lee would open one for himself and one for Hamlet, pour it in a bowl, and Hamlet would lap up the beer, lie down and burp and snooze until he heard the next beer open. Then he would open his eyes, stand up and position himself over his bowl and wait. The boys loved it—another drinking buddy!

Hamlet could open doors with his teeth and let himself in or out at will, always politely closing the doors behind him. He would go for a run without any supervision whenever he felt like it and give the police a merry chase, always making it back into the house, and closing the door before the police caught him. Once, I watched as he came in with the police in pursuit. They sat in their patrol car and watched him open the front door and close it by himself. The look on their faces was priceless.

Hamlet also liked to ride in the car. By now, we had a new MGA that was black with a red interior. We traded in the old faithful Plymouth and bought the MGA new off the showroom floor. It was the cutest little convertible you have ever seen, and this great monster of a dog loved to ride in it if he knew we were going somewhere—and he always did! He would go out and jump into the passenger seat. Now this car was a two-seater, and I had to share my seat with this massive body with a giant, lolling tongue and drool dripping from his eager mouth. It became a game to try to get out of the apartment without him, slipping out the back door or putting our belongings in the car an hour before take-off. But most of the time, he outsmarted both of us and was waiting in the car with his cropped ears straight in the air, excited and ready to go. That old dog had more personality than some people. He slept on the bed between us, on his back with his feet in the air. He sat on chairs with his butt on the seat and his long legs on the floor, looked you in the eye when you spoke, and listened to you with rapt attention. He became a big part of our life until, at thirteen years of age, Lee found him dead on the kitchen floor one morning.

Our life settled into a routine. Lee went to work with a lunch in hand that I had packed, came home, drank a six-pack, went to bed, and we had sex. In the morning, I fixed his breakfast, did housework, and waited on him hand and foot. I was more like a geisha than a wife but had none of a geisha's music, dance, and other finery. On Saturdays, Lee would wash the car. We now had a huge black Chrysler with fins. He would pick up Glen, get a six-pack, and cruise the main. He spent Saturdays with Glen, mostly drinking, and talking about cars or sports until it was time for dinner, if he managed to make it to dinner. Mostly he passed out in the late afternoon. I cannot count the number of dinner parties where I had to call the host and be excused because he was drunk and passed out, not to mention the countless movies we missed because he did not feel like going out. Usually, he would barely make it to dinner and then pass out on the couch. Sometimes, we would get in the car and start to drive to the movies, and then he would turn around and come back without a word, and go to bed. I was living with a twenty-year-old alcoholic who felt he did me a favor marrying him, treated me like a slave, never complimented me, and never said thank you for dinner. He generally ignored me, except in bed.

On Thursday nights, he played poker with his friends. My job was to provide food, refresh their drinks, and empty their ashtrays. They smoked cigars and the sweet, heavy stench cloyed my senses. I was to stay out of sight except when needed. Lee had a whistle on a string around his neck. For the amusement of his friends, when I was needed to perform any of these tasks, he would blow the whistle, and I would come out of the bedroom where I was reading, to empty ashtrays. It was great fun for them. This was not a happy marriage, and yet I adored him, looked up to him, and waited on him like a servant.

CHAPTER 3

*Graystone manor
and finding religion*

On the way to visit my mother, there was a house on Kilkare Road called Graystone Manor that you reached by crossing a small bridge over a creek, driving passed an open field. Built of gray stone with walls that were two feet thick, the house nestled into the side of a hill. It had been a hunting lodge at one time, and before that, I think a winery. I was fascinated with the place and drawn to it like a bee to a flower. Stopping there, I took time to make myself at home.

Photo 5 - Graystone Manor

Sitting on the second story stone deck daydreaming, I started pulling weeds and tidying up the garden. Somehow, someday, I was determined to live there. After numerous weeks, the owner, Mrs. Walsh, showed up there while I was there gardening. She was an eccentric old woman, accompanied by a noticeably gay, middle-aged bald man, Chris. She did not seem surprised to find me in her garden. She engaged me in conversation while Chris served us iced tea. Once she had satisfied herself with who I was, she told me about herself. She lived in Oakland with her companion, Chris, and visited her family home, Graystone, occasionally. She asked me if I would I like to see the inside of it. Boy, did I!

After climbing the terraced stone steps where I had been pulling weeds, the entrance was on the second floor. A window facing south over the second story deck reflected a beautiful blue floral pattern in stained glass. Upon entering the fine glass door that I had pressed my nose against more than once, we stepped onto barn plank floors that were polished to a fine red finish. With Navajo rugs thrown end to end, the massive living room was eighty feet in length with huge beams running across the ceiling. Every twelve feet, lights were set into the beams.

The furniture was oversized and comfortable, something you would expect to find in a hunting lodge. The fireplace was big enough to walk into, and at the far end of the living area, there was an oak plant table with a lustrous shine. Large windows were set into the gray stone all along one side facing the meadow, providing ample light. Since the house was built into the side of a hill, the other side was all rough stone. The kitchen was small and workable, and through a door at the far wall, the servant's quarters faced the lovely stained-glass window. At the entrance, I now noticed the library I had never seen while peering through the glass door. It was built into a staircase that went down one flight to a landing with built-in leather seats and reading lights. I was in heaven.

At the bottom of the stairs, a substantial door opened into the master bedroom with blue Persian rugs spread expansively across the room. A huge bed backed up to the stone wall where more reading lights were set in stone facing large windows that looked out on to a cement patio to a little fence with climbing roses. I knew this would be my place.

The bathroom was set with golden Italian tile, and the bathtub was big enough for four people, square with a ledge for sitting because it was three feet deep. Oh my god, I was in love. The next room was equally as big and sparsely furnished, visibly not used much. I had a plan. Back on the deck, I told her how much I loved the place and had been drawn to it.

"When you start gardening on someone else's property, that's obvious," she said, laughing.

I blushed but went on, saying, "I would really like to live here. I would take care of the place and tend the garden, and of course pay rent." I rushed on. There was no stopping me now. I was determined to make this place my home.

After not too much discussion, Mrs. Walsh agreed to rent me the place. She said she rarely came there and that she would stay in the servant's quarters when she did. I told her I was prepared to pay eighty-five dollars a month.

She snorted and said, "Eighty-five is nothing for this place, but I will take one hundred."

"My husband would not pay a hundred dollars."

"Then tell your husband it's eighty-five dollars, and you pay the rest out of your allowance or wherever you get your money."

Hmmm, a novel approach—lying to Lee to get what I wanted, and we would all be happy. And so, I went home and told Lee that I had found this great place to live, and we drove out to Kilkare Road. I had the key, and Mrs. Walsh had gone back to Oakland. I could tell he was impressed, though all he said was, "Well, it's closer to work." We moved into Graystone Manor the next weekend.

Blissfully happy I had a garden, I immediately planted tomatoes and finished weeding the terrace garden. Then I bought a BB gun and set up beer cans on the back fence above the terrace garden for target practice off the deck. I had a good shot. But after having to climb the hill many times to set up the beer cans, I came up with the idea of hanging can tops by strings at different angles, and when I hit one, they went *ping* and spun in circles.

For more fun, I attended a horse auction and bought a horse. On the inspection before the auction, the owner, a rough old cowboy thinking that I could not ride, said to me, "This is not the horse for you." I bought the horse anyway. His name was Joe, he was eight years old, and had good confirmation. He was a chocolate brown with a sweet face. Didn't all horses have sweet faces?

Had I asked questions and listened, I could have learned something. But no, I had to find out the hard way. I rented a trailer and picked him up and brought him home the very next day. I dragged a saddle and bridle out and proceeded to saddle him up. As I mounted him, he immediately threw me to the ground. Getting up off the ground, spitting dirt and checking for damage, nothing was broken. So, I walked over to him, stroked his nose, talked to him, and proceeded to mount him again. This time there was no problem; he was a nice ride. We rode up Kilkare Road until we found an open spot with no fences and rode to the top of the mountain. It was spring, and the wildflowers were blooming; I was thrilled. After our ride, I rubbed him down and put him back in the small corral.

The next day I got out the tack, saddled him up, and as I mounted him, his rear end hunched; he kicked out, and I flew into the air, hitting dirt again. What was wrong with this horse? I talked to him, got back on, and we had another good ride. On the third morning, I was a little more careful when mounting him. I talked gently to him, at first mounting slowly. But as soon as I was in the saddle, his body buckled, and with one giant thrust, I was on the ground again.

This continued to happen for weeks. Old Joe would throw me every day, and then we could ride. It became a ritual no matter what I did, how ready I was, or how hard I clenched my knees. This horse would not be ridden until he had dumped me first. Sometimes it took a few minutes, a few twists, and a few bucks until he got me on the ground. Then he would stand patiently and wait. He did not run. He was not afraid. He just had to dump me before we could go for our ride. The man had been right. This horse was not for me. After a few months, I put an ad in the paper and sold him at a live horse show.

Graystone Manor kept me busy gardening, cooking, and entertaining. The living room was big enough to hold eighty people, which I know was true because I gave Lee a birthday party there and invited all his co-workers. I roasted a turkey and had the bakery make little sandwich buns with roast beef and an assortment of salads, and of course a huge sheet cake with yellow roses and "Happy birthday Lee" written on it. I set up a bar on the outside deck with plenty of beer and hard booze for those that wanted it. My party was a great success and my initiation into party-giving. After that, I gave smaller dinner parties for six or eight, trying out recipes from magazines. As I mentioned before, Lee never ate anything except meat and potatoes, and his damn salad with Girard dressing, but his friends loved my cooking—and he loved his friends. Funny looking back, I did not have any friends. They were all Lee's, so when I left the marriage, I was friendless.

It was at Graystone Manor that I discovered theology. I would lie awake nights wondering about death. What happens when you die? I was afraid of dying, so I turned to my old friend, the library, and took out every book I could find on religion. I read the Bible, I studied Buddhism and even joined a non-denominational church. In Sunol, I finally settled on reincarnation. It made the most sense to me. Nothing ever really died.

Flowers died down and became dormant and then were reborn in the spring. It explained so many things to me such as a child prodigy being able to play the piano, like Mozart, with no lessons. He must have been a musician in his previous life. Or why there are people you meet who you know immediately or places you have never been but for some inexplicable reason, know the roads there.

One day, I discovered that I was truly pregnant. The smell of Lee's bacon frying in the morning made me leave the room. I could not keep anything in my stomach and spent more time in the bathroom than any other room in the house. I kept the toilet sparkling clean because I was holding on to it all the time. Throwing up everything I ate, I tried soda crackers and 7-up, to no avail. I lost weight, dropping down to 98 pounds, and grew a raccoon mask on my face: It's called a pregnancy mask.

Lee's mother, stoic as usual, said I would only need one or two dresses because I would never wear them again and it was only for a short time. So, I was reduced to two outfits, one navy with a white collar and one pink two-piece. I wore one while I washed the other, dutifully doing whatever Great Nancy thought I should do.

Pregnancy did not suit me. I was sick and miserable the whole nine months, and Lee was anything but the doting husband. He hated me being pregnant, acted like I had leprosy, and complained the entire nine months that he could have bought a Corvette for the price of the child—I hate Corvettes to this day. He did not want to be a father. Traveling with him in the car was hell: I would have to go to the bathroom, and he would refuse to stop, so sometimes I would have to hold it for up to two hours. He was not about to let his wife use a public restroom, by god. I would have peed alongside the street if he had stopped. It went beyond uncomfortable; it was painful. But I suffered in silence, never once complaining, simply waiting, reading, and waiting some more.

Then there were the baby showers Great Nancy's friends gave. Once again, my mother and family did not attend, and I had no friends. But there were lot of gifts anyway. Great Nancy picked the baby furniture while I painted the room next to ours a light yellow and decorated it for the boy or girl I was expecting.

Since I did not have a doctor of my own, Great Nancy insisted that I go to their family doctor, Dr. Shanks, who had delivered Lee. I went to him once a month and on the ninth month he said, "Well, let's schedule this birth for eight o'clock tomorrow morning."

I laughed and replied, "That would be nice, but how do we know the baby is coming?"

Still looking at my chart and not glancing up to look at me, Dr. Shanks said, "We're going to do a cesarean section."

"What? Why?" I asked, befuddled.

Dr. Shanks explained, "I've known this for months. You are too small for a regular delivery."

All those months I had been reading about natural birth and preparing myself for it, and my doctor knew that he planned to do a cesarean section and had not breathed a word of it to me. I was outraged! He said, "I didn't want to scare you." Now this scared me! Who else knew? Did great Nancy know?

Packing my bag at home, I lay down on the bed and silently cried. Then I went to the library and read about cesarean sections. At eight-thirty in the morning, Bo was born. I was unconscious and heavily drugged for the next five days. Dr. Shanks had made an incision from below my navel to the top of my pubic area. So why did he have to shave my pubes? The hospital staff kept me so heavily sedated with morphine that I was unable to function at all. They would bring me my baby and put him in my arms at my breast and I would fall asleep (pass out) and drop him. He would roll down to the middle of the bed.

Once I was so drugged that I thought I was under the bed looking at the mattress over my head and asked the nurse to help me back on to the bed. After four days, the staff decided to get me up and walk me. The pain was so excruciating that I passed out. Knowing what I know now, this old horse doctor did not know what he was doing. He was operating in the dark ages.

Rather than going home right away, I went to Great Nancy's and was put in the back bedroom. My son was kept in the front room where friends and neighbors could come and visit Lee's son. Lee the proud parent, carrying his boy on this shoulder like a badge of honor. Now he was the proud happy father after making me miserable for nine months. Meanwhile, I was kept in the back room and only saw my baby when they brought him in to breastfeed. I was kept out of sight and visitors were told I was resting. I cried, slept, and developed a urinary tract infection. I have never had such pain; I rocked and cried and rocked and cried. The doctor was called in, I drank glass after glass of water, and he gave me more drugs to sleep. Great Nancy brought me soup and told me I must keep my strength up so I would be able to feed my baby. That was the only time I saw my baby. He was kept in the living room on display for the neighbors in the bassinette that I had worked so hard to build.

Meanwhile, Great Nancy held Bo and sang to him, Lee walked him around, and after a week of this, I demanded to go home. I wanted my baby to myself. By now, Great Nancy had bonded with Bo and did not want to let him go. She thought we should stay at her house for at least a month. For once, I stood my ground and insisted that I was well enough to care for my son. So, finally after dinner on that Sunday I was given permission to hold my son in my arms in the passenger seat of the giant black Chrysler and we went home to Graystone Manor.

CHAPTER 4

Motherhood and monkeys

Bo weighed seven pounds, fourteen ounces when he was born, and was round, blonde, blue-eyed, and cute as a bug's ear. Lee named Bo after Beauregard Burnside General Electric Oxen. Lee was a company man. Bo's real name was Timothy Lee Oxsen, named after my brother. Lee liked that until he found out that my brother smoked marijuana, after which they were not friends anymore. Hmmm.

Little Bo moved into the room next to us, sleeping in his crib. I had read Dr. Spock and raised him by the book. Dr. Spock would later apologize for his book, years later. Now, it's too late!

According to Dr. Spock, when your child cried, you were not supposed to pick him up. Simply, you turn him over and leave the room. Bo cried a lot, and I followed Dr. Spock's instructions and just let Bo cry. It is heart-wrenching now to think that I did that, but I was going by the book like thousands of other mothers who were reading it.

Bo had colic a lot, and I spent many sleepless nights walking the floor with him until I discovered Jack Daniels—one sip for me and a finger suck for him. We both then slept; it was wonderful.

I nursed Bo in a big rocker in the bedroom. My breasts were swollen tight like watermelons, and I leaked so bad I had to put Kotex pads in my nursing bra to sop up the leakage when I would get dressed to go out. I could get as far as the car before I would have to turn around, go back in, and change my clothes.

In the third month, I developed an abscess on my breast that made it too painful to nurse, and Bo was put on formula. He grew rapidly, growing out of some of his clothes even before wearing them. He had lots of clothes, darling little suits, that were gifts from the same people that had given us wedding gifts. Great Nancy's friends were very generous—and Great Nancy never stopped buying clothes for Bo, who she loved with all her heart. Her whole life revolved around him. Great Nancy, as it turned out, had lost a son in infancy from an infection on his foot from new socks before Lee was born. She had been overly protective of Lee, and now she was overly protective of Bo. I shared my newborn son with her. She would not have it any other way.

Great Nancy also bought me clothes and continued to buy Lee his clothes: even his underwear and shoes. She would show up with several pairs of shoes that he would try on. He would then take the pair he liked, and she would return the ones he did not want. This man was the crown prince: his mother filled any needs or desires that I did not. All he had to do was verbally wish for something, and it appeared. I was every bit as susceptible to filling his every whim as his mother was, too.

Poor Bo, I was an eighteen-year-old mother and had no idea what I was doing, with little maternal instinct. Yes, I dressed him and fed him but was missing any subtleties of childrearing. As moms go, I was living in the "basic lane." As there were no car seats back then, I would hastily strap him into an infant seat: a little plastic contraption that sat on the car seat, not secured by anything. So, when I hit the brakes, it would fall off the seat with him in it, face-down on the floor. He would yell, and I would pick him up, dust him off, and put him back on the seat until the next stoplight. When I would hit the brakes again, he would fall off the seat again face-down on the floor. This was repeated many times because I was a bad driver.

Lee had taught me to drive a stick shift on the MG, taking me out to a county road at night to instruct me in the fine art of clutch and shifting gears. I was not a quick learner, but it did not help that he used a rolled-up newspaper to hit me on the head when I did it wrong. He was not a patient teacher.

After weeks of unsuccessful instruction, I went for my driving test and failed. I practiced and went back a second time and failed again. After the third time, I drove to Hayward, where I was not known, and barely passed.

Another example of my imperfect motherhood was running the pin through Bo's skin and closing it when I changed his diaper. His little yelp would signal my failure. Maybe it would have been better for Bo if Great Nancy had raised him.

A deeply researched novel that I read about the Lakota Sioux, *Hanta Yo,* explained that in the late 1700s these First Nation mothers allowed their babies to crawl around the cook fire and to keep them from getting burned, they would take the baby's hand and put it in the fire. After that, the babies kept their distance. When hiding from their enemy in the woods, mothers would hold the babies' noses to keep them from crying, so as not to give away their hiding place. Well, I did not do that, but when Bo was a toddler and would reach for something on the coffee table, I would say in a soft voice, "No" and then I would slap his hand. It did not take long. All I had to softly say was "No!" and Bo would blink and take his hand back.

When friends visited, they were impressed with what a good baby Bo was. He was! I never had to raise my voice, nor ever shouted. He never had any temper tantrums. This was a perfect baby. To this day, if I quietly say "No", Bo blinks. Think I did any damage?

Bo was such a good, sweet baby. Everyone loved him, especially Brown. Brown was what he called Great Nancy. Who knows why, but his first words were not "mama" or "dada". It was brown, directed at Great Nancy. From that day forth, Great Nancy was known as Brown.

Bo was a toddler when we moved from Graystone Manor. Checking the water because the well always ran dry in the summer, we would have to wait overnight for the spring-fed well to fill up. I had heard the county did it for free and decided to find out about the water quality. The county sent the report to Mrs. Welsh, and it pissed her off so much that she wrote me an eviction letter. I did not question it, but just started looking for a home in town, and found a new, two-bedroom apartment on a quiet street in Pleasanton, California. We moved. It was not Graystone Manor, but it was lovely and sunny with beige carpets throughout. We settled in.

Lee was attending UC Berkley, taking extension classes, and holding down the job at Vallecitos. There was no garden to tend, no horses or animals. I started reading more and turned my attention to my son.

Bo was a quirky kid. He spent most of the nights up. Awake and doing things, he could jump his crib to the wall, turn on the light, and pull the mattress apart. He would pick at the mattress until he got a hole in it, then pull the stuffing out and throw it everywhere. We went through three mattresses—cloth, plastic-covered, or even wrapped in double sheets and pinned down, it did not matter. He found a way to pull them apart. When he was not pulling mattresses apart, he would take off his diapers, defecate, and then fingerpaint the walls and rungs of his crib. When I came into his room in the morning, his shit would be everywhere including his hair, which he spiked with his shit. He was quite creative. Lee started calling him shit-head, which stuck well into his teens.

By the time he could walk, he was out the door every chance he got. I would be in the kitchen while he was playing with his toys. When I would notice it was quiet and go and look for him, he would be gone. He could unlatch the front door and be out so quietly I did not hear him leave. Then the frantic, running, calling search would begin. Clad in shorts, and a t-shirt, I would find him a block away running in his little red tennis shoes. Twice, the police were called. Once, they found him six blocks away, pulling his red wagon with all his toys in it. He was such a happy child, always laughing as he had just pulled off something, and he did! It was embarrassing for me, especially when Brown found out. Why wasn't I watching him?

When Bo was two, he became sick with a fever that ran too high for too long. He was admitted to the children's hospital in Oakland, where he spent several days while the doctors tried to figure out what was wrong. I spent my time hovering over his crib while they packed him in ice, his little face aflame. After a few days, it disappeared as quickly as it had come, and we were able to take him home. This was the beginning of something that would plague him for life. But for now, he was okay, and we continued our life.

One day while we were walking across the UC Berkeley campus, Lee saw a guy who had a spider monkey perched on his shoulder. Lee was positively delighted, and raved, "Did you see that?" He turned and dragged me back to where he had seen the monkey. He stood in awe like a kid in a candy store, with a huge smile on his face. Well, you can guess what I did. I went on a hunt for a spider monkey for Lee and special ordered one from a pet store in Fremont at a considerable price, picking it up just before Lee's birthday. The owner assured me the spider monkey was young and could easily be trained, giving me a pair of very heavy gloves along with a cage, saying, "the monkey might try to bite you."

Expecting Lee to be thrilled and thankful, his initial response was one of surprise: not glee. The novelty of my gift lasted for only a few moments. Placing the monkey's cage in our living room, I became the little devil's keeper.

Living with that little monkey, as it turned out, was less than sweet. Our fridge had to stay stocked with cartons of mealworms—icky—to be fed to the little guy as a treat. And yes, he did bite, grabbing onto my arm and sinking his teeth into it until he drew blood. Lee only had one run-in with him and threw him across the room shouting, "Little Bastard!" To my memory, this was the only name the monkey would ever get.

Biting was not the only thing this little devil did. Pressing himself hard against the cage, he would pee on anyone that came close. "Oh, how cute," Lee's friend Glen said as he walked right over to the monkey and got down eye-level with him. In response, the monkey grinned and peed right in Glen's face. Glen had enough of a sense of humor to think it was funny.

Nancy, however, was less amused when the monkey peed on her dress. "Oh, you nasty thing!" she cried.

Determined to housebreak the monkey, I tried holding him and talking to him. I hand-fed him mealworms, which he snatched from my hand, and turned his back on me to eat alone. Like a petulant child, he escaped from me one day while I was trying to bond with him. He ran around the house, breaking everything that he could get his hands on, throwing teacups and vases at me, chattering wildly, and cursing me. I finally took the broom and chased him, swatting at him while threatening to kill him until he ran back in his cage and slammed the door.

After a month of this, I called the pet store and requested they take him back. Spider monkeys can live 20-40 years, and I was done with this one in one month! "Nothing doing," the manager retorted. "No exchanges, no returns!"

In protest, I put the damn monkey and his cage into our big Chrysler's back seat and drove him through the Niles Canyon toward the Fremont pet shop. Nervous because a big semi-truck was in front of me, and another one was following me, I carefully kept my distance with both eyes on the road—my attention on my driving, and not the monkey. To my dismay, suddenly I heard that damn monkey chattering his evil chant and felt something warm sliding down the back of my neck. Realizing the nasty little thing was pressing up against the cage and peeing on me, I contemplated stopping, but with those big trucks hemming me in, pulling over was impossible.

Arriving at the pet shop, I wrestled the cage into the store. Throwing it up onto the counter with that nasty damn monkey in it, I glared at the storekeeper. Without saying a word, I continued to glare as I walked out, never to return. Monkey motherhood was not for me. After driving home, taking a hot shower to get that monkey piss off me never felt so good.

Only later would I learn essential facts about living with a spider monkey that would have been nice to know ahead of time. They are wild animals. No amount of training will stop them from destroying your home, biting, scratching you, throwing feces on the walls, peeing on you and your guests, and destroying anything breakable they can find. They do not like domesticity—and do not love you. Given the choice, despite a few similar challenges with my adorable "shit-head," I heartily recommend human motherhood. They love you back.

CHAPTER 5

Disillusionment

Lee and I were not happy, or maybe it was just me. After five years, I felt unloved, unappreciated, disenchanted, and restless. I wanted more from life.

I asked Lee, "Don't you ever want to go somewhere? Do something?"

He looked at me like I was from another planet. "No," he said. "Why would I?"

He was happy living in a small town, washing his car on Saturday, and reading *Nucleonic*, a magazine about nuclear power, and *Car Life*. Then John, a friend of Lee's from Harvard, entered my life.

John had come to town to visit his folks and his old school buddies. Of average height, dark-haired, with brown eyes and flashing white teeth, he had a smile that knocked me out. He smiled a lot at me. He came to dinner that evening and kept coming back. He paid attention to me, engaged me in conversation, and helped me in the kitchen, things no one had done before. He told me his mother was a gourmet cook and suggested we try some recipes together. He brought over Strauss and Bach albums, classical music I had listened to in my childhood. I had a new friend. Lee ignored us.

One Saturday, he showed up with two bicycles and suggested we go for a ride. I was overwhelmed. He treated me like a person! At the filling station where we stopped to put air in the tires, he overfilled the tire and it popped, blowing up with a bang that knocked us both over. We laughed so hard we cried. As he wiped tears from his eyes and gazed into mine, he hugged me. Oh, my God. I felt something deep inside me turn over.

John spent two weeks in Pleasanton, mostly with me, while Lee was at work or with his other friends. We would go on walks together, talking about books, music, and cooking. We stared intently into each other's eyes. Before he left to visit his father, who was a captain in the Navy stationed in Japan, he told me if I were not married, he would have taken me with him. He kissed me lightly on the cheek, held my hand, and looked into my eyes for a long time. He told me that he would call me when he came back to the states and was gone.

The fact that my life was not happy with Lee was only magnified by those moments with John. He'd never told me he loved me, and certainly never acted like it. My birthdays went unnoticed, as did our anniversaries. The only compliment he had paid in five years was on one of my birthdays when he said, "You've got a nice ass kid!"

After John left, I sat in our empty swimming pool and wept. I had met someone kind, gentle, smart, and fun to be with that saw me as a person. Still, I had said "Until death do us part" to Lee, and I had a good marriage when it came to a home and security. And then there was Bo. I thought about my life long and hard. I imagined what it would be like being with a man that liked me. John was in my thoughts every day. He would return in a couple of months, and if I were single, I could be with him. I finally decided I did not want to live the rest of my life in Lee's world and went to see Great Nancy. Sitting across the long dining table from her, I said, "I'm not happy. I want a divorce."

She looked at me long and hard, drew a deep breath, and let it out slowly. She said resolutely, "Well, I've born my cross for twenty-six years. I don't see why you can't bear yours!" Good lord, she thought of her husband as a cross to bear! I was stunned. She suggested a marriage counselor. A family conference was called, and his mother informed Lee that I wanted a divorce. Lee said nothing—just shot me a look of hatred. I agreed to a marriage counselor, looked in the phone book for one, and made an appointment. When the time came, Lee and I drove in silence to the office of the counselor, Dr. Bardilini, in Oakland. We sat in silence, leafing through magazines until a door opened and a small woman with her hair drawn back in a tight bun, wearing a tailored suit came through it and said, "Lee and Carol? Who wants to go first?" What? Not together?

"Alright," Lee said, "I will." He was in the office for maybe twenty minutes. Then he came out without looking at me as Dr. Bardilini held the door open for me. Once inside, she motioned me to a seat across from her desk. I sat. She sat. Neither of us spoke. Finally, after a long silence, during which I studied my hands, she broke the silence.

"I just wanted to see what the perfect wife looks like," she said, a kind benevolence shining in her eyes. Continuing, she noted, "Lee says that you are the perfect wife: a good housekeeper, good cook, good mother, and good in bed. He has not one bad thing to say about you. What's your story?"

I broke down and cried.

"I don't think he loves me or that he ever did or ever will. He treats me like chattel. He tells me I am stupid and could not get across the street without him. He has never given me a gift unless you count my wedding ring, or a compliment for that matter." I sobbed, and she handed me a tissue. It was all out now. I continued, sobbing, "I didn't know how much I was missing until I met a man who cares about me."

"Oh," she said, "another man!"

"Yes, a friend of Lee's," I confessed. "But we haven't done anything." I rushed to explain how John and I only talked and had fun together. I told Dr. Bardilini that I wanted a life different from the one I had, and I didn't think that I could do it with Lee. "He doesn't even like anything I cook except his damn meat, potatoes, and salad. We never go anywhere. I want to travel and experience life. He wants to drink and cruise the main like he did in high school."

My words came bursting out. All the hurt and anger I had been holding in for five years erupted.

"He doesn't compliment me or tell me he loves me. I don't think he does. He's never given me a gift or flowers. We don't do anything together. He doesn't read, so we can't discuss books. He thinks he honored me by marrying me. And his mother never calls me by the name. I am always 'that girl', or 'she.' All our friends are his—I don't have any friends of my own. They are all his. My life is not mine." Tears streamed down my face. She handed me another tissue.

Finally, I stopped talking and just sat there and sobbed. I was through.

After a while, she said, "I think you would benefit from some therapy. Would you like to come back and see me alone without Lee?" I looked at this kind older woman with compassion in her eyes and nodded. She handed me another tissue and said, "Very well, come back in next Wednesday at four o'clock."

She called Lee back into her office for a moment, and that was it. We left in stony silence. Not a word was spoken on the way home. The silent war was on.

Lee bought me a gold watch and handed it to me a few days later, a belated birthday gift, five years late. I thanked him politely, but at this point, it meant nothing to me. I felt like a tube of toothpaste with all the paste squeezed out of it. We went through the motions of our daily lives, but it was over. Then it turned ugly. Lee sneered at me, glared, and said cruel things.

Meanwhile, I saw Dr. Bardelini once a week for the next six months. She hypnotized me. She told me it was not important to have a college degree and that it was nobody's business. "If anybody asked," she told me, "tell them you have a degree in humanities." She told me I was not stupid and ugly, that I was bright and beautiful and could do anything with the life I desired. She said it was a first for her but that she recommended I get a divorce. I filed. After five years, I decided "till death do us part" was too much to ask; it could not be done unless I killed him. The honeymoon phase was over.

Now Lee loathed me, and I was the enemy. No one in his family got a divorce. I was torn between my wedding vows and wanting a life. I loved Great Nancy. Cold as she was, I admired her spark of humor and silent strength. But then there was John who would be returning in a few months, and if I were divorced, I could see him freely. Picturing a life with John, based on the little time that we'd had together, I felt I could be very happy.

After I filed for divorce, Lee openly hated me. He didn't talk at all. We still went through the routine of life, only now it was with a vengeance. He took my toothbrush and used it to clean the aquarium and hung it back in its usual place with green scum on it. I, however, went out into the yard and scooped up some "shit on a shingle" and put it in the middle of his boring salad. He stopped flushing the toilets. I peed in his aftershave, and while sitting on the edge of the tub, took great pleasure in watching him slap it on his face until he smelled it. I died laughing. We were not nice, nor civilized. We were mean, vicious people.

One day the phone rang, and it was John; he returned from Japan. I told him I had filed for divorce. He asked if I would like to meet him in San Francisco.

CHAPTER 6

John, finding love

Aiming to look ravishing, I dressed selectively, slipping on a black garter belt, black silk stockings, and a form-fitted black lace bra. Quivering with anticipation, I looked at myself in the mirror. Yes, my little black chiffon dress with spaghetti straps and swirling, a full skirt was the right choice. It dropped perfectly over my head, clinging to my tiny waist. Finishing the ensemble, I slid my feet and perfectly polished red toes into a pair of black patent leather five-inch pumps. My shoes glistened in a slant of fading light sifting through the window.

Running a brush through my long auburn hair and applying a quick dab of cardinal-red lipstick, I pulled my pink wool coat from the closet. With its mandarin collar, bell sleeves, gored panels, fullness at the bottom, and fitted waist, I was pleased with the image I saw. Balanced on my tall pumps, I skipped down the stairs and out the front door.

Climbing into my black Chrysler, I grabbed the wheel. As its engine turned over and purred, I eagerly headed for San Francisco. After months of dreaming about him, I was finally going to see John—I was floating on a cloud.

As I stepped into the lobby of the Saint Francis Hotel, John was waiting for me. As if in a dream, all I could see was him moving slowly toward me, his hands outstretched.

Originally built in 1904 by architects Faville and Bliss, the Saint Francis was designed after the Ritz in Paris and other European grand hotels in the hopes that San Francisco would become known as "Paris of the West." With its massive colorful murals, spacious rooms of travertine marble, burnished oak columns, gilded ceilings, and sparkling crystal chandeliers, this historic landmark hotel had all the grace and elegance of palatial five-star hotels in Europe.

But the scope of that grand place was not what caught my breath and sent my senses into a whirl. It was John, taking my hands at arm's length and holding on to them, standing there looking at me. He whispered, his eyes glistening, "Even more beautiful than I remember." He had missed me too. Smiling broadly, his compliment was music to my ears.

Hand in hand, we left the hotel and walked the streets of San Francisco. Though we had yet to kiss, we leaned for hours into each other with the familiarity of lovers. As we walked, I confessed, "I've been deeply unhappy with Lee."

He replied, "I have never met anyone I have felt so connected with before meeting you. Do you know how hard it was for me not to kiss you knowing that you were Lee's wife? I thought of you the entire time I was in Japan, and saw you in every graceful, delicate movement of life there. You were everywhere I looked. Wandering down paths bordered by cherry trees in bloom or passing through gardens filled with purple hydrangea and lush roses, I saw your face. Eating chicken toasted in honey and soy sauce late at night in the yakitori grills, I felt you sitting next to me. Sleeping in my room, you were with me in the shadows."

Smiling so long and hard that my face hurt, I thought to myself, This man is straight out of a romance novel, but he is real, and he loves me. He hadn't said it yet, but I knew. I felt loved. We never once let go of each other's hand. Despite the five-inch heels cramping my feet and the foggy cold around me, I felt nothing but warm elation. I was in heaven.

Several hours later, John guided me into a small French restaurant, seated me, and briefly let go of my hand to take my coat. Seating himself, he reached for both of my hands and held on to them.

"I don't want to ever let you go again," he said, as his eyes sparkled and danced with joy. We were joined, we knew it, and neither of us could take our eyes off the other. He was clearly the most handsome man I had ever seen. Though he ordered, we ate little, and no alcohol was consumed. Intoxicated with each other, we didn't need it.

After dinner, as we resumed our walk, John became serious. "We need to make a plan," he said. "I will be going back to school next week. We can write. When is your divorce final?"

Blinking painfully as reality set in, I muttered, "Nine months. But I can't live with Lee anymore." And, though I had not worked during the five years I'd been married to Lee other than a short stint with Sarah Coventry jewelers, I added, "I'll move in with my mother and get a job."

John assured me, "I can't move you into my dorm but I will start looking for a place for us to live. My parents will have to be told, but they will love you. How can they not? We will work it out. It will just take time."

For a moment, a shadow fell over me and I shuddered. We would be apart again.

John slipped his hand gently into mine with certainty, and we continued to walk through the streets of Union Square in San Francisco. It was an exciting city but when you are in love, anywhere is the most romantic place on earth. I was in love with a man who loved me back.

Much later, feeling excited and not at all exhausted, we went back to the St. Francis and he took me to his room. We were perfectly comfortable with each other. He had told me earlier that he was a virgin, which only heightened our passion. I was the first woman he had ever been with—and would be his last.

The next day we parted, with tears in both our eyes. That was the last time I ever saw him. On the Fourth of July, he jumped from a plane and his parachute did not open. Back living with my mother and working as a waitress in a truck stop, my heart was shattered. I began to drink.

SECTION 2

San Francisco

CHAPTER 7

Turning twenty-one

Working as a cocktail waitress in Livermore, California, I celebrated my twenty-first birthday in a bowling alley. It was uneventful other than a coffee pot exploding on me. When I announced to the management that it was my birthday, he asked how old, I answered proudly, "Twenty-one!"

He said, "And you've been working here for two months underage? You're Fired!" I took off my apron and went to the bar and proceeded to do shots with my friend. A young man I had found attractive earlier came in and walked over to me. I spun my barstool around and fell out of it onto the floor, at his feet. I woke up the next morning in my friend's house. Total blackout. That is how I started out my twenty-first year.

I was living with my mom back in Sunol. She had moved out of Kilkare Woods and into Charlie Chaplin's old house on Foothill Road. It was a two-story Victorian country home with seven bedrooms. I made myself at home in the first bedroom at the top of the stairs next to the bathroom. Bo was staying with Brown while I got my act together—and that was not happening. My divorce was final. John was dead. I was drinking. In all the years I had spent with Lee, I did not drink—and now, I drank like a fish. VO whiskey and water or straight VO out of the bottle that I kept in my room. I had seen Elizabeth Taylor in "Butterfield 8" and would rinse my mouth with whiskey when I got out of bed in the morning. I had bought an old Dodge with my wedding ring as a down payment and put a pillow and blanket in the back seat in case I drank so much I could not drive home. My day started with drinks at the Sunol Lounge until it was time to go to work as a cocktail waitress. Then I drank after work until closing and came home and passed out. My life was a mess.

One day, a person I had gone to high school with—someone I hardly knew—stopped me on the street, grabbed me by the shoulders, looked me in the eye, and said, "What are you doing to yourself? You used to be so beautiful. Where are you going with your life?" Thank you, Chris, wherever you are. You changed my life.

Twenty-one and single, I packed up my things and moved to San Francisco. I found an apartment at 222 Hayes Street, a block from the Filmore on the second floor of a four-story building. It had hardwood floors, a Murphy bed in the living room facing bay windows that looked out over the street, an old-fashioned bathroom with black and white tile and a clawfoot tub, and a small kitchen with a window faced to the next apartment building. I had sheets, towels, blankets, one lamp, and my good china and silver. I paid one hundred dollars rent and started job hunting. Bo was with Brown—happy, safe, and well-cared for. I needed to get my life together.

Applying at restaurants and bars, the only work I had done, they would not even take my application because I was not a member of the union. Union? What union? When I went to the union to apply, they said I had to have a job first. Huh? Catch 22! No job: no union, or no union: no job. How I did get a job is an interesting story.

When I lived across from the fairgrounds in Pleasanton, I would hang out at the racetrack when I was not stealing roses from their garden. One summer I was at the races alone. Usually, I went with my father-in-law

Al and sat in his box. But that day I was at the post. I had bet on a horse named Galacappi, a sleek-black gelding. The reason I had bet on that horse is that I had ridden it myself. Our apartment was near the train tracks, and within shouting distance of the fairgrounds and the horse races. I used to gather roses from the park and make huge bouquets. I also hung out at the track watching the jockeys exercise the horses.

One day, while watching the ponies being worked, I was offered a ride on a beautiful black gelding named Galacappi. Having never ridden a racehorse but ridden all my life, I accepted the offer, finding myself on a little tiny saddle with my knees under my chin on a great big powerful horse. The galloping was exhilarating, but one thing was missing: I could not stop the horse. I did not have enough strength or know how to stop a racehorse a second time around the track. It took two pony horses to stop me. When I dismounted, everyone was laughing, and my legs felt like Jell-o.

I went to the races when the fair opened. I was at the gate when they paraded the horses, and an Asian man, Alex Wong, was standing next to me.

"I would bet everything I had on Galacappi."

His face lit up as he asked, "Do you know something?"

Boy, did I.

Well, I only had forty dollars. But Alex believed me for whatever reason and bet a lot. Galacappi was a long shot, and Alex won $3,200 when Galacappi came in first, six lengths ahead. Alex was so excited that he grabbed and held me as he jumped up and down excitedly. He gave me his card, said he lived in San Francisco. He said to call him if I were ever in San Francisco, and he would take me to dinner and the theater. That is how Alex became my first friend in San Francisco. We saw *The Sound of Music* at the Curren and, after listening to my union saga, told me to go to Janet's Travel Service on Waverly Place in San Francisco and apply for a job.

Janet's Travel Service on the corner of Waverly Place, was in the middle of Chinatown one block up from Grant Street. One of their services was busing gamblers to Reno. I worked as a "bustess," which is like a flight attendant, only on a bus. We took gamblers to the holy city of Reno, where I served chicken wings, the Chinese kind where they push the meat down on the bone, making it easier to eat like a pop stick. I also poured tea steeped in a lot of lukewarm water and provided customers with warm wash cloths, sweets, and drinks. The Chinese did not drink anything hot or iced as they believed it was not good for the system. Also, I found that they are incredibly insular, and would not book a white person if you had the last name of Johnson and not Chang. "Sorry," they would say. "We all full. No not tomorrow, not next week. Sorry." And they would hang up. However, they hired all white girls to serve the Asians.

The job was fun. We loaded up in the morning and made the four-hour trip from San Francisco to Reno, where our customers were dropped at a casino with coupons in hand to gamble all night. In the morning, we boarded our charges and headed back to San Francisco, supplying them with pillows. Most of them slept on the way home. I did too; rather than sleeping in the motel provided for crew, I roamed the casinos and drank hot brandy with a twist, played blackjack, and found a jazz club in the sleazier part of town where top jazz musicians jammed all night long. I was addicted to jazz. That is how I met Flip, a tenor sax player. Tall, skinny, with a long nose and freckles on his mulatto skin, he was not handsome. As a matter of fact, he was ugly, but so ugly as to be comical. His laugh was a snort and a giggle. He laughed a lot. He would humorously say, "I'm so ugly, I look like twenty miles of chopped up donkey dick!" We became friends. Then, on my next trip back, lovers. His dream was to come to San Francisco and form a band. Of course, I could help because I had a job and a place to live in San Francisco. As the adage says, "What do you call a musician without a girl friend? Homeless!" Ha-ha!

I got fired from the job at Janet's Travel Service for sleeping on the job. Janet did not say that was why, she just said, "We don't need you." But I knew.

Flip came to San Francisco, moved in with me, and I became entwined with his dream of forming a band. He gathered people together from as far away as Sacramento. Living in the Filmore in the fifties, I learned a lot about black people. I remember picking up Sylvia, the trumpet player, from a ghetto home about the size of a shoe box where she lived with a family of eleven. She had a look on her face like she was anticipating something bad would happen at any moment and was constantly looking over her shoulder. She was a light-skinned mulatto, sometimes called "high yellow." She was also a lesbian; two strikes against her as far as society at that time was concerned. Boy, could she blow a mean trumpet! Later, she was picked up by Sly and the Family Stone. But back then, she was with our band, Little Bobby and the Flippers.

Photo 6 - Little Bobby and the Flippers

Small in stature, Little Bobby was a Mexican lead guitar player from the Mission District. His guitar was nearly the same size as him. Joe, black as his shoes with large lips and white teeth that had shown in the dark, was another band member that played bass. His hands were the size of meat hooks.

Charles was the lead singer, tall with a pompadour, and equally dark as Joe. He had a day job as a hairdresser straightening hair. He was fascinated with my hair and asked if he could do it. He said, laughing, "I ain't never touched no white girl's hair before." Charles and his wife, Maxine, became my friends long after the band was gone. I stayed at their house, and they babysat Bo. I tasted my first chitlins there. Tripe is one thing I have never learned to like.

So, the band came together and practiced at my apartment. This eventually got me thrown out, but we had a band. I found I had credit in Lee's name, went to Montgomery Ward, and bought the entire band matching black suits, white shirts, and ties. I insisted Cynthia wear a dress, which she hated. While I was at it, I furnished my apartment with a new couch, table, and four chairs.

We needed photos of the band, so I talked a photographer into doing it for free, telling him when we got big, he would get paid, and I would send him other business. Flip decided I was going to be their agent to get them gigs. I began my career as a booking agent. I went out and hit the clubs looking for a job for my band. Meanwhile, Flip and the band found their own gigs in after-hour places, playing all night for fifteen dollars each. But they were musicians and playing was their life, except for Charles who had a day job and a family.

After I arranged an audition at the Condor on Broadway on a Sunday afternoon, the band spent the morning primping in front of my mirror, pressing their slacks, and shining their shoes. We all piled into Charles' car—six people packed in that big old clunker—and drove to Broadway, finding a place to park one street over in an alley.

"You go in first, alone," Flip said, licking his lips, big-eyed with anticipation.

"Yeh," said Charles, straightening his shoulders and pulling himself up to his full height, "check out the scene."

The Condor was on the corner of Columbus and Broadway, the center of entertainment on the strip. A popular song "On Broadway" played on the radio. The place was closed, and I knocked on the door. Opening it slowly, the owner let me in, looking quizzically at me. "Where is the band?" he asked.

Smiling, I said, "They will be here in a moment." Then there was a second knock at the door. Flip was sweating, carrying an ax in his hand, just in case. His Saxophone and the rest of the group were gathered behind him.

"Are we late?" Flip said smiling.

"Not at all," said the owner swinging the door wide. A short Italian in his mid–forties, his clothes and jewelry attested to his wealth. His teeth shown white.

The band entered nervously and looked around. Spotting the bandstand, they headed for it like homing pigeons, quickly set up and began to play. Just then the phone rang, and to my surprise, it was handed to me. A gruff male voice was on the other end demanding to know what I was doing there.

"An audition," I replied.

"You got a license?" he inquired.

Bemused, I asked, "A license for what?"

"A booking license. You got a booking license?" he said impatiently.

"A booking license for what?" I repeated. My ignorance was profound.

"You can't book a band without a booking license from the local," he said. "Be here tomorrow morning at ten."

"Be where?" I said naively. I was really in the dark.

"Local 6, musicians union on Hyde," he answered.

"Okay," I stammered, and hung up the phone. Who was this man? How did he know me or that we were auditioning?

The next morning, I put on my most professional suit and found the Musicians Union. I was ushered into a meeting room where about twelve old fogies were smoking cigars, sitting at a long table. A seat at the end was reserved for me. It felt like an inquisition with the mafia.

"What makes you think you can book musicians?" I was asked.

"Musicians, though talented are generally not good at business and cannot sell themselves," I explained. "Therefore, I felt I could do it for them."

Hump, the man with the cigar at the other end of the table, grunted. They asked me my age and background. I lied a little and said I had some selling experience. A few more questions, and I was squirming on my seat. Then the man at the end of the table said to the others who had remained silent during the interview.

"Well, whatcha think boys, shall we let her in?" There was a slow nod of approval from each of them, and it was over. I was directed to the outer office to fill out papers. As a result, I became the first and only woman at twenty-one to become a booking agent with San Francisco Local 6.

CHAPTER 8

San Francisco and the music

Being a booking agent had benefits. I could get in free and go backstage at any concert. I got to meet a lot of now icons.

Photo 7 - Me and The Blues Brothers

The record company I was working for sent me to listen to a new group at a small club: Big Brother & the Holding Company. Their lead singer, was a scrawny, frizzled-haired, barefooted girl in a potato sack dress shouting into the mike with a raspy voice. I went back to the record company and told them, "I don't think so"—boy, was I wrong. The singer was Janis Joplin. We became friends and shared more than one bottle of Southern Comfort. When I came into one of her concerts, she would say, "Carols here, and now we are going to play some dance music!" Dave Getz, her Drummer, would smile at me and raise his drumstick and begin. Did I ever mention I love to dance?

Another artist I came across was Jim Morrison, lead singer in The Doors. Backstage, he invited me to meet after for a drink. He was a very confused person. He did not consider himself a singer. He would say, "I just stand up there and shout the lyrics." But boy, was he sexy. He had a stiffy in his pants that never went away, and this was natural—before there was Viagra. On our second date, he went through my purse and stole my drugs while I was in the bathroom. Really!

Photo 8 – Me with Jim Morrison

Donovan, a Scottish singer, songwriter, and guitarist, was performing in California at this time. Once, I met him after a concert. He was a lovely person, so I gave him some beads, and to my great surprise and pleasure, he was holding them on his next album, *A Gift From a Flower to a Garden*.

Once in Big Sur, I was privileged to attend a private party where Quicksilver Messenger Service played. I swear they made lights pop in the room like fireflies. And I was not stoned.

Someone I stumbled into was Mick Jaggar of The Rolling Stones at a sit-down concert in Hawaii. I could not stay in my seat. I got up and started dancing while I pretended to be on my way to the ladies' room as I got to the aisle. Mick jumped off the stage and danced with me through "Sympathy for the Devil." Wow! What fun!

★★★

Becoming the first and youngest woman at the age of twenty-one to become a booking agent with Local 6 in San Francisco, I could now book bands legally. Setting out each afternoon with my briefcase containing pictures of my groups and tapes when available, I soon had actual jobs for my guys. My nights were spent in the after-hour joints listening to music. Every musical performer that played in San Francisco would show up to jam after hours.

One of my favorite haunts was the Streets of Paris Club on Howard Street in the Tenderloin District where strip joints and hookers and drug dealers prevailed. After their big-time paying gigs, people like Gerry Mulligan, Elvin Jones, and John Coltrane would drop by. The club was open from midnight to six o'clock in the morning. Once I even saw Billie Holiday perform there. She was beautiful.

A small blue neon sign blinked on and off over an entrance that led down a dark stairway. Dark green, heavy velvet drapes hung at the bottom of the stairway. Once you pushed your way through them, you entered a cavernous, dimly lit room with a stage, a long bar, a scarred wooden plank floor, and utilitarian chairs and tables. There was nothing fancy about this place. You could get whiskey in a coffee cup if you could afford it. Otherwise, there was only coffee. Two lights shown over the doors: one red, and one green. The green was on regularly. But when the fuzz came strolling in, two of them usually once a night, the red light would go on. Though I never saw anything illegal going on because I was not looking, behind curtains in a second, more dimly lit room, all kinds of unlawful dealings were going on. I was only interested in the music.

Every wannabe musician came to the Streets of Paris and jammed with the stars. There, I met and added other musicians to my stable. One good, clean-cut, young piano player I booked into small clubs around the city, was the piano man. He put his bowl on the piano and played for tips. I did manage to get him contracts with real paychecks but there was a catch. Part of it went to Local Six. I worked for ten percent, but sometimes did not take it. I felt sorry for the guys trying to make a living doing what they loved.

One of the bookings was for Little Bobbie and the Flippers touring Pennsylvania—a six-month contract playing in colored clubs. Back then, it was nearly impossible for a black group to get jobs in white clubs. I would later break the color barrier. But for now, the band was happy as clams. They were sure that they were on their way to stardom. One of them, Flip Wilson, was headed that way, but I lost track of the others. Flip bid me a tearful adieu and said that he would write and send money. That never happened. I guess when he got out on the road, he forgot about the little patty girl (slang for white girl) that had helped him on his way.

Kicked out of my apartment because of loud rehearsals, I moved into a one-room studio on Hayes Street into one of the Victorians you see on the Rice-a-Roni commercial on television. Owned by two gay guys across the street from the park, it was a great apartment. Now I could have Bo. Grudgingly, his father delivered him to me, looking at my small apartment and sniffing in disgust. Without a word, he turned and left, leaving my little blonde son standing in the doorway blinking.

Dropping to my knees, I scooped him up. It had been a long time. Tears sprung to my eyes. He hugged me, looked puzzled, and said, "Why are you crying mama?"

I nuzzled him and whispered in his ear, "Just glad to see you. Let's go to the park and see what we can see."

Taking his hand and leading him across the street and up the cement stairs to Pacific Heights, there was a great view of the city. Lifting him high to see it, he exclaimed, "Pretty mommy!"

We spent lots of time in the park across the street but first, he needed to be registered in a day school. I had found one in the Marina District, a short bus ride away or a long walk. Working at Kaiser Hospital during the days and doing my booking at night, like any working mother I still found time in-between for my precious son. Weekends were reserved for Golden Gate Park and the San Francisco Zoo.

Another after hours place was Bop City, a place I had discovered while still in my teens. The greatest of jazz artists performed there. The owner was a gentle giant with a smile that turned on like a flashlight. Once I tried to get Lee to go there with me, but he said, "Are you Crazy? Black people go there!" Great musicians, both black and white played there: Stan Getz, Mose Alison, John Coltrane. That the audience was black did not bother me a bit. I was there for the music.

One night I was there by myself next to the bandstand sitting with my back against the wall and my feet in a chair listening to John Coltrane with my eyes closed, just grooving to the music. When he left the stage, he said to me, "I do not know what you are on, girl. But I wish I had some!" I had no idea what he was talking about. I just loved his music. I would figure it out later.

Wilbur Dean Couey was a drummer extraordinaire who tutored me in the ways of the music world and black culture. A Scorpio who always flew his colors, dressing in a deep murky maroon, usually with a knit cap on top of his dreadlocks, and burgundy wide-wale cords, he walked like a cartoon in slow motion. Everything about him was slow except his mind and his fingers. He talked slowly, choosing his words carefully, frequently pausing to roll his eyes around finding the right word. Sometimes he would start his sentence over, saying, "No, it's more like this." His voice was deep and musical. Couey became my friend. He became a frequent visitor at my apartment.

Once one of my straight white friends was sitting in my window on a hot summer day looking out onto the street. "Wow," he said. "You should see this dude on the street. He's all dressed in dark red, has dreads, and walks like he is moving to music."

"Yeah," I said without looking. "That's Wilber Dean Couey, and he will be at my door in a moment."

Couey also became a mentor for Bo and babysat him sometimes while I was out gigging. One night, Couey came into my kitchen with a sly smile on his face. "Girl, I got something I want you to try," pulling from his coat pocket a small bottle of tequila and from the other, a couple of limes.

"Get your salt-shaker and come sit down," he said, pulling out a chair at the kitchen table. Yes, it was a black man in the Filmore who first introduced me to tequila shots.

"Here's how you do it," he said after slicing the limes. He licked the back of his hand and then sprinkled salt on it. Licking the salt, I took a shot of tequila, and sucked the lime slice, and followed suit. Wow!

Years later, I would refine the art of tequila drinking. But this was a great start. Couey also introduced me to "Mary Jane," as he called it. He came in looking sly, always with an overcoat in the winter. He may have been poor, but he was always well put together, color-coordinated, and looking cool, always with a hat of some kind, usually a burgundy beret. He reached into his coat pocket and withdrew a matchbox from one pocket and some rolling papers from the other pocket. He sat at the kitchen table and rolled a joint, or "reefer" as he called it, and told me to sit down across from him.

"Now," he said, "here's how you do it." Looking slyly at me with slanted eyes, he lit the reefer and took a long slow drag and held his breath, then passed it to me. I followed suit but ended up coughing and coughing.

"Now here is the thing, mama," he coached, eyes twinkling. "You gotta take a slow hit. Hold it in as long as you can, then let it out slowly. Try again!" He blew smoke out of his broad nose and passed the joint back to me. "It won't hurt you. Just make things a little bit shiny and funny—and here's the thing. You'll get hungry—it is called the munchies. Got anything to eat?"

Reminiscing, I said, "Oh, yeah." I remember when I smoked my first joint back in the Hayes Street apartment with Flip and the band. They were passing around a joint before going to a gig, and I was horrified. They were smoking marijuana, but after they left, I picked up the roach and took a toke. Then I called Flip at the gig and told him my legs were paralyzed and that I had smoked the stuff he had left. He laughed, and I could hear him telling the band that I had smoked their weed and thought my legs were paralyzed. I could hear them all laughing. He said, "It's alright, baby, you can walk," and still laughing, hung up the phone. Yes, I could walk, and went into the kitchen and ate a whole box of saltines with syrup on them—I knew what the munchies were.

But now Wilbur Dean Couey was explaining and showing me the proper way to smoke dope—and in his company, I enjoyed it as I started pulling out peanut butter and jelly to make open-face sandwiches.

Couey was a class act. He started to teach me to play conga drums the next week. He said it was easy and spent sunny afternoons sitting on the kitchen floor. He brought an extra set so we could play together. Couey became my mentor in many things. He taught me about life in the city and about people of color. He called himself colored. "Black," he said, pointing at his shoes. "My shoes are black. Colored is the colors of the rainbow. Ever notice how many different shades people of color are, starting with looks-like-white but admits to having colored blood, therefore, is colored."

I tipped my head quizzically and he said, "Yeah, some are black!"

"Couey, what color are you?" I asked.

"Honey brown," he replied without hesitation. "Smooth and sweet like honey," smiling his slow, knowing smile. A Scorpio, he described himself as sexy, secretive, and sinister.

I said, "No, not you! Sinister?"

To which he retorted, "I can be, mama." He winked.

I never visited Couey at home, and never knew where he lived, or if he lived alone. I never asked, he just showed up at my doorstep when he felt like it and never asked anything of me. He was just my friend—and Bo's too. He would take Bo to the park, play drums with him, and talk with him on a grown-up level. When I saw him at Bop City or on the streets, he would nod to me, knowing I was conducting business. Wilbur Dean Couey. I will never forget you.

Charles, the singer in Flip's band, and his wife Maxine lived with their family two streets above the Haight. Maxine babysat Bo and cooked the most divine ribs I had ever had, though I could have done without the chitlins. Later, when I moved away and would come back to the city, they always had a room for me. They were family, and I loved them. One day, Charles got his chance to do my hair. He did an upsweep and needing something to hold it in place, he used a toilet paper tube. It fell out in the middle of an audition at the Fairmount hotel. Thanks, Charles!

I spent a lot of time in the Filmore. Back then, it was an entirely African American neighborhood. Walking the streets at night after a gig or returning from work, I was the only white girl in lots of clubs and felt welcome and at home. If people talked, I didn't know it, and there were no unwelcoming looks there. But when I took Flip to the Fairmount, we got the cold shoulder.

Flip said, "I told you, girl, this wouldn't work. White people don't like to see white women with a black man." I was shocked. I didn't know anything about racism. I hadn't been raised with it or taught about it. I just assumed everyone was equal.

During the days, I worked at Kaiser Hospital and at night, roamed San Francisco streets in and out of clubs. I especially loved to go out on full moons when the city was alive with lunatics. What fun!

The Spaghetti Factory owner off Broadway, an old man with white hair and one of the original beatniks, would feed me and ask, "What, you hang out at the Streets of Paris? There is nothing down there but pimps, whores, and drug dealers. A nice girl like you? Stay away from that place." After his fatherly lecture, he would send me home in a cab with a few dollars. Usually though, I walked everywhere from the Filmore to Broadway.

Enrico Banduchi, the owner of the Hungry Eye was another friendly, fatherly figure. I booked a jazz combo there to back up New York's stand-up comedian "Professor" Irwin Corey. Enrico would ask me to "babysit" the professor to keep him from wandering off before he was to go on stage. His stand-up was not an act—he was the real deal, crazy as a loon but highly entertaining.

Another place I hung out was a jazz club in Chinatown where a combo played regularly. The man who played bass was a regular at the Streets. Always wearing a suit, he looked like a businessman and had the reputation of being the best bassist in San Francisco. I decided to take him to a recording company, Capitol Records.

While there with a tape, one of the executives heard me talking and asked me if I would mind speaking into a mike. They were looking for someone to read for a religious record. This being a possible paying job, I started to read. What luck! I read and made a mistake.

"Start over," he exclaimed!

I started again, "So the Lord gave his only begotten son . . . " Stumbling on the next sentence, I muttered, "Oh shit," started over, and got to the same sentence and blew it again. "Oh, Damn!" I said, frustrated.

Well, by the third time I read, stumbled over a word, and uttered, "Oh, fuck," the reading was over, and I was out of a job. However, the record executive still had faith in me.

"We're looking for a gospel group to record. Go find one," he said.

Well, this was right up my alley. I asked my black friends and was directed to several storefront church groups. On Sunday afternoons, where I attended lively celebrations of the gospel, a band was set up next to the pulpit. Sometimes there was no pulpit. Everyone was wearing their best. The colors were vivid, and the choir was dressed in bright yellow, red or blue robes, singing, clapping their hands, and praising the Lord, hallelujah!

Recording it, I took the music back to the record company along with the names, addresses, and descriptions of the groups, upon which I was paid a finder's fee of fifty dollars. Not bad for spending time in church!

Though the music business was my life, I still held my job at the hospital. However, my salary was not enough to get us by. When I started using laundry detergent to wash my hair, I knew I had to get another job. There was a place in North Beach called Najia Baba, located down dark stairs like the Streets of Paris, opening into a very dark, open room with little round tables circling a dance floor and a bar against the wall. They featured Turkish coffee so thick you could stand a spoon in it.

Applying for a job as a cocktail waitress, I started work at Najia Baba's that night. The coffee was delicious and the belly dancing inviting. Later, I would take lessons. But for now, having money in my pocket at the end of the night was enough. I bought Bo a cute little red wool bathrobe and slippers, and he looked every bit the little man in it. The job also enabled me to keep more food in the apartment. I took Bo to day school at eight in the morning and went to the hospital to work. Picking him up at five-thirty, we would have dinner together, he took a bath, and I would put him to sleep with a bedtime story soon after. I went to work at nine in the evening at Najia. It was there that I met Ricardo.

Small, dark, and handsome, with golden-brown skin and jet-black hair, Ricardo would come in and sit next to my wait station. His teeth were perfect and very white. He dressed casually but tastefully. It was obvious he was interested in me by the way he smiled a lot and made small talk to me. A native San Franciscan, he was a hairdresser, picture framer, artist, and studied karate. After several nights of small talk, he invited me out to dinner. I had not had a date since I had been in San Francisco. Flip was out of my life, and I was flattered, so I went. Ricardo took me to an expensive little candlelit restaurant and ordered wine like he knew what he was doing—and so began our relationship.

Since he was infatuated with me, Ricardo talked me into letting him move in with me on the pretense that it would save money. He said he had done the math and splitting the rent and utilities, made sense. I cannot say I was in love with him, but there was an attraction, and we became a couple, moving to the top floor in a Victorian on Clay Street, a two-bedroom flat on the third floor where Bo would have his own room. With a charming view of the park, I decorated the kitchen walls with menus from San Francisco restaurants.

One night, I gave a party for staff in the record industry and, of course, musicians. Hosting with appetizers and a French 75 champagne punch with a touch of bitters and brandy, the French 75 punch recipe claimed that it was "good with stiff and formal crowds," which meant it immediately made everyone social and friendly. Ricardo refused to attend the party and went to a karate class instead.

The party ended early and was deemed a success, at least by me. I cleaned up and went to bed, only to wake up suddenly with someone slapping me. Shocked more than scared, I realized suddenly that it was Ricardo. In a jealous rage imagining me with a lover, he had climbed up the fire escape and came in through a window. Rather than using his key to the door, he thought because it was dark that I was in bed with someone. He had worked himself up to the point of anger, and then when he found me asleep and alone, he still grabbed me and hit me.

The next day he came into my work at Dun & Bradstreet on Howard Street and got down on his knees in front of the elevator and apologized, crying. Now I was embarrassed and sad. This man had a problem. He promised it would never happen again and I forgave him. That is, until the next time. Taking a job at the credit reporting agency, Dun and Bradstreet, located in a large office building on the sixth floor of Third and Howard, I had lied about my qualifications and experience in the interview. I got a great job on the reporting desk reading credit reports over the phone. I loved the job. The women who trained me had been there since World War II. No kidding! She wore her hair in the old style and dressed like Doris Day. Later, comedian Lily Tomlin brought her to life as Bernadette. She knew her business and trained me well. Wearing a suit and heels and sitting at a desk with a headset on, my only problem was that I could not read large numbers. There were just too many zeros behind the two. Two million or two-hundred million? I could not tell the difference. And, when I stumbled over the numbers, "Bernadette" would cut my line and take over. This happened often. After three months, Mr. Jones, a dried-up little man with a perpetual sneer on his face who sat at the end of the row of desks overlooking all the worker bees, called me to his desk. He had my file in his hands.

"It appears, Ms. Flemming," he chided, "that you miss informed us of your background. Therefore, I have no choice but to demote you."

Just like that, I was kicked out of the reporting desk and demoted to a file clerk. I hated filing. The next step down was the mailroom where I had a friend who made even less money than I did. I found out from her that people had worked there for years making less money than people on the report desk, and even less than a file clerk. They didn't complain, so they did not get paid more. In my eyes, it wasn't fair. Perhaps I should have been happy with being a file clerk, but I wasn't. After a couple of weeks of filing, I just started to stuff the files anywhere: A in Z, B in W. I laughed to myself as I finished my work in record time because nothing was in the right files. It would be years before some files were found.

One day after a two-martini lunch with my friend from the mailroom, I walked in purposefully late. You could hear my high heels clicking on the wood floor as I marched up the aisle to Mr. Jones' desk and stood right in front of him. When he looked up from shuffling papers, I said, "Fuck you, Mr. Jones, I quit!"

The entire typist pool quit typing and the file clerks quit filing. Dead silence filled the room. What I had done, they would only have done in their wildest dreams. As I turned and sauntered out of the room, you could hear the determined *click, click, click* of my heels. With a satisfied smile on my face, I was finished with Dun and Bradstreet.

CHAPTER 9

Life in the Fast Lane

After quitting Dun & Bradstreet, Ricardo and I moved to an apartment on Laguna Street in the Marina District. I continued my job as a receptionist in physical therapy with Kaiser Hospital working during the day, going in before sunrise and leaving after sunset. I hardly saw the light of day.

Photo 9 – Carol and Ricardo's painting

Cocktailing at a pub called The Bus Stop on the corner of Laguna and Union, I was exhausted. Waking up before dawn, I would reach over the side of the bed, light a cigarette and exhale deeply, while the other hand would grope for the vial of little green-and-black pills the friendly pharmacy had given me to pick me up. I did not know they were addicting or how bad they were for me—they just got me through my day and kept me awake during my night job. They also gave me little yellow ones to put me to sleep at night.

I was a mess living in the fast lane on cigarettes, alcohol, and pills—and did not even know it. I would drop Bo off at daycare, take the number thirty bus to Van Ness and High Street, cross the street in the breaking dawn and stumble to my desk in physical medicine.

One day sitting down, I noticed my feet. Oh Lord! I was wearing two different colored shoes, one red and one green, instead of the heels that matched my white uniform. Apparently, groping around in the dark closet, I had picked the shoes by texture, not color. It was too late to go home. My plan was to pretend I planned it as a joke or, if I got lucky, maybe no one would notice. I was wrong there!

Honey Brown, a cocoa-colored girl with almond eyes sat down beside me, nudged me in the ribs, and chuckling said, "Lord girl, you gotta stop dressing in the dark! Turn on the light!" Boy, did she hit the nail on the head.

At the hospital, my days were spent scheduling appointments for Dr. Zach and Dr. Jones, answering the telephone, and trying to avoid the germs that patients spread as they stood over me at the desk and coughed on me. Trying to stay healthy at a hospital was impossible. On our breaks, Honey Brown and I would go into the mail room and sort through the drug samples that arrived daily from the pharmaceutical companies.

Honey would say, "I wonder what this one does?" as she popped a pink capsule into her mouth, giggling. Lord, we were clueless. We ate handfuls of pills each day and worked through a blur of chemicals. That relieved our boredom but at what cost?

At the time, I was training to become a physical therapist and learning the benefits of hands-on treatment. Concluding that the hospital's process of rolling patients' bodies in a machine lacked compassion and was ineffective, one day a woman came in late to an appointment with Dr. Zach. Doubled over in noticeable pain, the woman was crying. Having had to take a bus route from a considerable distance, she had miscalculated how long she would have to wait at bus stops in between bus connections—she really needed to see the doctor.

Stepping into Dr. Zach's office, I said, "A woman who is in considerable pain is in the lobby. She is late but I wonder if you might see her anyway. She has been trying to get here for three hours."

Slouched comfortably in a reclining chair as he munched an apple, he answered me nonchalantly, "Just tell her to make another appointment."

Walking back into the lobby and approaching the distraught woman, I looked at her stricken face as I told her she could not be seen. I got so upset, I went back into Dr. Zach's office and slammed my keys on his desk. "Fuck you! I quit!"

-COP KARMA-
San Francisco Cruzan Confusion

Another night in Marin County, I drank one, no, two of those drinks that come in small bathtubs called *Cruzan Confusion*: one and one-fourth light rum, one and one-fourth tequila, one-fourth Benedictine, one and one-fourth lime juice, one-fourth coconut cream and the kicker, a 151 proof Virgin Islands Rum float. Add a gardenia and two straws and it looks good and is faster going down, tasting like a summer's eve. Ordering a second before the first one hit me, I left my party, got into my 1963 Chrysler, and headed for home in San Francisco. Halfway across the Bay Bridge, I noticed the red light behind me. Oh shit! Highway Patrol! Clocked at eighty-five miles per hour, I slowed to pull over. The officer was polite and charming, and so was I. He told me to slow down and have a good evening.

Continuing across the bridge, as I was exiting on Oak Street, I hit three parked cars doing severe damage to all three—I would have a hit and run, but my car tires had exploded. Oh well, I thought, and climbed the steps to the nearest house and asked a large black lady with a pink hair net and fluffy pink slippers if I could use her telephone. I called my babysitter and explained that I would not be picking up my son that night as I would be spending the night in jail, and please contact my friend to bail me out. Then I thanked the nice lady and returned to the crime scene to wait for the police. It did not take long.

One patrol car with two officers arrived. They surveyed the damage, called for tow trucks, and put me in the back of their car. I waited. After a few moments, they both got in the front seat and asked me my address. I told them, and they drove me there.

In front of my apartment, one got out and opened the door for me, offering his hand to steady me. He said to take some aspirin as I was surely going to have one hell of a headache in the morning, as he was seeing me to my door and helping me with my keys. He tipped his hat and said good night. My car was totaled, but no report was ever filed that I know of as no one about the accident ever contacted me. That is when I started taking the bus.

CHAPTER 10

Crash and burn

A month after I quit the hospital, I found out what "crash and burn" meant. Around that same time, I met Tamar. I had heard so much about her from Ricardo that I was fascinated and went with him to meet her.

Tamar lived in a flat on the corner of Pine and Filmore. Her place was an unassuming walkup until you stepped into the deep rich carpeting inside and sunk to your ankles. The flat was light and airy, sparkly but elegantly furnished with light beige walls, sofas, and carpeting all blending into one another. Seductive classical guitar music with drums flowed from hidden speakers. That day, no one was in the room. Ricardo and I looked at each other and sat down, sinking into the soft sofa. Ricardo stretched his hands back over his head and extended his lanky legs, grinning at me. Reclining as if he were waiting for a performance to begin, he announced, "She will be out in a moment."

Straightening myself as much as I could in the deep cushions, I recalled what I had read about Tamar in the *San Francisco Chronicle*. She had been married to a popular folk singer, Stan Wilson, who performed at the Hungry Eye. Due to a nasty divorce, the couple had caught the eye of the media. Tamar's pictures had been on the front page. She was a stunning blonde with a come-hither smile that promised something special. She had hidden a tape recorder under the bed while her entertainer husband entertained more than one lady, and the tape had been played salaciously in court to the titillation of the judge and jury. Tamar had been awarded a large settlement and sole custody of their daughter. I had followed the trail in the paper while it was happening. Now I was sitting in her living room with my now boyfriend, her ex-lover. Small world! But where was she?

Time passed and Ricardo folded his hands loosely in his lap and closed his eyes, taking a nap while waiting for Tamar. I looked about the room. Fresh flowers graced the coffee table and a large crystal ashtray invited smoking. Getting up to browse the black and white photos of Tamar on the wall, I recognized ones from the *Chronicle* that had obliviously been taken in a studio. Then I remembered something Ricardo had told me. Tamar had been a movie star in Mexico City. He said that they loved blue-eyed blondes. He also told me her father had been a doctor and was currently a diplomat.

Photo 10 - Tamar

After admiring the photos, I returned to my seat on the sofa, only to rise again and wander over to the window facing Filmore Street to watch the goings and comings of the people on the street. There was a Mexican market on the corner, and I wondered if they had dark cinnamon chocolate there. Maybe I would buy some on the way out. I was beginning to wonder if we should leave. What kind of a hostess invites guests over and leaves them unattended for so long? What was she doing? Why were we waiting?

Glancing at Ricardo, I noted that he was still in the same position with a slight smile on his face, eyes closed. What was he thinking? I was annoyed and pondered leaving quietly. Though I was not wearing a watch and there were no clocks in the room, I sensed we had been waiting for at least an hour. As I pondered my predicament, I heard a rustle and two giant doors slid open. A vision in lilac stood there smiling. What an entrance! What a performer! Her blonde hair was swept up in curls on top of her head like Little Miss Sunshine in the Wonder Bread ads. Her vibrant-blue eyes, framed in long black lashes, flashed above her brilliant, perfectly white smile. Yes, she was a beauty, but I was not prepared to be charmed.

She opened her arms in greeting. "You must be Carol. I am delighted to meet you," she gushed—and looked like she really meant it.

Ricardo had bounced off the sofa and came forward all flashing white teeth himself. "Tamar," he purred. "You look lovely!"

And indeed, she did. She was wearing a top-to-floor lounging gown in the softest violet that complemented her startling blue eyes as she stepped forward to embrace me, smelling like expensive perfume. Though I had taken pains to dress elegantly, I had been outdone. She was the queen. I was only a hand maiden.

"Sit, Please," she commanded. Maybe it was only a suggestion, but it felt like a command that could not be disobeyed. I perched on the edge of the sofa, not wanting to be sucked back into the depth of it. She took the only straight back chair in the room. Wouldn't you know it? In my mind I had already excused her for keeping us waiting. I was in the presence of royalty, and I waited with bated breath for her to speak.

She opened her perfectly painted mouth and inquired, "Would you like to smoke some hash?"

This began my relationship with Tamar, and my introduction to drugs, sex, and literature—Tamar style. She also introduced me to Gavin Arthur, the grandson of President Arthur, our twenty-first president, and not a noteworthy one according to Gavin. Gavin was an astrologer. Tamar made me an appointment with him on a rainy Thursday afternoon. At four o'clock, I found myself trudging up Turk and Hyde in the Tenderloin, the most unsavory part of town where the old man from the Spaghetti Factory had cautioned me pimps, whores, and drug dealers hung out.

Gavin lived on the second floor accessed by a small metal cage elevator, the kind you see in old French movies. I wondered how safe it was as I closed the door behind me and pressed the up button. It smelled of cigars and urine. I rapped on the door of 206 standing in the dark, musty hall, wondering, Is this a mistake?

A voice calling from within told me to enter, so I turned the door handle reticently and slowly opened the door. A lamp on a small reading table cast a warm glow on a room cluttered with books stacked in piles on the floor and on every flat surface, including the bed. This was the home of a scholar.

In a straight-back chair at a small desk sat a white-haired gentleman. His bright-blue eyes examined me closely. "Come in. Come in," he commanded. "Close the door. Take a seat. I am slightly incapacitated, or I would stand to greet you. Please, not that chair. Here, by me at the desk. We have work to do! I'm Gavin Arthur," he said, extending his hand. "Grandson of our not-so-illustrious twenty-first President," he said peering at me over his glasses. "Wasn't much of a president. Bet you've never heard of him?"

"Ah no," I replied, seating myself in another straight back chair, this one with a worn velvet cushion.

Still peering at me over his glasses he noted, "You're late. I expect you to be on time when you make an appointment with me." His eyes twinkled in a face worn with age and wisdom but few wrinkles. He was wearing an extremely wrinkled white shirt and tie. The shirt looked like it had been ironed with a hot rock. "Did you bring cash?" he asked. "I don't like checks—too much trouble."

Reaching for my handbag to extract two twenties, then carefully unfolding them, I said, "Forty-four dollars, correct?" Maybe he didn't like them folded either. Maybe he also had ties with this president.

"Thank you," he said politely. "Now, let's get to work. Please select a pencil from the jar on the desk. Choose a color you like." I reached for the jelly jar with the colored pencils and selected a green one. Leaning toward me intently, he asked, "When is your birth date and when were you born? The exact time, if known, is important. Astrology is an exact science. We must be precise." He took the green pencil from me.

"Appropriate," he exclaimed. "Virgo's color is green. Copper is your metal, and copper oxidizes green. Your birthstone, emerald, is also green."

"Oh, really," I said, surprised. "I thought it was sapphire."

"No," he replied emphatically. "Jewelers got together and to sell precious stones, they changed everything around. No, your birthstone is emerald." Then he bent to work over his papers, drawing lines across a circle that represented my natal chart. He checked his Ephemeris often and drew more lines crisscrossing the horizon and the heavens. Only then did he stop and turn to look at me, pointedly.

"You almost didn't make it past five years old. What happened?" I was puzzled and searched through my childhood years. He persisted, "You almost died you know. What happened?"

"Oh," I said brightly. "My brother gave me ant poison and I had to have my stomach pumped."

"Hmm," he muttered and turned back to the chart. Bent over his desk, white hair shining in the lamp light, he went on. "Then, again at ten years you came close to losing your life. Tell me about it."

Shivering, my skin began to crawl.

"Well," I said taking a deep breath, recalling the incident instantly. "It was a gray, gloomy day. I had stayed after school for a Girl Scout meeting, so I was walking home alone rather than with the usual bunch of Hill road kids. Hill road was just that—a hill with a bend in the road. From our house at the top of the hill you could see the entire road except for the spot where the road bent. As I approached the bend in the road, something in my head started to go off like an alarm system. *Clang! Clang! Clang!* I became extremely frightened, so much so that I crossed the road. It was as if someone was taking me by the shoulders and pushing me. I scrambled up the embankment about ten feet, dropped my schoolbooks, and used the tall weeds to pull myself up. As I did that, I noticed an old faded-blue Chevy parked in the bend of the road. My heart was in my mouth as the car began to roll and came to a stop just below me. There was a man in the car, and he had a gun in his lap. He hollered up at me, 'Come down here. I am going to kill you!'

My eyes widened in terror. My pulse was racing, and an inner voice shouted, *Run! Run!* I was frozen with fear like in a bad dream. My feet were rutted to the ground. I called back to the stranger, 'I can't get down there! I slipped getting up here. I will walk to where it is easier to get down and then come down there.'

Run! Run! The voice in my head shouted. I took a couple of steps, threw my books down and ran like the wind, never looking back, shouting, 'Mama! Mama!'"

"Close call," said Gavin. "Your alarm system is in good working order. Always listen to it in the future. It will protect you." He bent his head over my chart and went back to work. I sat there with adrenaline pumping wildly through my veins from reliving the incident.

"Well," said Gavin, "most of your planets are above the horizon so you will have control of your life, but you have stymied lines everywhere, so nothing will come easy for you. You will have to work for everything."

Sighing, I said, "That is the story of my life."

"This is exactly what we are looking at, only you have some control. You can make a difference," he assured me as he peered at me over his glasses. His intense black eyes met mine. I thought his eyes were blue when I arrived! I made a mental note in the back of my head: Hmm, eyes that change color and are not hazel. Interesting!

"You will live to be a ripe old age and become very wise," he said, smiling. "But there is a rocky road between here and there. For instance, this fellow you are living with—what's his name?"

"Ricardo," I volunteered.

Gavin's eyes became even more intense as he warned me, "He is an extremely bad fellow. Bad temper. No control. He will hurt you! You must get away from him now!"

More than a bit stunned, I knew Gavin was right. Ricardo had hit me more than once, but how did Gavin know? Then I was given the real stunner. Gavin's eyes pierced mine, pinning me to the chair.

"Are you pregnant with his child?" I bit my tongue. "Maybe, I thought. I was late in my cycle."

"You must get away from him," Gavin ordered.

My head swam, and I flushed. How did this man know so much about my situation and me? Everything he had told me was true. He bent over my chart and studied it some more. Pondering the chart, he added, "You don't have another exit until age eighty-five. You will live to be a wise old lady. Come back and see me again just to visit." He stood up, rubbed his lower back, removed his glasses, and dismissed me just like that.

As I made my way home on the number-thirty bus to Laguna Street, I contemplated my situation. I had been living with Ricardo for almost two years since he had suggested he move in to help pay the rent so that we could get a bigger place. He had lived in the Tenderloin in an apartment that was no bigger than a shoe box. Ever since I had met him at my cocktail job in Naji Babas where he was a frequent customer, I had liked and learned to trust him. He did not drink and only ordered a strong Arab coffee. At first, I thought he was gay! He reminded me of mighty mouse because he was no taller than me. His small stature had bothered me a little and it was my first experience with "little man syndrome." But he was charming, generous and a typically sexy Scorpio. We hit it off in bed. But the moment our feet hit the floor, we fought. He was jealous of everyone.

Though he always apologized profusely, crying on his knees, swearing he would never do it again, it happened time after time; I would go to work with a black eye and split lip. He was an abuser. I had never dealt with anything like that before and kept feeling sorry for him and hoping he would stop. Gavin had opened my eyes. It was not going to stop!

My last incident with Ricardo happened after we had been out to dinner across town. Walking to the car he began a senseless argument that turned ugly. He slapped me. As I ran away from him, he chased me. I am a fast runner and even in five-inch heels I could out-run him. But once he gave up chasing me and sped away in the car, I had no money, so I was forced to walk a couple of miles home. When I got there, he was waiting, quietly sullen. He gave no apologies that night. His temper was uncontrolled. There were regular clashes, usually because of his jealousy.

One time he was doing my hair at the saloon where he worked. It was owned by an aging homosexual, Herb, who was a great guy with a sparkle in his eye and a dance in his step. Ricardo, railing at me, said I had shitty hair as he combed through it, letting it fall straight. He was trying to put it in a French roll, and it was falling out. Herb came over and stood behind the chair looking into the mirror at me he said, "Why don't you just let it fall free, wild and free, like Carol?"

Ricardo's eyes glazed. He did not take criticism well and was offended and took it out on me, chiding me because he was trying to do something for me (for free), and I was ungrateful. I had not said a word. If he had wanted to shave my head, I would have sat there quietly. But Herb's comment set him off, and now I was "an ungrateful bitch." He pulled my hair tighter and tighter, and backcombed it till it stood on end by itself, sprayed it until it was stiff, and tied it in a French twist.

"There!" he said, his eyes glistening with menace. "You're finished." My head hurt, my eyes were watering, and it would be days before my hair would return to normal. But I thanked him, pecking him on the cheek, and turned to leave, catching the look of total amazement on Herb's face, who shrugged sadly. Turning to Ricardo as I went out the door, I heard him say, "Why did you do that to her?" I did not hear Ricardo's answer, but I bet it was a good one.

Counting the good points, Ricardo did pay half the rent, and he was clean—oh, extremely clean. He even wiped the inside of the catsup and mustard bottles. Doesn't everyone? In the shower he scrubbed every inch of his body like he had been contaminated with radiation. He was responsible and worked hard. He painted like Picasso and someday would have his own show. He did not drink or do drugs. Ah, but that Latin temper! I could not live with it anymore.

When I discovered that I was pregnant and knew by past conversations that Ricardo did not want a child, and realized he would be a bad father, I packed my things one day when he was at work and moved out. You guessed it. As ironic as it was, I moved in with Ricardo's ex-lover, Tamar to escape Ricardo's wrath.

CHAPTER 11

Tamar and astrology

Living with Tamar was a trip because she spent most of her life in bed, which was a large affair with many pillows and a comforter in her favorite color, violet. On small tables were stacked many books on astrology and metaphysics. Her canteen, a bottle of water and crystal glass, was always nearby, alongside an assortment of prescription drugs in small vials. The room was a large sunny one with overstuffed chairs for her visitors to relax in. The drapes were heavy damask and let no light in so she could sleep in the dark during the day. From the street, you knew whether Tamar was awake and holding court or not. If the drapes were drawn, you could not visit. Her food was ordered out and usually paid for by whatever male friend was visiting at the time. She spent late hours entertaining from her bed. Conversation was intellectual and covered history, politics, music, books, sex, drugs, and intergalactic travel. Never current events. Sometimes there would be as many as eight men in the room as Tamar held court from her bed. Always coiffured, her blond hair was done up magnificently by one the many gay hairdressers that waited on her hand and foot. They filled her water glass, fussed over her hair and makeup, and rolled her joints.

In a January 2019 *Cosmopolitan* article, Michelle Phillips from the famed The Mamas & the Papa's was quoted as saying, "Tamar was the epitome of glamour. She was someone who never got out of bed until two p.m., and she looked it. It was late afternoon, and she was dressed in a beautiful lavender suit with her hair in a beehive. I took one look and said, 'new best friend!'" It is true. Tamara was a magnet.

Let me tell you more. This beautiful intelligent lady who spent most of her life in bed surrounded by books and people was, I have decided, completely amoral. She told me about her childhood living in a Frank Lloyd Wright house in Los Angeles with her beautiful mother and doctor father. The house contained secret passages and rooms where unspeakable things went on. She told me she had sex with her father and his friends and became pregnant at the age of fourteen. She told on her father, but her mother refused to believe her. There was a trial; her father said she was a compulsive liar. He skipped town and she was branded for life. Her child, a daughter, was put up for adoption. Tamar was banished and sent to live with an aunt in San Francisco.

Just recently, I read that children who have sex with relatives grow up thinking that their only value is sexual and continue down a path offering their bodies to everyone and anyone in exchange for acceptance and affection. Tamar expected and accepted things in return. Her lush carpeting came from a tryst with a carpet layer. Her sound system, same thing. Her ex, Stan, still contributed alimony and her friends brought food from good restaurants. Tamar was taken care of. She did not work. She had everything she wanted but love.

Tamar dropped names like John Huston and other Hollywood notables that were friends with her famous father and frequent visitors to his home. She said there were orgies that she witnessed and took part in as a teenager.

As I spent more time with her, she told me jaw-dropping stories about her father. She said he was a sadist and had killed people, one in particular: the "Black Dahlia," actress Elizabeth Short. In 1947, the actress was found murdered in a vacant lot near Leimert Park, Los Angeles. Her murder to this day has remained officially unsolved. Years later in 2003, her brother, Steven, wrote a book accusing their father of the murder, called *Black Dahlia Avenger: The True Story*. Steven was a detective in the Los Angeles Police Department and now I believe she was telling the truth. Tamar was also involved with a doctor in San Francisco that did abortions when they were totally illegal.

One day, it was near Christmas and Tamar had what she thought was a great idea. She said she would order stuff from I. Magnin and Macy's and charge it to rich people's accounts; they were so rich that they would not notice. Way back then before charge cards, you could just do that by phone—put an order on your account and have it delivered to whatever address you wanted. I told you she was amoral. In my book, this is stealing. However, she assured me that these people were so rich it was like Robin Hood. So, she ordered, of course, lavender towels as a gift and had them sent to herself. Then she ordered two cashmere camel coats, one for each of us. When they arrived, I answered the door and was promptly arrested and taken away in handcuffs; a humiliating experience to say the least. I was fingerprinted, mugged, strip-searched, given an orange jumpsuit, and put in a cell with six other women, mostly black. I got the standard question, "Hey new girl, whatcha in for?" I was in shock, but I had been able to reach a friend, my "Daddy Jack," who rushed to the jail and posted bail. More about him later. When I returned home to Tamar's, with great composure, she told me that she had a record and would go to jail if I told on her. She told me that she had been involved in an abortion ring. However, she pointed out, I had a clean record, and all I would get was a slap on the hand. If she went to jail, she would lose custody of her daughter and the flat, and I would have nowhere to live. She had a way with words and was very convincing.

So, I took the rap, big-hearted, stupid me. I was given a five-year probation sentence and ordered to pay restitution. I paid for the sheets Tamar slept on and the towels with which she dried her body. She never paid me a cent though she promised she would. With friends like this, I did not need enemies! Apparently, Tamar had been using this scam for some time. In court I found out the most horribly damaging news of all. Tamar had gone through my address book and charged things to my Aunt Patty, leaving my aunt to believe I was a thief. Aunt Patty never spoke to me again, and I was too embarrassed to try to convince her otherwise. Though I told my mother what really happened, I don't think she ever bothered to clear my name. I have carried that stigmatism for the rest of my life. Thanks Tamar! Boy, was I naive!

Daddy Jack was the guy who bailed me out of jail. An older man with a Boston accent, he was a printer by trade. I met him at the Bus Stop where I worked. He didn't drink but would stop in for coffee. He always sat next to the wait station and talked to me. Mostly, he listened to my problems and offered advice. He was wise, kind, and gentle. He had a daughter my age somewhere who was living like a nomad in cars. He worried about her and sent her money when she asked. Jack would take me to dinner sometimes, and bought me small things he thought I might be able to use, such as hair barrettes and shampoo.

"It was on sale," he would say. He was a good friend and I stayed in touch with him for years. He took the place of my father who I had not heard from since I left the ranch, so it was Jack I turned to in time of need. He was always there for me. When he gave me money, he always said, "I don't expect you to pay it back to me. Just pass it on when you can."

Years later, I remember meeting a photographer on a bus once who needed film for his camera. I gave him twenty dollars knowing Daddy Jack would have wanted me to "pass it on." Jack did not approve of Tamar, but he never said anything negative. He just listened and asked questions like, "Do you think she is doing the right thing?" or "What do you think she is teaching her daughter?" Jack stayed in my life the entire time I lived in San Francisco.

My questionable friendship with Tamar would then lead me out of the frying pan into the fire: one of the men who visited Tamar—another one of her ex-lovers. Wasn't everyone? This one was a handsome, charming Merchant Marine named Dale Patrick Gleason.

CHAPTER 12

Dale Patrick Gleason (aka psychopath)

Shortly after I left Ricardo, I discovered I was pregnant. Tamar said, "You could do worse than Dale! He adores you and will take care of you and the baby. He makes good money as a Merchant Marine."

I was at a loss as to what to do. I was pregnant with Ricardo's baby, but he was violent. I knew it would not work, and I did not want to marry him. Nauseated most of the time, I never thought once about going to his family. That was out of the question. Aborting the baby? Unthinkable. Public assistance? I did not know it existed at the time. So, as Dale courted me with fresh strawberries, he took a taxi across town to fetch for me and used gentle words. I began to think maybe this was not a bad idea. Also, he was kind to Bo, who was spending most of the time with his grandmother Brown, who, of course, knew nothing of my situation. When he asked me to marry him and promised to take care of the baby and me, knowing the baby was Ricardo's, the wheels were set in motion. He said he would find us an apartment and two days later took me by taxi, neither of us having a car, to a three-story walk-up on Broadway just below the tunnel. It had hardwood floors, and the front room faced south on Broadway through a bay window. Afternoon sun streamed in, warming the room. The old, varnished floors had shown in the sunlight, and the walls were a soft creamy color. Down the long hall were a bedroom, a dining room, and a kitchen. It was well-lit, with a view of the San Francisco Bay. It was lovely.

"You like it?" Dale beamed! And enthusiastically peeling off hundred-dollar bills from his pocket, he said to the old Italian landlord, "We'll take it."

It happened so fast. With the help of some longshoreman, Dale got me out of Tamar's and into the apartment on Broadway. We set up our bedroom in the sunny front room, reserving the bedroom for Bo and the baby to come. Within two weeks of knowing Dale, I was setting up housekeeping with him.

Someone I hardly knew arranged for a wedding in Tahoe. I bought a cream-colored lace dress for the occasion. Eddy, Tamar's hairdresser, did my hair, and the next thing I knew, Dale and I were on a bus headed towards a casino in Tahoe to be married. We were transferred there by a gambling bus for older adults, and we were the entertainment: a nice young couple getting married. Dale was handsome and charming. Everyone liked him immediately, old ladies and truck drivers alike. He exuded boyish charm. The arrangements had all been made, even the marriage license and wedding cake. We were guests of the tour company. This had all happened because I applied for a job with the tour company and then explained to the manager that I could not take the job because I was pregnant. He was a compassionate young man and pressed me for details when he found I had no job, no money. He offered to set up the wedding for me as a promotion. I accepted, and here we were on a bus with sixty white-haired people who would attend our wedding.

We were ushered upstairs to a ballroom where the guests assembled around a makeshift altar. I was handed a bouquet of flowers and motioned forward by the clergyman who appeared as anxious to get this over with as I was. In the blink of an eye, I became an honest woman, married to a man I had known less than three weeks. The audience applauded and departed after eating their cake, but not before presenting the newlyweds with a bag of silver dollars.

A sweet white-haired old man said, "Good luck from all of us," and disappeared out of our lives. Never to be seen again.

So did Dale! I looked around, and he was gone. Maybe, I thought, he had gone to the bathroom. Minutes slipped by. Then I found myself alone with the minister. He wanted us to sign the marriage certificate to make everything official. Where was Dale? Certain that he will be right back, we waited and made small talk. Twenty minutes went by. No Dale. Both of us were uncomfortable. He went to check the men's room. I went downstairs. To my annoyance, there at the first gaming table was my new husband throwing the dice. He was deep in concentration and losing. He looked up at me and sheepishly grinned.

"Oh, there you are," he said as if I had been the one missing.

"The minister is waiting to sign the papers," I told him, in a monotone, not wanting to show my irritation.

"Just a moment," he said, pushing the remainder of the silver dollars on the pass line and throwing a seven. The croupier collected the last of our wedding gift, setting Dale free to return upstairs and sign our marriage certificate. He had gambled away our gift in twenty-five minutes. Without asking or telling me where he was going, it was kiss the bride, and hit the tables. Dale had lost the money, our gift, all of it, so we returned to our room. I was happy to sleep.

When I awoke, he was gone. He had gone through my purse, found the twenty dollars I had brought for an emergency, maybe food, and I lay on my back wondering what I had gotten myself into. The key turned in the lock, and Dale appeared looking like the cat that had eaten the mouse. He ran nervous fingers through his hair, a gesture that would become familiar. He said the obvious, "Oh! You're awake, and I almost won. I was up to three hundred dollars, and then I went for broke. And broke I finished," nervously laughing, running a hand over his head, not really touching his hair, just the gesture.

When we got home, I said, "You left me alone after the wedding and I was embarrassed. You didn't say anything to me. You lost the . . ." I didn't even finish the sentence as I saw the terrifying transformation on Dale's face. All color drained from it, and his eyes narrowed, with hard lines forming around his eyes. What happened next was so swift, I didn't see it coming. He slugged me so hard that it lifted me off my feet, dropping me flat on the floor. He had cold-cocked me. Oh lord, what had I gotten myself into?

Dale stormed passed me towards the kitchen, the click of his heels hitting the bare floor. I wasn't seriously hurt, but it happened so fast that I was stunned into silence. I lay where I had fallen, studying the ceiling. I could hear him turning on the water in the bathroom. What now?

He came back and pulled me to my feet. I touched my jaw lightly, amazed, and dazed. He said calmly, "Why don't you take a hot bath? I'll find something to eat." He acted as if nothing had happened, and as I soaked in the hot bath, I wondered if I had imagined. He hit me. What?

Dale shipped out soon after our wedding. He was on a six-week tanker. I spent quiet time reading in the sunny front room we had turned into our bedroom. I walked the neighborhood through Chinatown. Dale had left me with enough money for food. Bo was still with his grandmother. Daddy Jack came and brought me a bag of oranges and sat quietly as I told him about the wedding, omitting everything unpleasant. I did not want him to know that I had made a dumb mistake. But his eyes told me different. He knew. The days passed. I read, slept and took long walks.

When Dale returned late one night, he had his pockets stuffed with money and insisted we go out to dinner with his shipmates. It seemed customary to celebrate, and we did it at the Fairmount Hotel with lobster and champagne. Dale was onshore for several weeks before his next ship. Therefore, he had time on his hands, and we spent it walking about town. He took me to the Tenderloin to a small cafe where his grandmother worked. The door was dirty with handprints and the window steamy.

Doris, as she liked to call herself (her real name was Hazel), was a tiny little older-than-dirt lady with orange-red hair, and bright-red lipstick. She wore clunky fake jewelry with her white uniform. She was a spunky old gal running up and back behind the counter that seated perhaps ten, dishing out her homemade chili and serving pancakes and eggs and apple pie to characters William Saroyan would have loved to meet.

Longshoreman and street people, each had their own story. She greeted me with a bear hug, and though her arms were skinny and her legs spindly, she had quite a grip.

"Sit down, sit down," she said, motioning to one of the vacant stools at the counter. "I'll be with you in a moment. Hungry?"

Without asking what we wanted, she bustled back up the counter with two steaming bowls of chili with crackers. I was hungry. It was hot, spicy, and good! Leaning on the counter with both hands, I noticed several dime store, chunky jeweled rings on her bright-red, polished, knobby fingers. This was a woman who had worked hard all her life and had seen better days. But she had taken it in stride and had a kind word for every one of her motley customers. I watched her work the counter. She knew all her customers by name: Lucky, Skipper, and Terrible Terry.

Terrible Terry was an ex-showgirl, meaning ex-stripper, now hooker with hair ratted a foot high in a beehive and sprayed until it stayed that way for days. She hustled on the streets and at a joint across the road. She would come in to get warm, holding a mug of coffee in both hands, leaning against the wall, her eyes watery under her thick mascara with bright-red lipstick smeared on her face. She wore a tattered fake fur, five-inch strappy high heels, chipped red polish on her toes that matched her lipstick, and a partially broken string of rhinestones. Her hands shook from drugs or lack of them, or from the cold because she wore no stockings and nothing under her coat.

Once she warmed up, she would become animated and social and visit with Doris, the red-haired waitress. When Terry really got comfortable, she would take off her coat. I know this to be a fact because one time when I was there, she opened the coat to flash Skipper, the sailor. He seemed to enjoy it, but Doris snapped to attention.

"Not here! Terry," she said politely but firmly. "Put your clothes back on. I'm working; this is my establishment, and I keep it respectable. There are ladies here," she said, nodding at me.

Terry had blushed. "Sorry, she'd said," buttoning her coat. But by this time, everyone in the place had seen her pale, thin naked body with sloping breasts and a shaved pussy. She had giggled as she slid back into her roadkill coat, and turning toward Doris, had said, "Can I get a cup of coffee, honey? It is cold outside. I'll pay you later."

Like always, Doris had handed her a mug of coffee, and Terrible Terry retreated to the wall behind her. Leaning on the wall cupping her coffee in both hands, she had smiled to herself, lost in her own thoughts, perhaps of better days.

The little cafe had become a regular stop for Dale and me. Doris always fed us, and the company was more than entertaining. We became a threesome: Dale's grandmother, and the sailor and I going to the movies together, and to Doris's home. Full of clutter and several cats, a mongrel dog she called monster, and a chihuahua, a hairless ugly little thing with bug eyes and a rat-like tail, the house reeked of animal odors. The stench was so bad in my pregnant condition I almost gagged on entering. A third dog, another heinz-variety, was a mostly black lab with sad eyes and a sweet disposition. All three dogs slept with Doris on her unmade bed. There were newspapers spread everywhere beside three bowls of water and food, and extra papers on the kitchen floor in case they didn't make it outside in time. Apparently, from the smell of it, that was a lot of the time. Living in the city there was little outside, and Doris was at the cafe most of the time. The temperature was set at a stifling eighty degrees, and between the smell and the heat, our visits to her house were difficult for me, but she was so sweet and funny. Her old eyes sparkled with joy when she saw us. Dale was her only grandson, so she doted on him and adopted me as her own.

One day I had a surprise visit—a knock on the door of the Broadway apartment. Dale was out. I opened the door to a red-haired, heavy-set, middle-aged woman. She appeared nervous but friendly and hurriedly introduced herself as Dale's mother, though she called him Pat. I quickly invited her inside in the hallway. She self-consciously hugged me in an awkward gesture.

"Doris told me you and Pat were married. I am Dorothy. Welcome to the family. Don is parking the car." Looking over my shoulder, she asked, "Is Pat here?"

"No," I answered, "he's out to see a friend."

"Oh," she replied, seeming relieved.

"Won't you come in and have a seat?" I said, leading her to the round table in the dining room. "May I get you something to drink?"

"Coffee would be nice," she said, seating herself at the table, still in her coat, and placing her handbag on the table.

There was a firm rap at the door, and I sprung to answer it. The man standing there was double the size of Dorothy and breathing heavily from the exhaustion of climbing the stairs. He wore a light-brown suit crumpled from the drive. His face broke into a huge smile. "I'm Don."

I stood aside; the door opened wide. He entered without hesitation and went straight to the table and seated himself beside his wife.

"I was just getting coffee." I said, "May I get you some?"

While I made coffee, they looked around our barren living quarters and apparently approved—at least we were clean.

"Nice place," Don said, "but those stairs are a little challenging."

"Dottie," she told me to call her that wasted no getting to the point. I think she wanted to spill the beans before her son appeared. Twisting her coffee cup back and forth in her hands and staring into it, she said, "You know Pat was married before? And has a child, a little girl named Bonnie." This was news to me. I had not asked, and he had not volunteered. She looked up at me shyly, smiling, "He's still married. But Doris says he is happy and that she is sure that you are the one. But we think Pat hasn't told you, and you should know." She smiled again. Don sat quietly, a bead of sweat appearing on his forehead though it was not warm in the apartment. Dottie continued. "Pat, well, he's had some problems. He's been hospitalized for hmmm, problems." She looked directly at me. Her eyes were blue and watery. "Has he told you? Ah. No! Well, occasionally, he's not quite himself." The light went on in the back of my head, and I encouraged her. "Well, he's not nice. His wife, ah his other wife, ah has a restraining order against him." But she added in haste, "We think it will be different with you. We think you are the right person for him. We think you can help! But it is probably a good idea that he doesn't know we've told you!"

All this came rushing out breathlessly. Don stirred his coffee, and then as if on cue, the key turned in the lock, and Dale Patrick entered the room. He looked surprised and then pleased as he ran his fingers aimlessly through his hair and came forward, kissing his mother on the cheek. Don stood, and they shook hands. The next hours were filled with pleasantry conversation about nothing, and then they took us to dinner, picking up Doris on the way. Nothing more was said about Dale's problem.

Photo 11 - Dale Patrick Gleason smoking cigarette

Months went by, and Dale was away from the apartment frequently. When he left, the phone ceased to work. I discovered he had disconnected the mouthpiece from the receiver, so I was unable to answer the phone or call out. Strange. His disappearances were never explained. He simply had to go out. Sometimes, it was early evening, sometimes late at night. I lived in a quiet world of reading and resting. Bo had joined us, back from another long visit with his grandmother. It was time for him to begin kindergarten. There was a school on the same block, an old brownstone with an asphalt yard and high chain-link fences surrounding it. I took him to register for school on a typical gray, foggy day in San Francisco. The building was old and smelled musty. Filling out the necessary papers, I saw him to his room and left with a feeling of apprehension. This was not where I wanted to see him spend his days. As it turned out, he wasn't there long. Dale put us on a train to Fresno to visit his parents. We were to stay the weekend. They met us at the train station in sunny Fresno and took us to lunch, then to their nice middle-class home with a swimming pool and a guest room. They treated Bo and I like family. Saturday morning, we went shopping, and they bought much needed clothes for Bo and new tennis shoes for me. Being a city girl, I had nothing but heels. They drove us around town, pointing out points of interest, the zoo, the library, and the school that Bo might be attending.

"Excuse me, but we lived in San Francisco," I reminded them. Dottie looked at Don. Don looked at Dottie, then back at the road. There was a moment of silence. They knew something I didn't know. Dottie laughed nervously.

"Well, I guess it was meant to be a surprise. Maybe I shouldn't have said anything, but Pat is moving you here so we can keep an eye on you while he's away."

Without telling me, he was moving me in with his parents. He was packing and bringing our possessions to Fresno without asking or even telling me. Hell! I was pregnant and due to deliver in a couple of months, and my doctor was working at the University of California, San Francisco, where he had agreed to deliver the baby free as a teaching case. We could not afford a C-section. We had no insurance. Plus, San Francisco was my home.

SECTION 3

Fresno

CHAPTER 13

The weight of change

Dale married me knowing I was pregnant with Ricardo's baby and then sent me on the train to Fresno to visit his parents. Unbeknownst to me, he rented a U-haul, and then proceeded to move me out of San Francisco to Fresno into his parents' home, where I was accepted and welcomed. They assumed the baby was his and when she was born with cool-black hair and brown eyes, it made no matter. Dale's mom cuddled and cooed and held her, bonding with her.

I had not agreed to move to Fresno and live with Dale's parents. They were nice people, but I was being treated like a little kid. Dale arrived that night with a U-Haul, and all our belongings were stored in the garage until we could find a place of our own. As it turned out for Bo, it was a good move. Don and Dottie treated him like their grandson and outfitted him for school in a modern, clean environment, and I found relief from the stifling heat in their swimming pool. I became their resident mermaid. The weight of the unborn child was nothing floating in the tepid waters.

Dottie would bring food to the side of the pool. I didn't even have to get out of the pool to eat. So, ultimately Dale's decision was not a bad one. I spent the last part of my pregnancy in luxury.

Despite my luxurious life at Dottie's home, I also discovered while working at the Fairmount hotel as a maître d', Dale was a criminal. He would seat wealthy customers and then call his buddy to burglarize their homes and rob them. Having been in jail several times, his life of crime had started at sixteen with theft of a car. Then, as I would discover, he had robbed his adoring grandmother, beat his first wife, and been in a mental institution more than twice. Talk about out of the frying pan and into the fire!

This man was also a sexaholic and needed sex several times a day, like brushing his teeth. Then he would disappear for days at a time, during which I prayed that he would not return. Away from San Francisco, he told me about his life of crime. It didn't change in Fresno. He was jealous and would accuse me of cheating on him, wake me in the middle of the night clasping me by my nightgown, slapping me across the face, calling me a bitch and whore because he imagined I was with another man. Besides being jealous, a psycho, and thief, Dale did a lot of drugs. This clean-cut, handsome man smoked marijuana with hash as a starter. He also did pharmaceutical drugs by the handful, and when he was at sea, it was heroin, or anything else he could find. I lived my life anticipating terror. The front he put on for his family and the life he led away from them was unreal.

Dale shipped out again, and I was left with his very normal family: breakfast, lunch, and dinner on time, simple but good food. Dottie worked with Don in his insurance office, and they went to work together in the morning, came home for lunch, seldom went out, and didn't seem to have very many friends. They cleaned the house together, shopped together, and gardened together. They were inseparable. Their conversations were about the weather and if they should put Draino in the pipes. They didn't read and had no hobbies, oh, except for the grape lamp that Dottie made. And Don was so proud of her gluing all those little purple balls together.

They were the most content couple I have ever seen and welcomed Bo and me into their world. It was peaceful and surreal.

Then Dale came home. He had money, so we started looking for a house and found one several miles outside of town, a two-bedroom farmhouse in the middle of a sea of vineyards. Don and Dottie helped us move in. Bo would now be going to school in the country. I was now seven months pregnant.

Dottie had taken me to the county hospital the first week I arrived. I wore my white maternity dress, the one I had designed myself with tiny white pleats down the front, a mandarin collar and long sleeves, and delicate rickrack trim between the pleats. My hair was now shoulder length and tied back in a bow at the neck. I wore white pumps. I was still a city girl and certainly looked out of place in the county hospital. While I was waiting, my head was turned by a very good-looking doctor. He stared at me and almost walked into the door. I stared back. Instant connection!

My little girl, Lisa, would be brought into the world by this man, one I fell in love with, Dr. Julius Gray.

My first visit to the maternity clinic at Valley General, I locked eyes with this darling young intern. Dr. Gray had eyes that had sparkled, and when he smiled, dimples pulled deep into his cheeks. During the examination, we got to know each other a little. Dr. Gray was an intern specializing in OB-GYN. I told him something about myself. He sat beside me, held my hand, and looked into my eyes. His were warm and brown with long lashes. He had curly light-brown hair, and, of course, good teeth. I was smitten. He told me not to worry, that I was in good hands, that the county hospital was a good one, and he would take special care of me. He did.

Most of all, he had warmth and kindness as he listened to me describing my distress around leaving my doctor in San Francisco. He assured me that I was in good hands. I told him about Dale, the abuse and feeling trapped. He was sympathetic, nonjudgmental, and only kind as he held my hand. We became more than friends. He called me regularly to check on me and when I called him at the hospital, I was put through immediately.

Later Julius would tell me that he'd prayed he would not get me as patient when I walked in. I had prayed that I would—and I won.

When I returned home to Dottie's, I received a phone call from the hospital saying they would not take me because I had not been in the county long enough to qualify. I was devastated. What would I do? I knew I had to have a C-section, so home delivery was not a possibility. I wept uncontrollably. Don took over. He called the hospital and somehow managed to talk to Dr. Gray. Between the two of them, I became his patient. He became my friend and confidant, and platonic lover. He was wise, compassionate, comforting, and consoling. We talked on the phone each day. He told me he loved me, and I told him the same. I told him everything. We decided because we loved each other but were not romantically involved, well not physically, that it would be okay to be friends, so he invited me to his house for dinner. Dale was at sea.

Dottie drove me there and dropped me off with a crooked little half-smile on her face. She thought something was up. Julius greeted me at the door with a kiss on the cheek. His wife, obvious with displeasure was immediate. She went into the kitchen and started whacking apart a chicken with a cleaver, *slam bang!* I tried to make small talk, but she was flaming mad.

Julius and I looked at each other.

"I'm sorry," he apologized, "about the bad vibes flowing from the kitchen. This is not going to work."

I called my mother-in-law, Dottie, and requested a pickup. When she arrived with a real smirk on her face, she said, "Really, well what did you expect?"

Julius and I remained secret friends and saw each other in secret, talking on the phone behind closed doors. I visited him at the hospital and once he came to my house and I turned him on to pot. He had never tried it before. He said he did not feel anything and left to go back to the hospital, only to return a few minutes later asking if I wanted to order a pizza. "Hah!" I said, "You are stoned!"

Upon learning that my birth would be cesarian, my astrologer friend, Gavin, did a chart, selecting the most advantageous time for my baby to be born. Dr. Gray honored the time and date, and at the exact hour, minute, and second Gavin chose that would give her the best advantages, Dr. Gray delivered her. To say Lisa has led a charmed life would be an understatement. She is pretty, healthy, and married to a great guy whose father is Jack Oneill, a legend who invented the wet suit. She has always had everything she ever wanted and is a great mother to three beautiful children. Rolling through life without a care, I will always believe she has had an easy time of it because Gavin gave her a wonderful chart.

One night after a particularly bad beating, I ran naked from the house and took shelter in the nearest church. Why did I stay with Dale when he abused me so? I will tell you. He threatened to kill me if I left him. He said, "If I can't have you, no one can!"

Still, between the mean, nasty times, life could be pleasant. He treated the children well and never got tough on me in front of them. It was always in the middle of the night or when they were not around. He named my daughter Lisa after the movie *David and Lisa*. I allowed it because he treated her as his own. Ricardo was never mentioned. His parents fell in love with her. Dottie and Don would hold her for hours. Cooing and talking baby talk, they bought her beautiful little dresses. I didn't have enough nerve to get out. I was a naive little girl the night I took shelter in the church. That was the night I became a Catholic.

Monsignor Singleton swept into our lives with his little beanie and long black robes lined in red. His wide girth and pleasant but strong face took over. He saw to it that groceries were delivered to our house in abundance. The utility bill was paid for by the church, and Dale and I went into consultation. I took it to heart and began the process of becoming a Catholic.

Monsignor got Dale a job at a tire company. That lasted two weeks. Monsignor was on a mission to save his soul. I hoped this would be our salvation.

But one day, Dale disappeared and was not heard from for several months. I took a job at a Mexican restaurant, and Dottie watched the children. Lisa was now six months old and adored by her grandmother, who believed the baby to be her own granddaughter. Relieved, I settled into a work routine. I liked my job and the Catholic family who owned the business. I would have been happy if I never saw Dale again. One day on my way to work, I did something strange. I stopped at a fortune teller's house on a whim.

I paid the fortune teller, a large gypsy woman with long colorful skirts, five dollars, and she looked at me for a long while, and said, "There were two women in your life, both with red hair who mean good but are your two worst enemies."

Hazel and Dottie both had red hair. I needed to get away from them. Who else could it be? It didn't take too much to figure out they tied me to Dale, the man who put my life in danger. She said that I would be receiving a communication that would change my life before I left. "Soon," she said, "very soon." I thanked her and left with my head in a spin.

When I got to work, there was a phone number written down with my name on it. Someone had called for me. I picked up the phone, never guessing who could be on the other line. It was Dale. He was in jail, caught in a burglary. He wanted me to visit and bring Hazel. The last thing I wanted to do was visit him in jail or any other place. But I owed it to Hazel, so I called and told her where Dale was and arranged to take her to him. Dottie would watch the children. He was caught red-handed by the owner who hung on to him and sat on him until the police arrived. It was an open and shut case, but he wanted a lawyer. I found one in San Francisco. Hazel sold her house to pay for his attorney, and moved in with me in Fresno—dogs, cats, and all that stench. The lawyer was good, and within days, Dale was out of jail and in a mental institution in Napa. He had been there before and was comfortable there. I took Hazel to visit him there and even stayed overnight. This is where I had sex in a place that beats everyone else's story. Of all the strange places to have sex, we did it under the bed, in a ward, in a mental institution with his grandmother on the bed sitting guard! Bet you can't beat that one! My daughter, Nancy, was conceived there.

The grounds at Napa were pretty, and we could wander them. We were also allowed to bring in food. Picnics were okay. This was a mental institution, not a jail. Dale spent six months there. Then he was out free and back home thanks to his grandmother generously selling her home of fifty years and handing it over to a smart attorney. Part of the thirty thousand dollars went to bribe a judge. Dale's freedom was worth it to her, but not me. My nightmare was continuing. Remember what the fortune teller said!

Dale moved in with both of us and the kids, five of us in a two-bedroom house. Hazel decided to buy herself a little house and went house shopping. Dale took a job at Cashion's shoe store selling shoes. He had done that before in San Francisco. Cashion's owned three successful shoe stores. Dale charmed the owner, a man with a wife and two children, and quickly moved up the ladder, becoming a manager with a key to all three stores. He brought home shoes every night. I had more shoes than Imelda Marcos. Of course, he stole the shoes, and at Christmas all my family got shoes. Everyone got shoes. Dale spent money on expensive clothes. After all, he was the manager of three stores.

One day Dale came home after a three-day holiday. He was wearing a red cardigan from Patrick James. It was bulky. His face was white. He started pulling out stacks of money bound with rubber bands. He had waited till after a three-day weekend and a big shoe sale to rip off all three stores. He hastily packed a bag, leaving me with one stack of money, and taking the old green Ford station wagon we owned, he drove to the airport and disappeared again. I had to call Don to drive me to the airport to pick up the car. Strangely he asked no questions.

I was free of Dale once again and continued my work at the Mexican restaurant, settling into a routine. The restaurant owners took me under their wing, especially the matriarch of the family, Cruz. Her two sons, Toby and Ralph, and their wives, children, and all of their aunts came in on Wednesdays to roll tamales. The food was fabulous, the best Mexican food I've ever had, to date. Every day, Cruz would cook the family lunch, sometimes tuna sandwiches, sometimes a casserole. Simple, but good. The hot tostadas were tortillas with beans and chorizo heated in an oven at five hundred degrees till they bubbled, served with a tossed salad and homemade vinaigrette. It was the waitress's duty to make the tostadas.

When they were bubbling, you tossed the salad. While still sizzling, you served the tostadas quickly. Years later, I met a man who remembered me working at Estradas, and we raved about the tostadas. I could eat one every day and almost did.

Mama Cruz discovered my children were not baptized, and taking matters into her own hands, called Monsignore Singleton. On a Sunday, she bought the kids all their clothes and closed the restaurant for the Baptismal party afterward. The children were assigned Godparents among the family.

Here is a laugh. Tamar came down from San Francisco and became Bo's godmother. I still have a picture of her at the church looking pious. Later, she seduced the priest. After mass and the baptism, we all went back to the restaurant to celebrate. Let me tell you, Mexican and Irish Catholics know how to do it. I drank margaritas with Monsignor, and Toby turned me on to Grasshoppers. Oh my, Cruz roasted whole chickens as no one else could. They were magic in a mole sauce. Oh my God, that woman could cook. It was a wonderful afternoon, and I was loving being Catholic and being with this generous, fun-loving, happy family. I stayed with them for two years.

Meanwhile, Dale Patrick called from Boston, wanting to know if I had read or heard anything about the robbery. "Had the police been there?" No, No, and No. He wanted me to come to Boston and said he would send me a ticket to fly there for a visit. Fool that I am! I think it was the love of adventure and curiosity that propelled me. I packed a bag, flew out of Fresno to San Francisco, and got drunk at the airport bar. I was so nervous about flying. This was back when flight attendants were stewardess, and passengers were guests and treated like royalty. I threw up in a barf bag, but later was served champagne and a wonderful meal with real linen on china.

When I arrived in Boston, it was below freezing, and my lightweight coat felt like a newspaper. My teeth were chattering when I got off the plane. Dale was there to meet me and took me by taxi to a house he had rented on Beacon Hill. He had gone through the money living his flamboyant lifestyle but had managed to rent a beautiful house in the best part of town and was working at, guess what? Selling shoes. The house was empty: no stove, no fridge, nothing. He was sleeping on the hardwood floor, where I sat while he told me this story.

Cashion, the shoe store owner, married and with two kids, pillar of the community, was gay—closet case, of course. Dale had an affair with him, robbed him, and skipped town after leaving a blackmail note. That was why there was nothing in the newspaper, and no police report filed. Dale had gotten away Scot free and came to Boston to spend his money on whores, drugs, and fine dining. Then he waited for me. Why? Because he wanted to start over and was lonely.

I looked at the lovely empty house and said, "How do you plan to furnish it? What about the children?" But these were hollow questions because I had no plans on living with Dale Patrick now or ever again.

I returned to Fresno the next day. As I write this, I think how stupid I was. I should have gotten as far away from Dale as I could the first time that he hit me. What was I thinking? In truth, I think I was fascinated by his life of crime. I did not take part in it but observed it closely, too closely. It wasn't long before Dale returned to Fresno and moved back in. I was still working at Estrada's. He was welcomed home by his family, with no questions asked. They did not want to know. While he was looking for a job—NOT!—I went about my life: the Mexican restaurant, my children, and even Dr. Gray. We met and played tennis once a week. We talked on the phone each day. He was my lifeline, and he knew everything about Dale, although they only met once at the hospital. We were very discreet. Dale came and went without telling me where he was going, and I did not care. Sometimes he would sit in front of the house in a car with a sleazy looking man who looked as though he would have stepped on the hands of babies as they crawled.

Late one night, I got a phone call. It was Dale telling me to come and meet him on a country road, miles out of Fresno. He had the car, so I called Don. We drove together to the place Dale had directed us to. There was a U-haul truck stuck in the mud. Dale got in the car, and Don drove us home. Don never asked questions. It was weird. He knew there was something not right. But he didn't want to know.

When I got home, I found out that Dale and a friend had stolen a safe, a very heavy, huge safe and had tried to get it open to no avail. He got stuck in the mud and gave up, then called for help.

That afternoon when I went to work, Toby told me, "We were robbed last night!" He was laughing. "The poor slobs hauled our old thousand-pound safe down the stairs, must have taken six of them to move it, and there was nothing in it but old papers. Bet they are sore today!"

I knew one of them was sore, not to mention pissed. How they rented the U-Haul and under whose name I never found out. I did not want to know. Stealing from my job and the family who had befriended me made me angry. Still, consider this is the man who stole from his own grandmother, and oh yes, he was crazy. So crazy, I was afraid of him, terrified. He threatened me, telling me he would kill me. Why not? He would go to a mental institution, be out in a few years. But, he said, "You would be dead."

-COP KARMA-
Just Another Down Day in Fresno

Feeling depressed and lonely, I stopped at a country bar in the middle of nowhere somewhere outside of Fresno. As I sat by myself, I proceeded to drink about ten Stingers (one and a half ounce brandy and a half ounce white Crème DeMint) within about an hour. Then I climbed into my blue and white 1956 Ford station wagon and began the drive home. It was winter, and a slow drizzle was fogging the windshield as I turned on the wipers. At an intersection, I made a left turn. My short left missed the street and turned onto a railroad track. Oops! There was a train coming with one big headlight bearing down on me! The engineer was paying attention, saw me, and threw on his breaks while making train distress noises. I thought, Oh shit, and threw my arms over the steering wheel and buried my head in my arms, bracing for the impact. The train slowed but did enough damage to the Ford to wrinkle the hood up to the windshield. Amazing enough, I was not hurt.

The next thing I knew, I was in the arms of a dark-haired, handsome man with bright-blue eyes, his face close enough to mine to kiss. "You're going to be alright," he assured me sweetly.

After radioing for a tow truck, he carried me to his car, put me in the back seat, told me to lie down, and put a blanket over me. He then asked me where I lived, drove me home, saw that I got in the house, and said he would call later to see if I was alright. Oh, did I mention he was in uniform? Yep, he was an off-duty sheriff who just happened to be behind me when I turned onto the train track. He did call the next morning to check on me and invited me out to dinner. In his report, he wrote that I mistook the train track for a street because of bad weather and visibility and turned onto the track. Boy, did I!

CHAPTER 14

Bass Lake and LSD

With no idea of what possessed Dale to do it, late one night we were packing and moving to the mountains. He had rented a cabin on the edge of Bass Lake in Madera County, about fifty-five miles from Fresno. Nestled in the Sierra National Forest, Bass Lake is about fourteen miles from the south entrance of Yosemite National Park. This was beautiful country, with craggy mountains, pine trees, and gorgeous lakes. But, winter was coming. Since I had to be practical right away, I got a job at snowline lodge cocktailing the first day we were there. Dale would drive me to work and pick me up. Thankfully, Bo was on a visit with his grandmother. Lisa was a year old, still in the crib, and an unhappy baby. How could she be happy? I think babies are intuitive. She instinctively knew what was going on: she cried a lot, clenching her eyes shut, opening her mouth wide, and screaming in rage. She did this often. I could hold her and rock her and talk quietly to her, but she persisted in screaming. I understood. I wanted to do the same thing.

Finally, Dottie came and picked her up for a weekend visit. Without question, she glanced around the sparsely furnished cabin, sniffed, gathered Lisa's things, and disappeared within moments.

Dale didn't even look for a job. He would wait until I had worked a couple of hours' pay and had some tip money, and then come in and demand twenty dollars. It was enough for him to go to the Pines and drink—and that is what he did. I was too scared to argue—I just wanted him to go away.

Dale made friends quickly. One night, he took me to meet a young couple at a junction near the Pines. As we sat in their tiny cabin, we smoked pot together. It was snowing hard, so they suggested we stay the night rather than try to drive. The guy, a young construction worker named Dave, and his young, pretty, blond wife suggested that if we liked pot, we would love LSD.

"What's LSD?" I asked them.

"Well," he answered, "it gets you ten times higher than pot. Want to try some?"

"Sure," I said. "Why not? We're snowed in and have nothing better to do."

With that, he produced a handful of sugar cubes and said, "Just take one and hold it in your mouth. You should feel something in about twenty minutes."

Slipping the sugar cube into my mouth, I felt it dissolve, totally unprepared for what happened next. LSD was a hundred times stronger than pot times ten! We are talking full-scale hallucination. With glue-like heaviness in my feet, I stumbled into the bathroom. Standing in front of the mirror, I watched as the skin peeled off my face until there was nothing left to my image but a skeleton and a hank of scraggly hair. Scary? Oh, my God. What was happening? I could not get out of that bathroom fast enough.

Coming back into the room, I breathlessly told them what I had seen.

"Oh, that's nothing," Dave said.

"Nothing?" I squealed. "I don't like this. How long does it take to wear off?"

Having never experienced full-scale hallucinations before, I wanted it to be over as quickly as possible. All I wanted to do was go home where I thought I would feel safer.

Dale and I walked out into the snow. Looking around me, it was as if Star Wars was hurling toward us with driving force in all the colors of the rainbow. Is it white that is all colors and black the absence of colors? The white snow around us glistened, flicked with rainbow light. It really was beautiful. However, after what seemed like several hours, I convinced Dale to drive us home. Getting there was a trip I will never forget. We seemed to pass the same curves again and again and again. Or it would seem as though we had arrived at a place before we got there. It is hard to explain, but LSD does that to you.

When we got home at about dawn, I walked into a room that was unfamiliar. The chairs were breathing. Unsettled by their pulsating, I went back outside, only to discover the trees were breathing too. In fact, everything was alive and breathing—and I could see it.

Venturing back into the bathroom, I saw a pool of blood on the floor. Bathrooms were not a good place to be on LSD.

Dale sat in one of the breathing chairs, staring at his hands. No guessing what he saw.

All in all, my entire first LSD trip was not a pleasant experience. It was positively terrifying, took about eight hours to wear off, and left me a different person. When it was over, I was so glad to be normal again. I was happy to go back to my routine. There's tranquility in routine. I started to write.

Dale disappeared again, and I spent days and nights with an old Royal typewriter in front of the fireplace. In between writing, I worked to clear a three-mile radius of the cabin looking for anything I could burn to keep warm. After exhausting all those possibilities, I burned most of our furniture.

After a week, Dale came back. Wherever he had been, he didn't say. But he was in an ugly mood and demanded money to go to Duce's Lodge. Emptying my purse, I thought, Just go away.

I was pondering running away, but where would I go? What about the children? I knew they were safe with Don and Dottie, but I wanted my children with me—and Dale was attached to Don and Dottie. As long as they knew where I was, Dale would also know.

One night as I was driving down the icy road, my brakes failed to work. It took me a few seconds of stomping on the brakes to realize nothing was going to stop me. I banked the car into the mountain, slowing it little by little by edging it along the mountainside, bringing it to a stop against the mountain just before a steep drop off. Gasping for breath and shaking, I got out of the car and looked at the damage. The entire side was crushed in, but I was alive. A car stopped behind me. An older man got out.

"Man!" he said. "At first, I thought you were crazy. Then I figured out what you were doing. Another few feet and you'd have been a goner."

He drove me to work where I called for a tow truck. Later, the tow truck driver told me that there was no brake fluid in the car. "Not a drop," he said.

Right then and there, I decided that Dale Patrick was trying to kill me. Several nights later, he nearly did. Tying me forcefully to the bed, with his mouth turned down and the lines in his face deeply creasing, wearing his "other self" evil mask, he gagged and raped me, beat me, hit me in the face and stomach, and punched me in the ribs. This was not sex play—it was dangerously close to homicide. He left the room several times; I don't know what he was doing, maybe drugs. He'd come back, rape me again, and beat me some more. When I was unconscious, he left.

Waking to silence in a freezing house, I listened carefully for a long while. When I heard nothing, I started working at freeing myself. When I was free, I got up carefully and quietly. The car was gone. As I passed by a mirror, my face, swollen beyond recognition, was something out of a horror film. I stumbled through the snow to a neighbor's cabin. They let me use their phone to call Dottie. Why didn't I call the police? I was afraid, shaking in my boots, and feared calling the police would ignite Dale into finishing me off.

Don and Dottie came and got me. Within a few hours, I had bathed and packed some clothing. I sat numbly in the back seat while Don went back to the cabin and gathered my stuff. They took me to their home. While driving with them, Dottie said something I will never forget, "Sometimes Don hits me. But I deserve it!"

Oh my god! Moving back in with them and in a safe routine again with my children, I went back to work at Estrada's. Don and Dottie didn't speak of Dale. Weird! They just went on with their life as if nothing had happened. Hazel had bought a cute little house in the Olive district and was at home with her cats and dogs. I usually saw her at dinner with Don and Dottie, who never went out, but Dottie was a good cook. The food was simple but good. The children were happy. Then I discovered I was pregnant with Dale's child.

For nine months, I worked through the entire pregnancy waiting tables in a fog. Then something wonderful happened. Hazel put up a down payment on a house for me and the children. She explained that with a growing family, we needed permanence, especially when Dale came home. I shuddered! The house was almost new, had three bedrooms and a large, fenced backyard. An initial $5,000 moved us in: Bo, Lisa and now Nancy. Delivered by Dr. Gray, Nancy was a blue-eyed, pale-haired, sweet-natured little thing. Gavin would do a chart for her, too, as she was also born cesarian. However, due to an unfortunate delay in her birth, she was not born at the time Gavin chose. There was an emergency and I waited in the hall on a gurney for two hours. Sadly, Nancy was not as fortunate as Lisa and has had a hard life.

Her grandmother, Dales' mom, also decided that she was Dr. Gray's child and treated her like a stepchild, heaping Lisa with tons of gifts and Nancy with nothing. At Nancy's birth, the nurses treated me with extra care too, saying "My, she looks just like Dr. Gray."

They could not have been more wrong. I wish that had been true, but Dr. Gray and I never even kissed. By then, everyone thought we were carrying on, except Dale Patrick Gleason. Thankfully, his mother had kept her thoughts to herself, or else I would have been beaten for sure.

We were together in a home. We had little furniture and less money, but I had my job at Estrada's and Don and Dottie babysat all the time. Their whole life was my children. I was as happy as I could be but still living under the cloud that Dale might return.

At Estrada's, I talked to Toby, who had become my close friend and confidant, and I finally told him what was going on. He had seen my bruised face when I returned, asking for my job back. Horrified, he told me I must file for divorce and get a restraining order. He called an attorney immediately and made an appointment, assuring me he would take care of the expenses. At about the same time, Dale called Hazel. He was in the Philippines and had shipped out again. She told him I was filing for divorce. He jumped ship, flew back to Fresno, and immediately went to an attorney to contest the divorce. His attorney called me and told me he would get me an annulment for free, that Dale was crazy and dangerous, that he would see to it that I got a restraining order, and that I should have someone to stand guard to protect me. As an added precaution, he would alert the police—all this from Dale's attorney. Finally, I was getting some help.

A friend I had met at the restaurant, an ex-marine, took up residence on my couch. He carried a gun. One day, while he was out, Dale appeared in my kitchen. I reached for the phone on the wall to call for help, but he beat me to it, ripped it off the wall, and wrapped the cord around my neck. He was strangling me with it when Jim, my ex-marine, came in. In two seconds, it was over. Dale was on the floor, and I was sent next door to call the police. That was the last time I saw Dale Patrick Gleason. I was free at last.

Chapter 15

Judge and the renaissance fair

Living in a tract house on Norwich Street with Bo, Lisa, and Nancy, they were spending more time at Don and Dottie's house than mine. It was summer, and Don and Dottie's swimming pool was a big draw for them as summer in Fresno could soar to 110 degrees. Besides, I was turning into a hippie, and Don and Dottie were concerned. Truth be told, I had already smoked pot and had dropped acid with their son, did not take drugs, and was a Baba follower into meditation and brown rice. Still a hippie at heart though, I was feeling freer and more alive than I ever had. Dale was gone out of my life forever, or so I hoped.

Having just turned twenty-five and quit my job at Estrada's, the Mexican restaurant, I had returned to working as a booking agent for musicians. My primary act was a solo guitar singer named Bob Rains. Handsome, charming, and talented, I had booked him at the Harrah's Club in Reno. He was my main breadwinner. I was also working with a local rock group that was bringing me no money.

As I basked in the Fresno, California sun, Cream's first album, "Fresh Cream" echoed in my head. Humming to the refrain, I felt quite free. Now recently divorced from my second husband and having dropped acid for the second time, I was feeling perfectly unfettered.

My neighbor and sometimes babysitter Lauren, with her light-brown shoulder-length hair and a beautiful creamy complexion was eighteen years old. She had decided to give up her virginity but could not decide which of her two boyfriends to give her "wild moment." She asked for my help.

Rocky was a charming, worldly Leo who was full of himself. Good-looking with a mane of dark hair and dazzling white teeth, he lived in San Francisco with his uncle on upper Powell. Lauren brought him to meet me. Laughing a lot, he bragged that he wanted to start a school for virgins and teach them how to please a man. Hmm—was I impressed? No. But he was cute.

However, when my babysitter introduced me to her boyfriend, Judge, that was a completely different story. Not good-looking in the classic sense, he had charisma coming out of his ears! Judge was wonderful in the true sense of the word; he filled me with wonder. With infinite energy, he played lead guitar in his band, wrote music, and flew an airplane. He could wire a house, build a door, or dismantle his red Porsche's entire engine, clean it, and put it back together, repaired. I watched him do this in my driveway one night. Also, he could cook, sew, and bake. Plus, he was a jeweler, dancer, skier, potter, and photographer. In short, there was nothing Judge could not do. Name something and this guy would excel in it quickly.

Falling in love at first sight was the last thing on my mind. It was only a matter of days until he found his way back to me alone, with Donovan's "Mellow Yellow" album tucked under his arm. Not much taller than me, Judge's long blond hair was pulled back to expose a solitary pierced ear. When he smiled, his moon face and pale-blue eyes crinkled so deeply that his eyes nearly disappeared. That was enough to instantly draw me in. I fell in love.

I became the agent for his band, traveled with them to gigs in distant cities, and took him to Los Angeles to meet my friend and songwriter Kelly Hodel.

A word about Kelly Hodel, Tamar's brother. He was as opposite from Tamar as one could get. He wasn't about the money—he was about life. A singer-songwriter, he wrote the famous song "Greenback Dollar Bill" with Hoyt Axton, but Hoyt took credit for it. Kelly didn't care. With dark hair and dark eyes, Kelly was as laid-back as they come.

Kelly lived in a large old house hidden from the street by an overgrown garden: a jungle of trees and fragrant plants with beaten paths that led through this forgotten piece of land in the heart of LA. All doors and windows were left open. Hammocks hung in the living room, and a soft, overstuffed chair cushioned against one wall. Old furniture from secondhand stores, scratched and worn but beautiful and comfortable, a painter's easel, musical instruments, and multicolored flowers planted in crockpots filled the room. The smell of musty books and floral scents from the garden filled the house. Previously, I had brought Bob Rains here to work on his arrangements with Kelly, and now I brought another musician, Judge.

Judge was my introduction to the spiritual leader, Babaji/Meher Baba, regular acid tripping, and a world of "having your cake and eating it too." We would talk about astrology, spiritual advancement, and Babaji for hours. Just being around him made me feel high. The three months I played at life with Judge were enchanting. While he cleaned the house, painted, and made something lovely for me to wear, exhausted by his inexhaustible energy, I often just slept.

Photo 12 - My psychedelic bedroom Judge painted

During one of these three blissful months, we drove to the Renaissance Pleasure Faire in Los Angeles in my beat-up '56 Ford station wagon. What begun in 1963 in Agoura, near Malibu, to create a "living history" for school children and their families, the Southern California Renaissance Faire was the first of many to sprout up throughout the country. At sun-up, we arrived at Kelly's house to find a dozen costumed people waiting for us. "Just in time," Kelly proclaimed, "we're going to the Renaissance Faire!"

Kelly supplied us with costumes. A Renaissance man, he did not need to add much to his usual costume-like attire; a leather loincloth, moccasins, homemade beads he tossed around his neck, and a headband to hold back his long blonde hair. With no idea where Kelly got the costumes, he found a weskit for me that laced tight up the front, coupled with a full-sleeved blouse and long cotton skirt. Judge was resplendent in tights, a leather jerkin, and a huge hat with a plume on it.

My crazy friend, Tamar, was traveling with us, along with her young daughter. Tamar, in her sixth month of pregnancy and third month of dropping acid every day, was so far removed from reality, she mumbled to herself as we led her by the hand. Her baby, incidentally, was born healthy, arriving in the middle of a rock concert at Griffith Park on a hot rock, while Tamar was receiving head. But I digress. Back to the Renaissance Pleasure Faire.

Limping from gas station to gas station, my station wagon needed repair at every stop. Charming the attendants into letting him use their tools, Judge would fix the car, including two flat tires. Our expectant mother, Tamar, also needed to stop frequently. We sang all the way, our throats sore but spirits high as we arrived at my friend's house in Los Angeles at six in the morning. The next morning, we abandoned my ailing vehicle and joined a caravan of costumed crazies headed to the faire, dropping acid on the way.

I have no idea what subsequent faires may have been like. That first one was so perfect, I was never tempted to go to another, knowing it could not possibly be as good.

Held on a beautiful, sunny spring day, the fields were lush with wildflowers and vast stretches of bright yellow-mustard bloom. I was high and in love. Dropping into the faire with that caravan of equally high, jubilant crazies was like turning the pages of a fairytale book. Leaving the noisy bustle of the Santa Anna Freeway far behind us, we parked in a dusty, straw-flecked parking lot overlooking the faire.

Trudging toward the festivities, from the hill we could see multi-colored tents, thatched huts, smoldering fires, and pennant flags flapping in the breeze below. People in period costumes were strolling about, and some sat playing instruments. Enchanting music floated up to us.

"That's really something," someone exclaimed.

Like Brigadoon, I thought.

Judge looked at me, grinned, and reaching for my hand, whispered, "Let's go," as he pulled me forward down the hill.

Coming closer, we were greeted by smiling people in Renaissance attire, dancers, jugglers, fortune tellers, craftsmen, and minstrels. Judge had his dobro along and would stop periodically to make music with a wandering minstrel. Tunneling through the dense fields of mustard flowers and tall weeds, we wandered about and crawled through handmade paths and rooms, meeting other crazies.

Toward the middle of the day, I borrowed a horse from a mounted policeman and went for a gallop through the hills. The horse was a lovely, spirited creature that enjoyed the gallop as much as I did.

Much later, when the afternoon shadows fell, Judge beat his guitar like a drum, scarring it forever, joining other drummers in a wild serenade to the setting sun.

Finally, as we walked across a swaying grass field, Judge made up a song from the rhythm of my hat swinging back and forth.

My point in bringing you into this part of my life, however, is not to wax poetic about Judge, although there was plenty there to admire. No, it is to take you back with me to a big turning point in my life, the day Damhara was born.

While we were wandering at the Faire looking at jewelry pots, bits of glass trinkets, and other "do-dads," Judge said, "I could make these things."

I replied, "Really? Let's open a shop!"

And we did.

CHAPTER 16

Damhara

Judge went right to work making jewelry, roach clips, and amulets. We borrowed a kiln and started making pottery—even I got into the clay and turned out little ceramic figurines. We found what seemed like an ideal location for a tiny shop. The rent was fifty dollars a month plus ten percent of the gross.

The woman who owned the space was a crazy old battle-axe, the spinster sister of one of the toughest superior court judges in town. It took some negotiation, but I finally managed to convince the old broad that she should rent her long-vacant shop to us—actually, she only saw me. Judge, with his long hair and pierced ear would have freaked her out, for sure. When I had the key in my possession and she had her first month's rent in hers, we moved in and went to work.

Judge painted giant psychedelic flowers over the walls in vivid colors. He also found an old showcase without any glass and made a spider web from embroidery thread for the front of it to display his jewelry. We let it be known that we were interested in consigning artists' works—and soon, the shop was ready to open. All we needed now was a name for our license.

Judge wanted to call it The Cosmic Junk Shop. Afraid of the connotation the words "junk" and "cosmic" might suggest to more conservative buyers in Fresno, I insisted that this was an artists' co-op. People were already starting to call it a psychedelic shop even before we opened. The last psychedelic shop in town had only lasted about a month before being busted holding a few pounds of grass. Not wanting that to happen to us, I decided when I opened the shop that I would refrain from using any drugs for my own protection. Also, I was ready to dry out for a while and encouraged Judge to do the same. But he had different ideas.

We named the shop Damhara, pronounced Dom-Har-Ah, because when we asked the Ouija board, "What has long hair and drives a red Porsche," it answered "Damhara."

Assuming the real meaning of Damhara was an Indian word meaning sun, I learned later that in the Kabbalah tradition it means originality and a desire to be different. True to its tradition, Damhara was different; It was becoming a head shop.

If I were prone to not being totally honest, I could say that Judge's intent to continue using drugs was behind why we split up. Or it was because we did not agree on how the business should be run. But the truth is, it was my jealousy. Soon after the shop was opened, Judge started seeing Lauren again. Flying into a jealous rage, fueled further by a bottle of Seagram's VO, a classic Canadian whiskey, and some reds, I smashed his pottery and cut his socks in two. I can be transparent about this now because I am a changed woman. Now when I feel hostile toward a rival, I just go quietly into the backyard and eat dirt.

SECTION 4

The hippie years

CHAPTER 17

Pete

Walking back from the store into the house on Norwich Street in Fresno in the summer of 1968, I found a ruffian stranger sitting in my living room. Casually slumped in a little legless black chair wearing surf trunks and a wrinkled t-shirt, his shoelaces were untied. Gangly and tall, with his knees drawn up under his chin, he looked like a giant praying mantis.

"I'm Carol, I live here. Who are you?" I queried.

The stranger smiled a goofy ear to ear smile, showing imperfect teeth. His cockeyed grin was disarming. "I'm Pete! I play guitar," he announced quite loudly, as if that would explain everything. "I live here now. When you walked in, a rainbow of colors was surrounding your head."

Blinking at him, I said a surprised, "Oh."

He explained. "I'm going to join the band. Hank picked me up in Santa Cruz, on the beach. He said you needed a guitar player, so here I am."

Pete stood up, his legs so long that they seemed to hinge and unhinge when he walked. Tall with stooped shoulders, he had a large nose with a hump on it, and one eye was larger than the other. A curious picture. We circled each other during the evening like two butterflies mating. Was he drooling?

Photo 13 – Pete

For some inexplicable reason, I was drawn to this odd looking man-child. After a while, I asked him, "Where do you intend to spend the night?"

Pete had not stopped smiling, and now he broke into laughter.

"I guess I'm going to stay with you!"

Smiling, I said, "Good."

But when we were at last in bed, we kissed once, and I felt a strange sensation of incest. Looking into his eyes, I felt as though I was kissing a relative.

I said softly, "This will never do." He agreed, so we just slept curled up in each other's arms and fell asleep. That confirmed my belief in reincarnation. We were past-life siblings. Pete stayed with me from that night on but moved into another room.

Since I knew Pete planned to play with the band in the park that Sunday, when the band was setting up, I was surprised to see that he was not there.

"Where's Pete?" I asked Mike.

"Your house."

"Why, what's happening? Don't you need him to play?"

"He's sick," Mike replied.

"Okay, he was fine this morning. I'll go get him."

Hustling back to the house, I found Pete curled up in natal position on the bed.

"What's wrong." I asked. "You sick?"

"Not really," he replied. "Just feeling down. Don't feel like playing guitar."

"But, Pete, everyone is depending on you. Without you, they can't play!"

I coaxed and prodded Pete until he got into the car and we were on our way to the park. Only then did he admit the real reason he had not wanted to play. Though he had great warmth and was an excellent guitar player, as it turned out, Pete was painfully shy and coming down from some bad drugs. At the last moment, he got cold feet.

"I am not going to do it."

"Oh yes, you are—you came here to do this, and you will do it!"

"Jeepers, Pete," said Mike when we arrived, relieved, "sure are glad you showed—we can't play without you. Hey man—let's turn these people onto some music! What-o-you say, Pete!"

Pete looked downcast but answered as he tuned his guitar, "I'll see what comes out." The day progressed and the crowd grew. Mike and Pete's band stopped after an hour set, collapsing from the heat on the lawn.

Pete played that day and felt better about himself, and for a makeshift band, they made some fine music. "Guess I could play after all," he said, grinning.

I had a lot more to deal with, not knowing much about the kind of drugs he had been doing. Speed? Or was it that kind of stuff I had been taking in San Francisco at Kaiser? Hmmm, well, both could make you depressed, so what Pete needed was a lot to keep his mind occupied.

Another group called Cream Puff materialized out of nowhere wanting to play. They took the stand, and we nodded our approval.

When Cream Puff stopped playing, Rick Chapman took the microphone to speak about the Indian prophet, avatar, and non-sectarian spiritual master, Meher Baba. Anti-LSD, Baba warned in his "God in a Pill" booklet that LSD was harmful physically, mentally, and spiritually, and that the so-called "spiritual experiences" generated by mind-altering drugs was superficial. "I have come not to teach but to awaken," Baba said, "I am the Divine Beloved who loves you more than you can love yourself." Some have called Baba a false prophet, but I cannot accept that because nothing Baba says conflicts with the teachings of Christ and speaks only of love.

That day, I heard Rick telling Pete, "The only thing you have to worry about is bread—I don't mean green stuff. I mean bread to sustain your body. Stay where you are and listen to your heart—it will tell you what to do."

I rejoined the two of them and we're all silent for a while. Then Pete turned to me and asked, "Is it okay if I stay with you for a while? I could help out in the shop."

The arts festival ended with people dancing on the grass. Joining in gleeful abandon, I breathed easy. The day had been a complete success.

A sweet fate dictated what followed: Pete joined the band that played at Damhara and became my roommate, my family, my constant companion, and a source of great joy. His cheerfulness was contagious. We lived together platonically, as brother and sister, and I maintained my sexual fast. I drew him from a deep, depressive well and he was a drink of water on a hot day for me. His unfailing good humor and positive attitude carried me through some of the most intense times of my life and eventually brought me to Santa Cruz.

In the meantime, Bo was spending some time with his dad and Grandmother Brown in Pleasanton. The girls were with Dottie for most of the summer, and I was having the time of my life running Damhara.

CHAPTER 18

Damhara and the youth center

On Sunday, July 16, 1967, Max, the coffeehouse owner next door, and I were surprised to see a newspaper article with the heading, DAMHARA GALLERY OFFERS PHILOSOPHY WITH ITS ART—and I quote:

Like a bit of Haight Ashbury, Fresno's newest art gallery, The Damhara, is at 857 Fern Street. A giant sun with a serene face and rays around resembling a woman's long hair blooms flower-like on the gallery's front window. On display inside are psychedelic posters, fanciful strings of hand-strung beads, handmade earrings, Indian headpieces, leather anklets with bells, spectacles with prisms for lenses, antique costume jewelry, sculptures, and paintings.

Photo 14 - Damhara

Either for want of space in the small shop or out of whimsy, some of the art is displayed on the ceiling. Not all the articles on display are for sale. Prominently displayed here and there are curious diamond-shaped pendants of bright colored wools, some with tassels hanging from the corners. Co-owner of the gallery Carol Flemming offered this explanation. "They are called God's Eyes, and because of their religious significance, may never be sold but only given away."

Gallery partner Forrest (Judge) Johnson, a local artist and McLane High School graduate who majored in electronics in Fresno state college, added, "This is not just a store. It is a love shop. We want to get the love movement started in Fresno. We want to get everybody smiling. Did you ever notice how most people walk around looking unhappy? The shop's idea originated in a desire to help a lot of kids who make things by providing a place to sell them and give persons who like beautiful tripped-out stuff an opportunity to buy at low prices. We want the kids to do the thing they do and to make some money doing it," concluded

Johnson, a clear-eyed earnest young man whose longish hair is confined with an Indian headband.

Since the gallery was opened June 16, Miss Flemming said she has been amazed by the number of artists who have called "with groovy merchandise." She said she now can take orders for handmade dresses that a local seamstress designs and makes. More than a gallery, and more than a store, the Damhara is a center for the distribution of anti-war and pro-Meher Baba printed materials.

Meher Baba, whose name means "compassionate father" is a non-sectarian spiritual master living in India. Among his more publicized messages is a booklet in which he states his anti-LSD views, *God in a Pill?* He warns that LSD is harmful physically, mentally, and spiritually, and that the so-called spiritual experience generated by taking mind-changing drugs are superficial and that continued use of LSD leads to madness or death. Miss Flemming admits that many of the Damhara habitués are former users of LSD but that they have rejected the drug and hope to convince other hippies to discontinue. Added Johnson, "The only real goal for anyone that makes any sense is God-Realization, but you can't get there with a pill. Stress on the word love, and slogans such as, 'Make Love Not War' are derived from the ultimate equation that God is Love, and that the only way to be a happy, good, and complete person is to be a loving one."

The gallery is causing considerable stir in the neighborhood—favorable and unfavorable. Staid shoppers in the area are disconcerted at the infiltration of the long-haired, bare-footed youth wearing Indian bands and bells. Miss Flemming, a petite and pretty young woman with long dark hair, said one woman asked her why she went around barefoot all the time. "I told her because it feels good. She seemed satisfied with that. Isn't that what most women like to do at home: get out of their girdles and take off their shoes?"

Johnson said a male visitor took umbrage at the fact the word "love" was plastered over everything. "I asked him, would you rather we wrote the word 'hate' everywhere? Why does that word love scare everybody much anyway?"

Earlier this week, passersby's were surprised to see a "happening" in front of the gallery. Some persons then visiting the Damhara decided Johnson's ancient convertible looked too drab and required some painting. So, they took up brushes and paints and covered it with swirls of bright colors and fanciful flowers. The flowers have become almost a symbol for hippies because they symbolized the beauties of creation, which are free to all. As one Haight Ashbury hippie commented, "Who was ever loused up by a flower?"

The Damhara also serves as a center for those interested in forming self-sufficient "tribal communities." The name Damhara was the answer given by an ouija board in reply to Miss Flemming's question as to the right name for the shop. She said she believes it is an Indian word referring to the sun. That is the reason for the sun painted on the front window. Among artists represented in the gallery are Larry Frank, Ken Feuerstein, Benita Funk, Marsha Boston, Randy Johnson, Chris Miller, Corky Vandersluis, Sammy Snell, Laudine Gome, Mike Clay, Jim Prime, and Marius.

After the article in the paper, Larry Frank should not have been surprised about why we teased him. He did not get the joke about his two first names but hung out so much I hired him. He worked afternoons in the shop so I could be home with my children. Larry Frank started hanging around Damhara, sitting on the sidewalk with the gang. I had noticed him because he looked like Judge, although at that time everybody seemed to look like Judge to me. My heart was aching. One of the girls in the gang said that Larry had sworn girls off for a year, so I immediately felt a bond with him.

A bashful, quiet guy, Larry never said much but was always there with a ready smile. He would sit on the curb, and when I went next door, he would say, "I'll watch the shop for you," and he did. If the phone rang, he wrote down messages, and if important, he would find me. One day, I asked him to paint a cardboard box and he did such a magnificent job, I suggested he paint cigar boxes and sell them. He made one that never sold, so we used it as a cash box.

One night as I was closing, Larry waited for me outside. When I came out, he shyly approached me and said how much he liked the shop. "It gives me a place to go," he said hesitantly. "Uh, I was wondering, uh, if I could . . . if I could work for you. You will not have to pay me anything. I just want to be a part of what is happening. All the kids think it's really something, and if I could be a part of it, I'd sure like that." What could I say? I said yes and gave him a key.

Larry came in and took over every day while I went home and took a shower. Fresno is a sweltering, sticky place in the summer, and our little shop was a hot box. He was dependable, honest, and eager to please. He spoke gently and his bashful smile charmed customers. Larry only made one mistake, but it was a beaut. We had taken some silver jewelry on consignment. He got the price tags mixed up and sold a twenty-five-dollar ring for a dollar and fifty cents. After that, we inventoried everything and started keeping books. That was Larry's idea—he was blown out by his folly.

We stayed open at night—and that is when I got a call from Max.

"Can't you do something about the crowd of kids out here? They are blocking my entrance and scaring my customers."

What? I called the shop. Larry answered. I asked, "What's going on down there?"

Larry answered, "Ah, Nothing much."

"But Max just called me. He says there's a crowd of kids."

Casually, Larry said, "Oh them! Yeah, there's a bunch of people just hanging out."

"Why?" I asked.

"I don't know," he answered honestly. "I think it's because they think we're cool."

"What do you mean, we're cool?" I probed.

"Well," Larry stuttered, "You know—the psychedelic sign!"

Going down to the shop that night there must have been seventy-five to a hundred kids just hanging out in front of it. They were sitting on the curve and standing in the street leaning against the building. It was like they were waiting for something to happen—but what? Why here?

Kids were starting to change: they were growing their hair long and going barefoot. Bell bottoms were popular, and beads were everywhere, circling necks, wrists, and ankles. There was a new revolution underway, and, at twenty-five years old, I was a part of it. Going into the street, unaware as usual, I talked to the kids, who ranged in age from sixteen to eighteen.

Photo 15 - Damhara and the group

"What are you doing here?" I asked.

The kids replied, "There is nothing else to do, nowhere to go, and your shop is cool." Most of them called it a head shop, but to me, it was an art gallery. We sold no drug paraphernalia, pipes, or papers—only posters and beads, and the walls and signs were defiantly psychedelic. But, in their minds, this was a head shop in Fresno. Now they did not have to go to the Haight in San Francisco.

★★★

It is true my manner of dressing had changed. under Judges' influence, I had quit wearing makeup. He insisted I looked better without lipstick—and while it was hard for me to give up, he insisted, and I gave in. My hair was now long and straight—and my favorite dress was a pair of wine-colored bellbottoms and a floral shirt, embellished of course, with beads. I had discarded my shoes as unnatural, needing to feel the earth under my feet.

One of the artists that came into Damhara had made me a couple of dresses of her own design. She wanted me to wear them to help her sell them. One was a sleeveless swirl of burgundy colors and so short, I could not bend over without showing my bottom. Rather than bending over, I did what is now called the "bunny-dip." Of course, wearing an anklet with a bell on it, you always knew where I was, and the beads I wore never came off, even in bed. Yeah, I guess I had turned into a hippie without even noticing.

Puzzled about what to do with the kids hanging around, I called Mayor Floyd Hyde, an agreeable little man with black hair, a round belly, and practiced smile. He readily agreed to meet with me concerning the kid problem but suggested we meet in the park. I made flyers, passed them out and posted them in neighborhood windows. All teens were invited to meet with the mayor concerning the lack of anything to do in Fresno. There were no teen clubs, YMCA, or skating rinks—nada, nothing.

Having become the spokesperson for these teenagers I was about to meet, one summer evening, the mayor and I, and about a hundred teens met in the park to figure out a plan. The meeting made good press for the mayor, and the kids were promised a place of their own. After the meeting, he took me aside and suggested that I look for a building that could house a teen center.

I thought to myself, Me? Why Me? Well, because I was there.

"These kids seem to have a connection with you and are causing you a problem." It was a good point. They were cluttering up my space, and I had called him. I agreed to look for a building, and meanwhile he would look for funding—and we parted with a plan. Doing as he directed, I found a building on the outskirts of town, the old Sun Maid Raisin building.

With nine offices, one vast central area great for bands, a huge area on the second floor big enough for dancing, and a sizeable basement, the old Sun Maid Raisin building was large enough to house several hundred kids. It had been vacant for a long time. Contacting the Sun Maid people, they agreed to rise to the cause and rented it to us for $500.

Recontacting Mayor Hyde, he invited some of the kids and me over for a swim. It was not hard to gather a few teens who wanted to swim in the mayor's pool. The mayor's house was in a quiet old neighborhood, a stately tutor. We rang the bell hesitantly and were welcomed by the mayor himself. Pete, Don, and Mary had come with me. We were shown through the house and to the backyard, where we sat by a pool built for swimmers. It had not ever been cleaned and was covered with green algae. All it needed to be a nature preserve was water lilies and fish—and maybe it did have fish! After introductions, Mayor Hyde began to speak, "Tell me what you've found and your plans."

Suddenly, I was in charge. Pete and I walked around the building and came up with some great ideas. The main room would be for dancing because it had lots of room. The three offices would be for the house bands to practice and store their instruments. One office would become the "Hip Job Co-op" where summer jobs could be found for teens. One would be turned into a free store where people could drop off their unneeded items and pick-up goods for free, something like the Goodwill but at no charge. The very front of the building would house Damhara—and the office next to it would be mine, with an art studio downstairs. With hopes of getting local artists to teach there, we would seek donations from local groups like the Lions Club and the Masons to buy art supplies. Upstairs would be a meditation and counseling room. I had already contacted a psychologist who had agreed to come in for free.

"Pretty ambitious plans," the mayor said. He smiled and added as he stood up, "I think we can arrange the funds and negotiate the rental contract. And we will have to put together a board of directors. You cannot function alone. However, you can help select them. I have a few good people in mind. Let's do this."

The meeting was over, and there were no milk and cookies. Oh well. As he walked us to the door, the mayor said, "I'll have my people call you." That was the last time I saw Mayor Hyde.

Pete was grinning ear to ear and gushed, "Boy, did you see that pool? Too bad we didn't bring our swimsuits."

Giggling because I did not have one, I said, "Maybe we could have skinny-dipped with the mayor?" The thought caused me to laugh out loud.

The people the mayor had call me to become my board of directors were outstanding and perfect in every way. Dr. Peal, the head of the Department of Psychiatry, was a rotund black man with the sweetest, happiest face I had ever seen. I would tease him about how he should dress in white robes with an olive wreath on his head, he was so kind and generous. That is just the way I saw him. But even though he sweat profusely in it, he always wore a distinguished, tailored wool suit with a white shirt and tie. Once we got to know each other better, he would come to my house and lie on my couch and tell me about his difficult cases, which we thought were funny.

Dr. Peal brought a young physiologist to our Board, Dr. Fox. He liked to be called Dr. Fox, but I called him Jim. He was studying the whole movement. I was still not aware that I was involved in a movement!

One day, Lou Trexler showed up at my door in uniform, with hat in hand. He was a sheriff. "Heard you could use some help," he said shyly.

"What?" I stammered, wondering what a police officer was doing on my doorstep.

"The youth center," he replied.

"Oh, of course," I said, relaxing. "Please come in."

Lou was easy to talk to and down to earth. Mellow, honest, and kind, we talked a while. He became my best friend on the board.

We decided we needed a clergy and, of course, artists. Where could we find them? No problem, I knew a local artist and thought we could get him to volunteer.

That is when I was struck with a thunderbolt idea. To raise money for rent, we asked the city to donate the building to us for a weekend to hold a dance. Proceeds from the dance would fund the building until the city could come up with the rent. The company that owned the building agreed—it had been sitting empty for two years—so after recruiting teenagers off the street to clean the building, we threw a dance party the very next night. Even Deputy Sheriff Lou Trexler from the local jail, donated commercial mops and a giant bucket. An easy-going, loveable man, Lou was also a pipe-smoking, bead-wearing hippie in his off-hours. He became an invaluable friend to me in my time of need.

We were moving fast. Within a week, we were in the Sun Maid Raisin building. The Damhara sign was hung, and kids were painting the windows with psychedelic sunflowers and peace signs. Judges' old band agreed to play for the opening and loved that they had their own band room with keys. Judge had left the band. A desk had magically appeared in my office, along with a table and chairs for our future board meetings. Damhara, the teen center, came together like magic. I was even given a salary of $500 a month by the city.

Our board worked to get financial backing from foundations and philanthropic organizations. One organization, the San Francisco Council of Churches, representing Glide Memorial Methodist Church sent a guy dressed in a button-down collar and black suit. However, as he swept into my office, his tongue-in-cheek smile, direct communication, and alert eyes belied his conservative attire. He promptly sat in lotus position on my couch and told me the Council of Churches had sent him to evaluate me.

"Let's talk. Tell me about your sex life," he said.

I laughed.

"Would you like to go to bed with me?" he continued.

"No, thank you. You don't turn me on," I answered, as we both laughed.

"You are a fine person. The Council of Churches will throw support your way," he said, handing me a $500 check.

CHAPTER 19

Two ciggys

Nervous about speaking at groups like the Lions Club, Chamber of Commerce, Rotary, Soroptimist, and Kiwanis, before speaking, I would say a small prayer and meditate that whatever came out of my mouth would be the right thing. I would usually sit on a desk or table because standing behind a podium made me uncomfortable. With no idea of what to say, I would cross my legs, take a deep breath, and launch into my speech.

At first, I was anxious, but became more self-assured as I progressed, and began to really enjoy telling club members about the work we were doing at Damhara—the kids with talent, the musicians, the artists, and the future executives. Kids there were finding their way, each one contributing the maximum ability of their skills to bring together a place of their own. I would share how Damhara had become a haven that was safe for their teenagers and ask them to contribute to us by supplying art supplies, paper, paint, and clay. Inviting them to come and visit Damhara so they could listen to their youngsters' music and see it for themselves, only a few came. Art supplies did arrive, and the room downstairs became alive with activity under the direction of a local artist who donated his time, Roger. Some fine sculptures emerged from those art sessions.

By this time, business had dropped off at the shop. People hardly bought anything anymore, but I did not care. Running Damhara, the teen center, kept me busy. Dr. Fox invited me to speak on his local talk show. He was nervous; I was not. Wearing a knee-length white shift, no jewelry, and my hair parted in the middle, falling straight, my feet were bare. I had not worn shoes since the first of summer, or underwear. What was the point? Summers in Fresno were blisteringly hot.

When Dr. Fox got into the car, he pulled out a pack of filtered cigarettes, shook one out, put it in his mouth, and then offered me one out of courtesy. Though a non-smoker, I took it. It seemed like a good idea at the time to light one up. Head rush!

We were greeted at the door of the TV studio like celebrities and asked if we wanted something to drink—a coffee, water, or soda. I opted for water. We sat in big leather chairs, waiting to be introduced. At the break, we were hustled into the glassed-in studio and had microphones strapped about our necks. Dr. Fox brought his cigarettes and placed them on a table in front of us. Someone rushed to get him a lighter and ashtray. There was a huge monitor on the wall in front of us. I could see myself on TV. Wow! Then the interview began, starting with, "Tonight, ladies and gentlemen, Miss Carol Flemming is the Hippie Movement leader in Fresno."

Expecting to be introduced as heading up a teen center, this introduction caught me by surprise. To calm down, I reached for a cigarette and lit it up. Not a good move. Then he introduced Dr. Fox as a physiologist for the young people at the controversial teen center run by Miss Flemming. Controversial? I was dumbfounded and lit another cigarette. Glancing at the monitor on the wall, I noticed two cigarettes hanging from my mouth. Then I went blank.

The interviewer asked me, "Miss Flemming, how did Damhara come about?"

Paralyzed by stage fright, I could not think or speak. He saw the glazed look on my face as I sat there with two cigarettes in my mouth, and the camera quickly swung to Dr. Fox.

"Dr. Fox," he asked, "what are the ages of the teens you see at Damhara?" He interviewed Dr. Fox for five minutes and then we went to commercial.

Dr. Fox turned to me and asked, "Perhaps some fresh air?" And once out the door, the blood rushed back into my head. Having not done my meditation or prayer before the interview, I was a wreck. I managed to pull myself together, and Dr. Fox carried the remainder of the show.

Arriving home, Pete was laughing. But when he saw how distressed I was, he put a hand on my shoulder and said, "It's all right, kid! You did your best." Then he started laughing again. People do chain-smoke, but doing it two at a time during an on-camera interview—what was I thinking? I had made a fool out of myself. All I can do now is laugh.

Damhara had become a living, breathing entity alive with activity and good vibes. Each night there was live music provided by one of five house bands for five-hundred kids. Bands were not hard to find as musicians popped out of the walls—and they were good, too. I danced every night until midnight. I had given up all drugs and become a Baba follower. And as Lou said it, I would need to be like Caesar's wife, beyond reproach, to run a teen center.

The kids embodied innocence: fun, open, and loving. They became my extended family. Also, I was getting the teen life that I never had—and Damhara was a safe place for them. Though I caught a lot of blame for it, I never hid a runaway child or helped anyone get out of town. What these kids' parents failed to see were the reasons why their children ran away. Sometimes parents called me asking how to tell if their kid was using drugs. My reply was simply, "Ask them." Plain and simple: communicate with them. Honestly, I can only remember one parent who had it together with their kid.

Several people lived with me that summer in Fresno, including eighteen-year-old Nancy. Petite and blond, she had chosen where to live by putting her finger on a map of the states with her eyes shut. Fresno had fallen under her index finger, so she arrived there with a wooden crate filled with clothes and a few plastic dishes. Initially, she had moved to "the bat cave," a communal living house in the country funded by dope. This was fine until the "daddy dope dealer" of the house decided to "tame the Hell's Angels" with LSD. However, when the bikers arrived, they were loaded on reds and beer, and demanded that "daddy" turn over the women at the house to them. A fight ensued, prompting the beating of one girl, and kidnapping of another. When Nancy tearfully told me this story, feeling removed enough from the scene to feel safe, I took her in and notified the police. They located the missing girl, who had been thrown on the back of a motorcycle. Hells Angels traveling on the road were easy to spot, so on the road to Oakland, California, the kidnapped girl was located.

CHAPTER 20

Summer of love

Becoming a full-time shopkeeper, I made trips to San Francisco to the Haight Ashbury to buy beads and posters to sell in Damhara.

It was 1969, the Summer of Love, Woodstock and San Francisco were abuzz with change. Despite the fact my heart still ached for Judge, times were good. By example, he had taught me so much. I was learning to be cheerfully positive, and from him, had inherited a tremendous amount of spiritual power. My thinking had changed. I loved Damhara and the people who frequented the shop. It had become a hangout for college students and teenagers. The coffeehouse next door was run by a liberal, elderly Jew, named Max, who lived through the Holocaust. He had seen a lot of life and talking with him was enjoyable. Neither of us were ready for what happened next.

Digressing, let me tell you about an old pilot from the coffee shop. His name was Ace (of course), and I expressed interest in flying. Within the hour, we were in a two-seater on the runway at the Fresno Airport. This was my first time on a small plane, and I loved it up.

We circled the airport, and suddenly Ace shouted into his microphone, "Mayday, Mayday!" Well, it was my first time in a small plane, but I was no dummy and knew we were in trouble. I wasn't really scared, only more interested. We circled the airport again and landed perfectly smoothly.

Then and only then did I ask what happened.

White as a sheet, Ace said sparingly, "We lost engine power and had to glide in."

"Oh," I replied, "guess you are a good pilot."

As he squared his shoulders and regained some color, he said, "Yes, I am—that's why they call me Ace."

Back to Damhara. Some nights there were so many kids on the sidewalk there that it looked like a mob from an Italian movie. One night I had to ask some of them to leave the shop so that potential customers could get in.

"Please," I pleaded. "I have to eat—allow me to make a living!" They left, only to return with a hamburger and a Coke for me. Ye gads! I was moved. I could not help but love these kids.

One day a boy of around fifteen came in and gave me a key ring with a peace sign on it. "Here," he mumbled apologetically. "I stole this from you yesterday. I just could not keep it."

That was the only incident of theft we ever had. I felt perfectly comfortable leaving the shop unattended to go next door for a Coke or sandwich. If someone wanted me, they would find me or leave money on the counter.

CHAPTER 21

Fun with Pete and Carol

It was mid-summer and HOT! You could cook an egg on the sidewalk. A Saturday night, the fair was in full swing, and Harvey and Darrel were going to take us to the fair. Harvey and Darrel had moved in with us for my protection. They were bunking in Pete's room, aka Bo's room, but Bo was on vacation with his father. It became late and they did not show up.

"Guess they went without us," Pete said, shrugging his shoulders. Looking down his nose at his hands, he then looked up with a cockeyed grin and said, "Boy, would they be surprised if they came back, and everything was different!"

"Like what?" I asked, taking the bait.

"Well," he said grinning mischievously. "We could glue all the furniture to the ceiling and turn the house upside down. When they come in, everything would be upside down, and they would be really confused."

"Great idea," I agreed. "But how are we going to do it?"

"No, wait," Pete said in a loud voice, pointing his finger for emphasis. "I've got a better idea. Let's move out, and the whole house will be empty when they return."

Smirking, we spent the next four hours moving all the furniture into the backyard. Every bit of it. We were on a mission. We passed each other hauling lamps and chairs, grinning at each other. We were having fun. Soon the house was completely empty, and you could hear our feet echoing on the hardwood floors. When it was completely empty, we turned on the overhead lights and waited.

It was eleven before the boys came in. Pete and I hid in the kitchen and listened. As the guys moved about the house, we crept about, staying out of sight, covering our mouths with our hands to keep from laughing out loud. Pete's eyes sparkled with merry mischief.

Shocked, Harvey called out, "What the fuck, Darrel! Are we in the right house?"

Darrel answered, stunned, "It's empty. What happened? They are gone! Harvey, are we in the right house?"

They had not moved from the doorway. Pete's body was starting to convulse with laughter. There was silence. We figured they must have stepped outside. Then we heard their footsteps coming toward the kitchen. We moved into the bedroom.

"Yeah, it's the right house," Darrel said. "Harvey, the stoves and fridge are still here. I wonder if there is any food—I'm hungry."

Answering Harvey said, "You ate six corn dogs. Darrel, do you suppose they took the food?"

As I looked at Pete, his eyes widened as he looked back at me, his hand over his mouth. His eyes said: *damn, we forgot to clean out the fridge—there's not much there anyway.*

Frustrated Harvey said, "We've got to find them."

He moved into the bedroom. We moved into the hall.

Calling out to Darrel, Harvey says, "It's empty in here, too!"

Crouched in the dark, I can imagine his face puzzling, like a dog that misplaced his bone. Darrel joins Harvey as they move to the next room.

Pete and I creep into the living room as Harvey, stupefied, says, "Empty! Gone!"

Unable to contain our mirth, Pete and I are now rolling on the floor, which is where they find us. Then we burst into riotous laughter. Tears are running down Pete's face, he is laughing so hard. I am gasping for air. Harvey and Darrel stand over us.

"Ah. You guys are crazy! How did you do that? Where is the furniture? We thought . . . never mind what we thought," Darrel said, still slightly dazed.

"Yeah, you didn't think anything because you didn't know what to think . . . we got you!" Pete said.

Then they start to laugh too, sitting on the hardwood floor laughing like hyenas.

"Now, where are we going to sleep?" Harvey asked.

I rolled over and sat up.

Pete said, "Hey, I've got an idea. Let's move the house to the front yard. We can sleep out there."

"You're crazy," Harvey said, "I'm not sleeping in the front yard. There could be a drive-by." Yeah. After a piece in last Sunday's paper, we had people driving by our house, sightseeing like at Christmas when a block is decorated with candy canes and lit up Santa scenes. Except, these sight-seekers were looking for hippies—us!

"Okay, I'm in," I said, and the boys helped me move two double beds to the front yard, and we set up a bedroom scene: two beds made up with a bedside table with a lamp in between. Pete took great pleasure in hanging picture frames in the shrubbery and putting books on the table.

"It's that special touch," he said, grinning. We put our pajamas on and climbed into bed.

When the sun rose in the morning, the neighbors had a sight to behold. Mr. Brown came out of his house, looked at us, scratched his head, picked up his Sunday paper, and went back in. It was not long before the procession of cars began . . . honest! People and their children were driving by to see the hippies and what a show we gave them!

Pete and I spent the entire day entertaining the sight-seekers without antics. We made our bed and brought out chairs and read! We also ate our lunch outside on the kitchen table. Pete insisted on eating with his hands and would stuff his mouth when the cars slowed down to gawk. Darrell and Harvey stayed out of sight and spent the day in the house hiding. Friends came over and gathered outside on the grass, played music, and genuinely enjoyed themselves.

That night we moved the furniture back inside and put the house back together. A lot of fun was had for free, but it didn't stop there. The next Sunday, traffic backed up on our block again as people cruised by after church to look at the hippies. This time Pete had another idea. The front of the house had a picture window, and he moved the coffee table over to front of the window and ordered me to work the drapes. He would peer out between the drapes, and when a car was almost in front of the house, I was to open the drapes, and Pete would stand on the table and play statue. After a while, he got bored with playing statue and would tap dance. I would open the drape. He would tap dance and then take a bow. Then I would close the drapes, wait for the next car, and do it again. After a while, Pete said, "Your turn," and I would get on the table and do a little ballet while Pete worked the drapes. We got positively creative with our little shows.

CHAPTER 22

Arresting development

Asleep on my bed and alone in the house, I heard a knock on my door. On that sweltering summer day, only half awake, I opened the door to find two police officers at my door.

"Miss Flemming?" the woman officer sternly asked.

"Yes," I answered sleepily, puzzled.

"You're under arrest," she said.

"What? Why?" I asked, wondering for a half-second if I was dreaming.

"Never mind, just come with us," the imposing male officer with her instructed.

"I just woke up," I said, "let me wash my face."

Following me into the bathroom, the woman police officer watched as I washed my face, brushed my hair, and glanced in the mirror at my stunned reflection. Did she think I had planned to make my "getaway" through the bathroom window? Why? Straddled in the doorway and steely-eyed, she seemed to take great pleasure in her work.

Before leaving the house, I scribbled a note that read, "Help! I'm in jail."

Riding downtown in the back of their police car, I was puzzled why I was being arrested.

Protesting, I said, "You can't arrest me without telling me why!"

Grinning maniacally, the woman police officer replied, "I just did. All I know is we have order to pick you up signed by Judge Unjust."

Then I smelled a rat. Judge Unjust was the brother of my landlady when I'd first opened Damhara in the small shop. He had even prepared the eviction notice for her.

By the time I heard the jail steel door clang and was being booked, I was panicking and kept repeating that I wanted to make a phone call. After a long, ignored wait, I called Damhara and told one of the kids that I was in jail, did not know why, and to alert the board that their fearless leader was in the slammer. Given a faded-green flour sack to wear, I was shown to a cell.

Sitting in the cell, I surveyed my new surroundings. Opaque windows let light in, but I could not see out. When the six other women in my cell asked why I was there, all I could do is shake my head and say, "I have no idea."

"Oh, yeah. I'll bet," said a three-hundred-pound woman who plopped down beside me on a bench. Wearing her dress dropped to her waist, fifty pounds of flesh spilled over a dirty white bra.

A young, pregnant Chicano girl was lying on a dirty, bare, stained mattress. She looked at me and said comfortingly, looking at her hands, "Scared? I was scared too. I still don't believe I am here. I've been here three months for shoplifting."

Swallowing hard, I screamed inside. This could not be real! Then my jailer came to the bars, and calling out my name said, "You're free to go."

Apparently, Lou, my deputy sheriff friend at the jail, had heard they were bringing me in and had rushed to bail me out. I threw my arms around him.

"Do you know why they arrested me?"

"They wouldn't tell me," he said quietly. "Apparently there is a county ordinance about having a cover on your trash burning barrel and you did not have one."

"Sincerely?" I lamented, "I don't even use the barrel. This is ridiculous."

"That's not the point," he answered. "The point is, the district attorney wants you locked up and will get you on anything he can. Why do you think you were picked up on Friday after four o'clock? The courts are closed. You are lucky I heard that they were bringing you in. I had to call the judge at home to set bail for you."

The next time I was arrested, it was for not having a dog license despite the fact I did not own a dog. Nancy had brought a dog home with her and the next day a dog catcher chased it, asking if it was mine. I said, "No, but it is sort-of staying at my house." He shoved a paper at me to sign. Shortly after, Nancy moved to Berkeley and took the dog with her. When I was sent a notice to appear regarding "my dog," I telephoned and said I did not have a dog and forgot about the matter.

But apparently, Mr. Brown, my two-hundred-plus pound, strawberry-complexioned neighbor, had taken to spying on me and turned me in. Though I had never done anything to him, he inexplicably hated me and Pete. While watering his lawn, Mr. Brown would call us names as we came and went. "Long-haired queer," he'd shout at Pete, to which Pete would throw his arms open wide and shout back, "I love you, Mr. Brown!" Blood rising into his face, Mr. Brown would yell back, "Dirty horse's ass hippie!" Brown made a threat one day to call my landlord, only to find out I owned the house.

To my dismay, I went to jail again. This time, I bailed out and went to court, pleading not guilty and asking for a jury trial.

Nancy was unable to come from Berkeley to testify on my behalf—and my neighbor testified against me, but failed to make his point when the judge asked him if he had ever seen me call, feed, or pet the dog in any way that gave the impression it was my pet. He told the truth—he had not. After three days of deliberation, lots of State of California money, and a big waste of my time, I was found not guilty of owning a dog without a license.

The following day, a stranger knocked on my door. Identifying herself as Carol, she said, "We have something in common. I own a small neighborhood nightclub downtown. I, too, am being harassed by the district attorney, but I have the goods on him."

"Ah," I replied, feeling a glimmer of hope. "Come in."

Anxious to spill her tale, she stammered, "I read about you in the paper and have been following your adventures. I think I can help you."

When I looked puzzled, she blurted out, "Don't you know why he hates you? He is a *faggot* and hates you because you are a woman and surrounded by young boys, where he would like to be. He cruises the Greyhound bus depot, honey. Hey, listen . . . the place I own is a gay joint, so that is how I know. The son-of-a-bitch . . . I was ripped off by a couple of gays and tried to press charges and the DA protected them. I lost my case. He laughed at me. It happened several times. I got fed up and set him up. I have pictures of him in action. He will not bother me again. Next time you need to deal with him, give me a call. I'll come sit beside you and watch the cocksucker turn green. He'll leave you alone after that."

Dumbfounded, my mouth dropped open—I could hardly believe my ears.

Carol reached over and patted my knee.

"I don't have anything against gay people, honey," she oozed, "but this bastard is sleazy, and only prosecutes those he has a grudge against. He is not fair or honest. And I'll tell you something else. He smokes dope and pops pills, better believe it." She stood up to head toward the door. "Do you want to see the photos?"

"Heavens, no." I answered.

"Okay then," she replied. "I'll be running along. Just remember if you need me . . ."

CHAPTER 23

There goes the neighborhood

One day I received a phone call from John, a young man I knew through Jaycees, who was mildly amused by the notoriety I had been receiving in the press. He told me that Mr. Brown was trying to form a vigilante group to run me out of town. As he asked me if there was any reason for Brown's animosity toward me, suggesting an unhappy affair.

"You must be kidding!" I exclaimed, nearly falling over with laughter at the suggestion. "I wouldn't have him at the end of a stick. Have you seen him? Really . . . he has a wife and family. And besides, he's fat and ugly . . . jeez!"

Another day, I came home to find a building inspector with a clipboard in my backyard. The man said he had received a complaint from Brown that I had removed the glass from a window and installed stained glass in its place.

"Yes, it is true. Is that against the law or do I need a permit to install stained glass in my home?" I queried.

"No," he said, obviously puzzled by the complaint. "It's just that we got a call. What would that matter to your neighbor?"

"Maybe it's because he can't see into my house that way if he's standing on his table trying to spy on me," I suggested wryly.

John suggested I listen on the extension while he phoned Brown. John said no matter what Brown said, to stay completely quiet. Sputtering, Brown told John that I was a terrible woman and should be run out of the community.

"Why?" John asked, but Mr. Brown would not be specific.

Coaxing him, John said, "Come on, Mr. Brown. You can tell me. I am a man and you told me you knew something about this woman. As a concerned citizen, I need to know."

"My wife and children are here, and it is too terrible to say in front of them," Brown sputtered, at which John suggested he go into another room and shut the door to talk with him.

"Now you've got me curious," John persisted. "You are trying to form a group to have this woman ousted and you know something. You should share it with me if I am going to be a part of it." Brown excused himself and went to another phone.

As he spoke, I could feel myself beginning to fume. "The things I've seen with my own eyes are indescribable," he muttered. "I'm embarrassed to repeat them." Then taking a deep breath, he salaciously drawled, "I've seen her in the backyard with a whole parcel of men swimming nude in her swimming pool. Naked, all of them naked! And doing things to each other, not just kissin' and huggin' like normal people," his voice rising in tone like an adolescent boy. "and . . . she was suckin' their dongs, and they were doin' it all over the yard, around the pool, in the flowerbeds, in all different positions. I tell you, sir, it was terrible!"

During this monologue of boldface lies, my eyes got wider and wider as I slid down my chair gasping, until at last I had to put the phone down.

John agreed if that was true, something had to be done—and hung up the phone.

As we looked at each other, I said to John, "That's completely untrue."

John interrupted me and said, "I know. The man apparently has fantasies about you."

"My God," I moaned, "the man's sick! I don't even have a swimming pool."

CHAPTER 24

Horror in wing-tip shoes

Late one night, when everyone was asleep, including me, I heard a knock on the door. No one else stirred, so I got up and went to the door in my birthday suit, which was how I slept. Something did not feel right. The slide lock was on. Cracking the door open, I saw two men standing there. Peering out at them through the cracked door, I could see they looked straight, with short haircuts.

"Yes?" I said, sleepily.

"We were told we could crash here," one of them said.

"Who told you that?" I asked.

"Someone at the bowling alley," the other replied.

Puzzled because I did not bowl, did not know anyone at the bowling alley, and didn't even know where it was. Still not yet awake or thinking clearly, I muttered, "You can sleep in the car. I'll give you blankets."

As I turned toward the linen closet, that is when my alarm went off. *DANGER*, it screamed. *CLING. CLING. CLING.*

Turning to go back to the front door to tell them no, it was too late. One of them had slipped his hand inside the door and unlatched the safety lock. They were both inside standing near the front door. Wearing black pants and jackets with black wing-tipped shoes, their vibes unfriendly. These were not hippies.

"We're going to have a little fun now . . . we're going to have sex with you," one of them sneered.

Though deeply alarmed, I didn't scream or run because I did not want to put Pete or the children in danger, who were asleep in the next room.

"I do not think that is a good idea," I said warily.

"Shut up, we know there are children in the house. You don't want them hurt, do you?" one said menacingly.

Starting to go into shock from the horrible realization of what was about to happen, I mutely nodded my head no.

As one of them pushed me toward the bedroom, the front bedroom where Nancy and Lisa were asleep, I was terrified. Throwing me to the carpeted floor in my babies' room while they slept in their cribs, I whispered hysterically, "shhhh . . . " Unzipping his pants, he threw himself on me, and entered me as I lay there muffled, crying silently, pushing up and down on me as though he was doing pushups.

"Move, dammit," he hissed at me. How could I move? I was frozen with fear.

After a few moments, he got off me and the other one took his place. I was terrified that one of the girls would wake up or that Pete would wander out sleepy-eyed and they would hurt him.

When the second one was through with me, he grabbed me by the hair and pulled me into the kitchen. The other one was standing there, looking around as though he was trying to decide what to do with me next.

As he let me go, I noticed there was a knife in the sink. I thought about grabbing it, but then what? I could stab one but then the other would attack and likely kill me—and the girls and Pete. Two large men against one small woman was not good odds.

Saying nothing, they were just looking around. Did they want to steal something or were they deciding whether to kill me? Edging toward the back door, I had no idea. When I got my hand on the handle behind my back, I turned it ever so slowly—and, once the door was open, flung myself through it in a dead run, never looking back once. I have always been a good runner, but that night I sprouted wings—I flew like the wind, naked as a jay bird, without knowing if they were chasing me. Running around the corner to my neighbor's house because I knew it would be unlocked, I leaped in, and bolting the door behind me, screamed for help. Joy and Tommy burst from their bedroom and found me in their kitchen, naked and shaking.

"What happened?" they asked alarmingly in unison.

"I was raped!" I exclaimed, in a flood of tears. "Someone please, call the police!"

Tommy immediately called the police, grabbed his gun, and headed to my house while Joy wrapped my shaking body in a bathrobe. Minutes later, Tommy returned, and to my relief said that there was no one there but sleeping children and Pete, and that he had waked no one.

Joy poured me a shot of vodka and said, "Here, drink this," and poured herself one too. We stood in the kitchen waiting for the police to come.

In about an hour, the police showed up. After I recounted what happened, the two of them took a routine report, and then left. They didn't offer to take me to the hospital—they just wrote in their notebooks and left.

The next day when I told Pete what had happened, he was at first dumbfounded and then seething with anger. Picking up the phone, he called Lou Trexler, who came over immediately, and called the sheriff's department. Discovering no report had been made, Lou's brow furrowed. He hung up and was silent for a while. Then he turned to me.

"What did the men look like?"

"They wore black pants, jackets, and wing-tipped shoes," I said somberly.

Lou shook his head. Without hesitation, he said, "DA's men. Carol, I don't know why but the DA is out to get you—and for your own good, I think you should leave town."

A slow tear rolled down Pete's cheek. White with shock and clenching his hands, he said, "Why? Carol has done nothing to hurt anyone. I don't understand."

Shaking his head, Lou answered, "I don't get it either, but something is terribly wrong, and I'm concerned for Carol's well-being."

Turning toward me, he added, "I can take you down to the police department and you can look at mug shots, but I don't think you will find them there. I think this was meant to hurt, humiliate, and scare you. Lord knows what will come next."

My voice cracking slightly, I answered, "Let me think about it."

Getting up, Lou hugged me and said, "I'm so sorry. You are too good. This should not have happened to you." As he left, he added, "I promise to look in on you."

Pete and I went about our business, but nothing was the same.

CHAPTER 25

End of era

The article began: "Mayor Floyd H. Hyde today called off a session with his youth advisory committee on the future of a youth center because several adult opponents of the center refused to leave his office."

As I read further, I learned the mayor had deliberated for an hour with half a dozen men and women who objected to Damhara. A Mrs. Muriel Jefferys, the most vocal opponent, had complained, "I don't want agitators to come from San Francisco and start a hippie house. All hippies are the same." When Mayor Hyde had asked her what a hippie was, she had retorted, "That's a ridiculous question."

Hyde had noted that he wanted to help young people, not run them out of town. "Most of them are our children," he had said. "I do not want to encourage a hippie house. We are not going to condone any lawlessness. I am the mayor for everybody, not just those who cut their hair like I do."

When Dr. Peal had called Damhara an asset a woman opponent had gasped.

That Sunday night, Lou came by the house, dragging his chin on the ground. His eyes met mine dolefully, and then shifted back to the ground.

"What's the matter, Lou?" I asked softly.

"There is a meeting of the board tomorrow morning. You'll know then." He turned and left, leaving me with a sense of foreboding. Pete and I looked at each other silently as he raised his eyebrows in a quizzical way.

Dancing Don raced in. "Are you okay, Flemming?" he spouted. Then Harvey rushed in, followed by Learch, one of the teens that hung around Damhara. Kissing my cheek, they joined the table. Five of us sat in silence. Harvey spoke first, "I was at the coffeehouse when I got the word. It spread like wildfire."

Pete turned to me and asked, "Shall we ask them or wait until tomorrow?"

Learch searched my face, and looked at Harvey, asking, "You mean they don't know?"

Pete threw his hands up and said, "Alright man, what's happening?"

Harvey, his head bowed with his hands folded on the table, said quietly, "The board held a secret meeting tonight and shut down Damhara. They fired you. Damhara is dead.

As it turned out, my "grand theft conviction," the one I had generously taken to protect Tamar, was central to my undoing. Admitting to condoning the act and receiving the merchandise though it had not truly been my crime, marked me as a criminal. Also, my friend, Dias, thinking my fence gave him privacy, had unwittingly sunbathed nude in my backyard. Welcoming young people and traveling guests into my home, my occasional use of "four letter words," and the fact I was an ex-drug user also made me undesirable. In testimony, even though Pete said that Damhara had helped him get off drugs and given him direction, District Attorney Daly countered with the claim that "she not only associates with young people who use narcotics, but with people who deal in narcotics." Plus, a ridiculous "labor violation" that occurred due to having given babysitting money to a friend to give to my babysitter which was never delivered, was cited. Also, my having had to appear in court for a trumped-up charge of stealing an art object from Damhara was mentioned. That incident had been coupled with the day someone I did not know came into Damhara and gave me a chunk of hash. Instinctively, I had flushed it down the toilet seconds before drug enforcement people arrived to search Damhara for drugs. It had clearly been a setup. Ironically, my generosity in housing homeless teenagers was also an issue.

The truth was the kids who frequented Damhara had goals, values, and morals. I was proud of them. All they needed was a little time to find out who they were—and Damhara gave them a place to do it. They also trusted me. Mayor Hyde and the ministers of several Fresno churches said it was a vital place to reach out to alienated youth. But the voices of Attorney Daly, City Councilman Elvin Bell, and two conservative Fresno radio hosts boomed louder. They presented it as a den of iniquity where curious teenagers were contaminated by the "psychedelic generation." Ultimately, their harmful words had impact. The final straw was that Richard had told the board that I was pregnant with his baby and to avoid scandal, they had decided to shut us down. Months later, when it became clear I was not pregnant, it dawned on a few board members that Richard had lied. Several asked for forgiveness but by then, it was too late.

I felt like I had been hit in the stomach with a basketball. Damhara was my world—it had been my baby, born of love. A secret meeting had been held without including me or the kids, shut down by the very people I had chosen, my board of directors. Why? It would be months before I would learn the details of what happened that night.

The next morning, Dancing Don and I cut twelve pink roses and took them to Damhara. At the board meeting, I handed each member a pink rose and a Meher Baba card that read, "Don't worry, be happy. For I am the divine beloved who loves you more than you can ever love yourself." The benevolent Baba smiling from the card reminded me that Damhara would never be dead. It lives to this day in the hearts of those who believed in it.

SECTION 5

Santa Cruz

CHAPTER 26

The house on Bixby street

It was a perfect day, the sky a summer blue over the glistening sea. Sitting in my car overlooking Pleasure Point, I could hear the murmur of happy voices from the beach below as I pondered my dilemma. Though I had been house hunting for two days, nothing had turned up. It was time to go back to Fresno.

"Oh well," I sighed to myself, "if God had wanted me to live here, I would have found a house . . . guess not!"

As I started my car and headed back toward Ocean Street and the highway towards home, so deep in thought, I missed Ocean Street. Instead, I turned on to the next street, Bixby Street. As I realized what I had done, I looked up to my right and saw a "For rent" sign on a ramshackle two-story Victorian home.

To say the house was neglected would be an understatement. Its paint was crumbling and weather-beaten into a yellowish gray. Its shabby bottom windows were boarded up, and dingy bay windows faced two scraggly, aged orange trees on a patch of forgotten lawn. There were scruffy overgrown rose bushes on the house's side with a narrow driveway leading to a wood frame single garage. I halted the car at the curb, jumped out, and ran up the stairs, two at a time, so that I could tear the sign off the door.

The realtor was located just around the corner, and it was still just before five o'clock. There in a flash, I was so excited, I blurted out to him, "How much for the Victorian on Bixby Street?"

He answered, "One hundred dollars."

It just so happened that I had one hundred dollars As I reached in my purse and pulled out the cash, I thrusted it at him. "I'll take it!"

"Not so fast," he cautioned me, "you haven't even seen the inside."

"I don't care," I repeated firmly, "I'll take it!"

"No," he replied, "I won't rent it to you until you've looked around and seen the inside."

"Okay," I said obligingly, taking the key he handed to me.

Dashing back down the stairs and around the corner, I fit the key in the lock and opened the door to my new home. There was no longer any question in my mind. God wanted me in Santa Cruz.

In a small entry hall, two massive doors opened into a front room with high ceilings and bay windows. Another door led to a second room containing a small Victorian fireplace with a huge, ugly, metal heater in front of it. As I rushed through that room, I noticed that tall windows looked directly into the neighbor's house. Curiously, I wondered who my neighbors would be.

One of the bedrooms opened into a bathroom with a clawfoot bathtub. A door on the far side of the bathroom led into another bedroom on the other side. I thought, Only one bathroom. I will make do.

With high ceilings like the rest of the house, the kitchen included a good-sized gas range, no refrigerator, and a pantry that overlooked a pint-sized backyard. As I looked through more long windows from the kitchen into the neighbor's backyard, I noticed abundant orchids flourishing there. Musing to myself, I thought, Maybe they grow them commercially.

Mangling the corner yard, a large, overgrown tree dripped with lemons the size of ostrich eggs. Amassed garbage was piled high in the middle of the yard. Apparently, the previous tenants had not wasted money on the garbage disposal. That smelly heap needed to be taken care of right away.

Since downstairs was boarded up, I had not bothered to look at it. Regardless, I wanted this house badly. As quickly as possible, I rushed back to the realtor before he could change his mind. I signed a month-to-month agreement and gave him the money. He asked no questions, and neither did I as he handed me the key. I went back to Fresno to rent my home and pack, thanking God on the way. Headed toward a new life, I had always wanted a Victorian to play with—and now I had one only a block from the river's mouth and the beach.

Bo was not as happy as I was about moving. Leaving friends is the end of the world to a sixth grader. Normally happy and easy-going, he became sullen and morose. After some thinking, I decided to make him a deal. If, after thirty days, he was still unhappy we would move back to where we started. The girls were not in school yet, and it was a grand adventure for them, no problem. We packed as much as we could into Pete's old Dodge Woody and made the trip back to Santa Cruz. Pete had already moved in and was waiting for us when we arrived.

As I took a closer look at the house, I discovered that not only was it filthy, but the last tenants had left behind their trash inside as well as out. Almost every closet was full of garbage. Assuming they had gotten tired of taking it outside, I guessed that they had just decided to store it in the closets.

I cleaned an area in the front room and set up my bed with clean sheets. This would be my oasis to fall back on when I became tired of cleaning. The children all slept with me that night, and in the morning, I began in earnest to make the house livable, starting with the kitchen and bathroom. Pete made two more trips with our belongings from the other house. We had left a box of pots and pans on the front porch that would not fit in the first load, and they were missing when he returned. So, we started our new life in Santa Cruz with nothing in the kitchen but my cast iron frying pan, and a Dutch oven. Those pans and I were old friends.

Our old car gave up on the fourth and final load as it turned the corner, hiccupping for the last few yards. It died as we came to a stop in front of the house. Pete pushed it into the driveway and unloaded it. For the next few months, they put new part after new part into that vehicle. It was practically a new car with all those replaced parts, but it never ran again, nor even turned over. That poor old car had given us all it could moving us and our belongings to the new home. We did not have the wherewithal to rent a moving van and had no friends with trucks, so we left all our large furniture that would not fit in our car in the old house. Also, I had decided to rent the house furnished so if we were to return in thirty days, I could keep my promise to Bo, if necessary.

Life went on at Bixby Street, the kids went to school, and Bo found new friends. He came in from playing one day, and I asked him what his decision was. He looked at me with a blank stare.

"Should we move back to Fresno?" I asked.

"Are you kidding, mom?" he shouted.

"No, the thirty days have passed, and I intend to honor our agreement" I reminded him.

He looked blank again.

"Remember I agreed if after thirty days you weren't happy here, then we would move back to Fresno?"

Eagerly wanting to return to his outdoor activities, he shrugged his shoulders and said, "Huh! Oh yeah, no—I need to go now. Donna is waiting for me, and we are going down to the levy—I'm gonna build a raft!"

"Okay," I said grinning. "Have fun!"

Then he turned and went bouncing out the door without so much as a glance over his shoulder. Oh, how quickly we forget.

Around this time, Bo had also decided to change his name to Beau. Guess he was starting to outgrow the true meaning of "Bo."

I hastily placed an ad in the newspaper and rented our former house to someone who answered the ad for a deposit of $300, without requiring references. Some of the furnishings included a walnut executive desk, a dining table with chairs, beds, kitchen appliances, and pictures on the walls. When their rent check bounced and I could not get them on the phone, Paul, my new friend, drove me to the house only to discover they had stripped it bare. Not even the electrical wall plates remained. They had used a screwdriver to undo everything that could come loose. Not a single light fixture or toilet paper holder remained. My furniture was all gone, and to add insult to injury, they left the house locked, so we had to call a locksmith to get in. I later discovered this was not the first time in a long series of dirty tricks these tenants had pulled on landowners. After a year, I put the house on the market, and by then we were settled on Bixby Street.

Within a week of moving, I was hanging out of the front window trying to clean it when a small, newer model car pulled up to the house. A tall, gangly man untangled himself from within. He wore glasses and looked straight but friendly. "Are you Carol?" He asked, smiling. He came up the stairs and offered his hand. "I'm Paul Bartko, Maia's friend. She called to let me know you were here. What can I do to help you? Would you like to come to dinner tonight?" he asked without taking a breath. Still smiling, I noticed a twinkle in his eye that in the years ahead, I would come to know well. I accepted his dinner invitation, and he came back to pick us up that evening.

Paul lived on 9th street near the harbor in a little cottage with his wife, Nuaha, a beautiful, black-haired Arab women who worked as a physical therapist. Paul was going to law school and working for the Economic Opportunity Commission during the summer. He was a perfect host, offering me a glass of wine while he rolled a joint. Nuaha was busy in the kitchen and did not join us. I found this to be routine after a few visits. Paul held court and entertained while Nuaha cooked and cleaned. Paul asked me what I intended to do in Santa Cruz, and I replied that I was looking for a job. He asked me what I could do, and I told him about my most recent experiences running a teen center. He asked me if I would be interested in a job at the EOC.

"Sure, anything," I exclaimed.

"Or," he said, "Nuaha could find you a job at a nursing home."

Agreeably, I said, "Either is fine."

We had a lovely meal of chicken curry, Paul's favorite. I learned he usually prepared it himself. Both Paul and Nuaha were excellent cooks, and there were always six to ten guests at their home on weekends, some of them spending the night. Paul always gathered conversational, interesting people together at his dinners. He took to calling me Carolee. One afternoon he telephoned me.

"On Saturday, I am cooking a curry or barbecuing salmon. We are going to have a few people over, would you like to join us? My buddy, Jim, is coming down from the city. He works for the IRS. I think you will like him. He is a little crazy. My other friend, Joe, who teaches political science at San Jose State College, will be there with his lady from Aptos. They are also both a little crazy. I think you'll like them, too."

According to Paul, everyone invited to his house was a little crazy, so I assumed he described me to others as a little crazy too. He was right, or likely a lot crazy. I always liked his guests, and the food was excellent.

Weekends at Paul's became a regular occurrence. Paul, like everyone else, was of draftable age. He had been trying to get Nuaha pregnant to stay out of the draft. It was not working, so he made excuse after excuse about why he could not make the appointments with the board. Finally, it caught up with him, and he decided to register. Another long period passed. Paul had managed to postpone the inevitable but eventually his luck ran out. He was sent off to boot camp. When he returned on leave and walked into my house, I did not recognize him. With gaunt cheeks that gave his eyes a deep, hollow look, he had the expression of a scared rabbit. He was painfully thin and seemed taller. His head had been shaved, and stubble covered it now. Army life had not agreed with him. He announced he was not going back. He said, "They are fucking going to kill me if I go back."

A sergeant had pistol-whipped him for disobedience. Though I could not imagine Paul being disobedient, I knew he was a free thinker and king of his domain. The army was not for him. "What are you going to do?" I asked.

"Not sure," he replied, "But I am not going back to that place. I have two weeks to think about it. One thing that is for sure, I am not going."

Paul shot himself in the foot the day before he was to return to Fort Hood. It seemed a rather drastic solution, but that was his choice and it kept him out of the service for a few months. He was ordered to report to the Presidio hospital in San Francisco for a physical exam that turned into a mental exam, resulting in his incarceration in the loony bin. Nuaha called and asked me to ride along to San Francisco; Paul was not there when we arrived. He had gotten out, stolen a car, and made a run for the Bay Bridge with the military police in hot pursuit. They caught him on the bridge and brought him back in a strait jacket. We were there when they brought him in, wild-eyed and flailing his body, screaming obscenities at everyone. As they dragged him passed me, he winked. At that point, I knew he was all right and was handling this in his own way. It seemed a difficult choice, but Paul had a sense of the dramatic and was enjoying himself immensely. Soon after, he was quietly sedated with drugs, which was just what he wanted. He stayed stoned on prescription drugs until they released him a couple of weeks later, all according to Paul's intentional plan.

Not long after, Nuaha got pregnant. Paul passed the bar, and they bought a large rambling house on Branciforte Drive in Santa Cruz, California. There, the weekend parties continued. My summer youth job ended, and Nuaha recommended me for a job as the activity director for a nearby convalescent hospital. Nuaha explained that my job was to keep the residents active, get them out of bed, play ball, bingo, crafts, etc. However, this was not what management had in mind. They preferred to have their patients in bed as this was less trouble for them since they were not "cluttering" the halls in their wheelchairs. I liked my job with the old people and loved listening to their stories. It seems impossible to live that long and to not have learned something.

Mrs. Brooks, a silver-haired, dignified lady with enormous blue eyes that magnified in her bifocals, was a favorite of mine. She had no family, her husband had died, and her cancer kept her in constant pain, waiting to die. I would stop at her bed when I was through working and sit and talk. It was not meaningless chatter but deep intellectual thought-provoking conversations. We talked about the meaning of life and the lessons to be learned. She told me about her life and asked me about mine. At the time, I was having jealousy attacks. She told me that "green-eyed monster" was a hard one. "I never did master that one," she said with a slow smile. We were both silent for a few minutes. She took my hand and spoke softly, "Remember, the best relationship is one in which your love for one another exceeds your need for each other."

After visiting with Mrs. Brooks, I always went home in a reflective mood, wanting to do something for her. Her only desire she had was to die at home. I was thinking daily about a way to get her out of that place. Meanwhile, I tried to bring some joy into her life and others at the home. Bringing in a box of kittens, I watched their eyes light up with pleasure and listened to them coo as they held the tiny, furry creatures in their old, gnarly hands.

Pete had a great rapport with the residents, so I asked him to come in and play his guitar, which he loved doing. Concerned that Mrs. Brooks might be bored since she lay in her bed day after day with only her thoughts to occupy her mind, I asked her if she was bored, but she replied, "Live a good life, then when you get older and think back on it, you'll be able to enjoy it a second time."

It was Pete's idea to bring Mrs. Brooks our television, and when she asked him about it, Pete nonchalantly shrugged his shoulders and said, "We don't need it." Smiling at me with her intense blue eyes, Mrs. Brooks seemed pleased that we cared for her—and it made me feel good, too.

However, Nauha called me that evening and told me I was no longer needed at the nursing home. I was devastated. "Fired?" I said, stunned, "You have to be kidding. Why?"

Nauaha explained, "Well, it's their position that you are causing disruptions by bringing in hippies."

"That would be my friend Pete," I protested. "He came in at my request and played his guitar for them. They loved it!"

As Nauha continued, she questioned, "Dirty animals?"

Distraught, I answered, "I only brought in a couple of kittens. You should have seen the elated looks on the faces of all those sweet old people."

"I know, I know," Nauha mused, "but they were particularly disturbed about you selling the television to Mrs. Brooks."

Now I was enraged. "I didn't sell the television to Mrs. Brooks. Pete gave it to her. It was his," I explained.

"Well," Nauha replied, "they took it away from her, put it in a closet, and want me to return it to you."

Heartbroken, I wept, hardly speaking as tears began streaming down my face, and I stifled an outright sob. How could people be so cruel? I felt empty inside and thought to myself that Santa Cruz was not any different from Fresno. There were petty, mean people everywhere. Defeated, I cried myself to sleep that night.

Several days later, Nuaha called me again, with hesitation in her voice. "I thought you would want to know, Mrs. Brooks died last night."

"Thanks," I said and put the phone back on the receiver, pensively catching my breath.

CHAPTER 27

George "Scooter" Kinnear

Georges dad told me he would sue me if I printed this.
Think he is dead now.

George "Scooter" Kinnear came into my life in the summer of 1970. He was eighteen—a blonde, wiry, rugged surfer from San Diego. Pete brought him home from the beach. He stayed, just kind of moved in because he was underage and technically a runaway.

His father, a captain in the Navy, was a strong disciplinarian; George was scared to death of him. Once, when he came to the house, George ran out the back door and hid in the basement. Essentially, this was harboring a fugitive. I insisted George register and attend school, which he did, sometimes dropping acid before classes and not going at all when the surf was up.

George loved surfing more than anything; it was his first and only love. One night, I helped him with his homework, an essay on hate, and

I asked why he was writing on this subject. He'd been given a choice between love and hate, he answered, and he didn't know anything about love.

At that moment, I decided to make it my mission to introduce him to love, starting with his love of the ocean (sea, sand, and sky), then love of beauty, puppy love (little dogs), and brotherly love (Kevin). As he began to grasp the feeling, his eyes widened, and his face lit up. "Oh!" he grinned, "I get it, but that mushy stuff, I don't know about that!"

"You will," I smiled.

George had a natural animal magnetism. I soon began calling him "George, George, George of the Jungle" because he was wild and could not be tamed or trained. He was as comfortable outdoors as he was uncomfortable in the house. He roamed the hills, lakes, beaches, and cliffs, bringing home shells and driftwood, which he carved and made into mobiles. He wore little clothing—ragged jeans and a t-shirt with no shoes or underwear. His sun-bleached blonde hair was straight and shaggy and hung over one side of his face when he was concentrating on carving a piece of wood or playing his guitar.

Finding delight in the simple things outdoors, George had great reverence for Mother Nature. His expression of sheer pleasure at the anticipation of riding waves was only exceeded by the experience of being in the tunnel. A perfect day for George was four-foot sets with wave after wave coming in. It was that south swell he prayed and waited for, and when it came, nothing could keep him from his love—not school, work, or family. He'd grab his board, throw a towel over his shoulder, and was out the door to pursue his passion. Many meals were left cold when one of his surf buddies stuck his head in the door and said, "Surf's up!"

On days when there was no surf, and the ocean was flat, stormy or mushy, his face, always so animated and alive, turned introspective and quiet, then irritable and restless. This was a tiger you did not want in the house. A caged animal is not a happy animal. George needed to be free and outdoors more than anyone I've ever met. It was this animal quality that attracted me to him.

When I was close enough to touch him, I could feel the electricity between us. Once, passing in a doorway, our eyes locked, and we held for a moment like magnets. George threw back his head and laughed his wild, insane, let-it-all-loose laugh: "Wow, Flemming, what was that?" Being a woman of the world, I knew exactly what it was. I also knew it wouldn't be long before George would learn about another kind of love.

One chilly evening in September, a rare occasion when we were alone in the house, we built a fire in the fireplace and sat on the floor in front of it. Our knees touched, and suddenly we were looking into each other's eyes. George had this strange, quizzical half-smile, reached for my hand, and slowly pressed my fingers to his lips. For an eighteen-year-old boy, this was a good start!

Knowing I wouldn't be rejected, I took the next step. I leaned into him and snuggled into his chest, turning, and lifting my head to his lips for a soft, lingering kiss. He held me wordlessly for a few moments. Slowly he got up, still holding my hand, and led me to my bed.

George turned eighteen during the height of the Vietnam War. We had been actively protesting for two years, lying under busses if necessary, to keep them from taking our boys. Scummy had gotten out by walking naked through the induction line. Bob and Paul shot themselves in the foot, and Pete was classified 4-F because of his flat feet. Others went to Canada, and some just didn't register.

George was at a loss, and of course, his father (the captain), thought he should join. He was willing to sacrifice his firstborn to "be the first on your block to have your boy come home in a box."

I wasn't willing to see this bundle of joyful energy sent to a foreign country to fight a war he didn't believe in, and I knew just how to stop it.

"Marry me," I proposed. "I have three children, which automatically makes you exempt." As the possibility sank in, George's face lit up with a slowly spreading smile.

"Boy, will my old man be pissed!"

I called Ted MacAvenney of the Glide Foundation Church in San Francisco, an anti-war activist and minister, and he readily agreed to marry us. So, on Saturday, we hopped into George's old truck, surfboard in the back just in case there was a swell on the way and took the coastal route north to San Francisco where we were married in the basement of the Glide Memorial Church on Hyde Street.

The floor was strewn with pillows in psychedelic colors, and a light show was the background for our nuptials. George wore a brown corduroy jacket (borrowed from Ted), and his only decent pair of jeans. I wore a brown jumper with a cream-colored satin full-sleeved blouse.

After the wedding, we went to one of my old high school friend's homes for dinner. George discovered they had a dirt bike and a hill out back to ride it on. He spent our wedding day riding the motorcycle up the steep dirt hill until he was tired and dirty, shouting, "Wow! What a rush!"

George beamed when he was finally coaxed into the house for dinner and exclaimed, "I've got to get one of those!" We stopped by my mother's house on the way home. George playing with the dogs outside, my mother looked out the window and proclaimed, observing my new husband, "Why, he's only a child!"

"Yes," I said, "that's why I married him."

On Sunday, a beautiful sunny day, we had a wedding reception at the house on Bixby Street and invited friends from work. George's surfing buddies were there, his boss Everett with his wife Jenny, his brother Kevin with his girlfriend Katie (who brought her mother), and a special guest, his grandmother Bobbie from Long Beach.

I wore a blue satin minidress, decorated the house with flowers, and laid out a buffet table with lunch, centered around a champagne punch. Rock and roll music was blasting from the stereo.

Everyone was having a good time until I heard Katie scream about taking her mother to the hospital. Unbeknownst to me, George had spiked the punch with LSD. Everett, his eyes bright and shining, said, "Oh, I've always wanted to try that." Ted quietly helped himself to a second cup, followed by the rest of the surfing crew. Katie dragged her mother down the front steps, screaming at me, "Why don't you grow up?"

"Me? I didn't spike the punch," I protested. Truth was, I didn't want to grow up; I was having too much fun.

Life with George was never dull. I followed him into the hills, exploring places he'd found he had to show me, extending my childhood. We rode his dirt bike—yes, he got one of his own—up Zyante Road into the Santa Cruz mountains, took a private road a few miles, and then onto a dirt path. When that became too overgrown, we climbed to the top of the mountain on foot. Here, much to my surprise and George's glee in showing me, we found sand dunes backed up to the mountain facing the sea. Miles from it was a warm, sandy beach with shells and sand dollars you could dig'out by hand. It was indeed an amazing place, proof that long, long ago, these mountains had indeed been covered by ocean.

I never knew how he found these places, but another spot George took me in the Aptos Hills on his dirt bike was Newt Lake, entirely covered with water lizards. At first, they looked like algae, but on closer inspection, everything was moving, like an ink spot on acid.

George made me climb into an old boat and rowed us across the lake. He loved it. I thought they were icky and pictured falling into the lake and those lizards crawling all over me. George fished one out of the water and insisted I pet its belly, asking, "Isn't he cute?"

"Yuck…"

To please him and disguise my repulsion, I petted the creature because I knew from experience that if I showed fear, I probably would have a handful of them slung at me. Boys being boys.

George loved to scare me. One of his favorite tricks was to get me on the back of the motorcycle and take me for a ride someplace I'd never been and then, without warning, jump a ditch or small creek, just to hear me scream. He found that hilarious and laughed his Woody Woodpecker laugh all the way home.

In the winter, George surfed River Mouth beach, located adjacent to the Boardwalk in Santa Cruz and within walking distance from home. Though the swell was often small, it was better than nothing. Sometimes, however, it was big, and he would surf until, he said, his brains fell out— even after dark. He would build a bonfire so he could find his way into shore near the wall of the Boardwalk.

As soon as spring came and the weather permitted, we headed for the beach. I also learned to surf but was by no means as passionate about it as George and his surf crowd. George's surf crowd consisted of Crazy Ted Kappa, Ad the Third, and Art the Gimp. Art wasn't really a gimp, though he told me he had been as a child when he'd had polio and limped. There was no sign of a limp anymore, but Art still carried that image in his head and always considered himself a gimp. As comfortable in water as on land, Art was what they called a "goofy foot"; he surfed with his right foot forward. Living alone in a small surf shack, Art dressed himself like a two-year-old, pulling on anything available—shirts inside out, pants with pockets turned out, mismatched socks or no socks at all, shoes untied, if shoes at all.

Art could have cared less about how he dressed or what people thought. He supported himself by washing dishes at night, so he had all day to surf. With a robust golden-tanned body, sandy-brown curly hair, and blue-green eyes, most of the time Art was shy and serious until a broad, unexpected grin would surprise his face, turning into a giggle that ended in a deep rumbling laugh taking over his entire body. He seemed to have no control over his hilarity.

What he found funny were things you had to think about twice, like words with double meanings. A favorite saying was, "Oh, we're all gonna die!" which he'd belt out wide-eyed, waving all ten fingers in the air. This was to emphasize the smallness of our problems.

I was waiting tables at the Pasatiempo Inn at the time, and Art was the dishwasher. One night I was cocktail waitressing a banquet, running in and out of the kitchen, and Art was not his friendly self, almost like he was mad at me, but I didn't have time to pursue it.

The next day Art stopped by the house and gave me a piece of his mind. After declaring he respected me and thought of me as a sister, he leaned in with eyes blazing and shaking his finger in my face and snarled, "You were dressed like a *slut* last night!" He looked like a jealous husband.

"Oh, my God! That's what's bothering you?"

"Yes," he stormed. "Every man in the kitchen was talking about your nipples."

I broke into laughter. "My nipples?"

"Yes," he fumed, "you weren't wearing a bra, and everyone could see your *nipples!*"

"Art, I never wear a bra. I don't own one."

"Well, last night I noticed!"

"And that's it? That's why you didn't speak to me all night?"

"Yeah! I was embarrassed for you."

"Well, Art, don't, because it's no big deal, and I don't care. I see nothing wrong with your nipples, and I see them all the time."

"Well, that's different!"

"How's that different?"

"I'm a boy."

"And . . ."

Art rolled his eyes, searching for the answer. His mouth opened, and he started to say something, but nothing came out. Then he turned abruptly and stalked out, and that was the end of that.

One night, George and company set out for the store to buy some milk and cookies. It was late, and they walked to Albertson's, open until midnight, instead of Shopper's Corner, which was closer but closed at nine. After an hour, when they hadn't returned, I grew a little concerned. I was waiting for the cookies. Then the phone rang, and I was more concerned. The police had George, Kapper, and Ted in jail for trespassing.

As the story came out later, on their way to the store they took a shortcut through a vacant orchard and around the Crystal Palace, a large Victorian home abandoned for many years. (The last tenants demoralizing its previous grandeur were crank heads, hence "Crystal Palace.") Well, George and group decided to go inside and explore. They were wandering around upstairs when George found an old lady's black hat with feathers and a veil. He put it on and was mincing about being the old lady when the police surprised them; the three boys were making so much noise they didn't hear them coming.

The police found George so amusing they handcuffed him with the hat on and took him in so everyone at the station could have a laugh too.

George's face was still red when he got home hours later. I borrowed the $200 for bail from Bartko.

Later that summer, we decided to take a surf trip to San Diego, George's old stomping ground. He wanted to surf Black's Beach and stop at the Hollister Ranch along the way, another Santa Barbara surf spot.

At the time, I was working for the Economic Opportunity Commission (EOC) as a summer youth director, a job Bartko had gotten me. It was a paper job, no work. My actual purpose was to drive James, another of Bartko's friends who didn't drive himself, so they hired me and gave me a trumped-up title. I took my job seriously and kept trying to work while Bartko kept reminding me not to rock the boat.

Our routine was to go to the office, have coffee and donuts, and read the paper to pass the time until lunch. I would drive James wherever he wanted to go. Sometimes I drove him to San Jose, where he was going to school the following semester. I waited for him while he arranged his upcoming enrollment. None of this had anything to do with our government paycheck.

Bartko called it free government money. Whoever wrote the program had nothing in mind but making money for friends, and it worked. About ten of us were on the payroll with our government offices, telephones, and cars. I even put together some summer dances for the youth and had a big blue bus at my disposal to pick up said youth. I drove it around the boardwalk seeking kids to carry off to my dance, but though I tried, they were all too busy enjoying smoking dope and hanging out to want to come.

After I drove James home that Friday night, I loaded the car with the only summer youth I could find: my husband and his surf buddies. They tied their boards on top of the old army gray recruiting car, and we set off for San Diego on another road trip equipped with LSD, black beauties, smoke, and a bottle of Southern Comfort. We drove the Pacific Coast Highway through Watsonville and Monterey, and finally Carmel before we hit the curves of Big Sur. We had dropped acid and were all getting high when George abruptly pulled over for a hitchhiker who looked like

Frankenstein standing on the ocean side of the road before I could say, "No, don't."

The giant, who introduced himself as Carl, climbed into the front seat. We all sat in the back, listening to the conversation. He asked George about the government license plate. George, forever the comedian, told him we had stolen the car.

"Alright!" roared Carl, thereby encouraged to share his story. Carl was an escapee from a mental institution. George laughed aloud with glee—he was creating his own comedy. Together, they conspired to dump our car for another one in Santa Barbara because Carl thought the government car was too risky. The back seat crew thought the whole thing was too risky. Our entire trip had turned paranoid as we were pulled into the scenario being concocted in the front seat by crazy Carl and George, who was laughing like a hyena, convinced we were all enjoying the joke as much as he was.

Finally, I snapped out of shock and suggested we stop for fresh air and a stretch. As soon as we were out of the car, I pulled George aside and said, "Are you mad?"

George, grinning from ear to ear, said, "Isn't this great?"

"No! We're bummed that he's ruining our trip!"

"What do you want me to do?"

"Get rid of him."

"Okay. Get back in on the driver's side and keep the engine running. I'll be right back."

He turned to crazy Carl. "Come with me. I have something to show you," and they walked off into the moonless night towards the cliffs.

We got back in the car and waited. The guys were totally bummed. In a few minutes, George came running ass-over-teakettle, hands in the air and laughing like a loon, the crazy giant following ten feet behind. Carl was big, but George was swift, and as he reached the car, I threw the door open, and George jumped in, yelling, "Go, go, go!"

I peeled out, leaving the now confused, crazy giant running down Highway One after us. George was still laughing, and the guys in the back seat were staring mutely out the rear window as the giant disappeared into the night. We never got our high back, but our relief was vast. Soon the bottle of Southern Comfort was opened and passed around. The sun was rising as we approached San Diego. Somehow, we slipped through LA without noticing.

We arrived at Black's Beach on a perfect Southern California day. I stretched out on the sand while the guys hit the water. It was hours later when they came in, George's face beaming. We set off to find food and shelter, stopping by a friend of George's house. Luckily, his parents were out of town, and we were invited to crash. I headed for the bathroom and had a lovely, elegant soak, then opted to nap while the guys went out to hunt for waves.

On Sunday, we all dropped acid at Sunset Beach. Perfect four-foot sets rolled in for miles. The water was warm as the weather and the sky as blue as a summer sky can get. We were happy.

George's San Diego friend, "Chicken Man," a tall, lanky, typical Southern California bronzed blonde surfer, had a longboard—a really long board. George decided it was time for me to try surfing, urging, "You'll never get a more perfect situation."

Under the group's watchful eyes, I hefted a board twice as tall as me and headed into the water. I managed to stand up the first time out. Exhilarating! On the second wave, when I stood up, I lost my top, and my boobs just jumped right out, much to the amusement of the guys onshore. The second wave was my last, I had done it, and that was all that was required of me. The ocean belonged to the guys, and I was content to resume being a beach bunny.

As the sun set, we packed our things, tied the boards back on the car, and headed north. We got as far as Santa Barbara before deciding to pull over for a nap.

So, there we were, all hunkered down amidst our wet towels, dirty clothes, leftover fast-food wrappings, and sand, when a highway patrol officer approached, shining his light in the window, and tapped the car's hood. Of course, he thought it was stolen.

We waited in the car while he got my boss out of bed. Paul, bless him, said, "Yes, she works for the government in the summer youth project and she's on a field trip with summer youth." The cop took one more look in the car at my rumpled cargo, shook his head, and got back in his car, probably wondering about government money.

Monday morning, I had some explaining to do. Paul made me write a report on taking urban kids to the seashore, and everything ended well, including my job, because summer was over.

One winter night, when a storm was rattling the old windows, a cold rain was beating on the roof. George, Kapper, and I were huddled in front of the fireplace, the only heat in the Victorian house beside the kitchen stove. There came a knock at the door. George and I looked at each other; we weren't expecting anyone. Though our friends stopped by at all hours uninvited, this was a bad night to be out, and our premonition was that it was not good. Without a word, George went to the door, and I heard a muffled conversation. He returned, saying, "Let me get my jacket." He was shaking his head, eyes downcast as he went passed me. He said slowly, "They found Art's body under the trestle. They want me to identify the body." It took a minute for what he'd said to sink in. Art's body? Was he dead? It must have been a mistake. I saw him yesterday.

Kapper got up from in front of the fireplace and said, "I'll go with you." Without another word, they left with the two policemen who were waiting in the hall. I sat by the fire, stunned, waiting for them to return, and to tell me it was not true. Soon they were back. "He's dead," George announced. "Either that or he is one hell of an actor!"

A man in a trench coat was with him. Yeah, a trench coat. Well, it was raining, and he was a detective. He was wanting to ask us a few questions. "Did we know anyone that had a reason to kill Art?"

Dumbfounded, we all looked at each other and shook our heads.

"Did he have any enemies or carry large amounts of money?"

We all laughed at once. No money was more like it!

The detective gave us a *you are all weird* look, and said, "We suspect foul play because all of his pockets were turned out."

We all laughed at once again. George explained that it was Art's usual manner of dressing: shirt unbuttoned, no socks, and pockets turned out.

After the detective left, we sat staring into the fire. Each one of us, with our own thoughts. Kapper said, "Art told me last week he didn't think he was going to live much longer."

George said Art had been in a lot of pain from an earache.

"Do you think he jumped from the trestle?" I asked, musing.

"Nah!" said George. "He loved to surf the north swell at the River Mouth. He was probably just checking it out, and maybe he leaned too far over and lost his balance. His neck was broken."

One thing that bothered me was George said his hat was missing, and he would never have gone out in that storm without it. He loved that hat. His sister knitted it for him. He wore it everywhere. Art did deal a little dope. Could there have been foul play? Nah, his hat probably floated out to sea.

George said, "I'm going over to his house to have a look around."

"No," I protested. "Don't do that. Too risky. The police will do that, and you don't want to get involved. What if he has grass there and you are over there snooping around? Let the police handle it."

For once, George took my advice.

The next night we had a farewell party for Art. His family had come down from the city to claim his body and came over. I cooked dinner for them, a pasta with clams, one of Art's favorites, and garlic bread dripping in butter. We had wine and some tequila for those who wanted something stronger. His family and friends sat around the fire telling stories about Art. I had never met his family before; they were very warm, loving people. Later I was in the kitchen pantry alone, when I felt a presence behind me and hands lightly touching my shoulder, a familiar voice said, "Thanks, Kid." I turned, and there was no one there. He was gone.

I went back into the living room, where everyone was suddenly quiet. "He was here," his mother said.

"Yes, I know," I said. "He thanked me."

His mother and I hugged and laughed through our tears.

She said, "Come on, I'll give you a hand with the dishes. Art would want me to."

CHAPTER 28

Manny Santana and the Mexican heritage center

One afternoon, Paul called and asked me, "You speak Spanish, don't you?"

Caught by surprise, I replied, "Yeh, a little, why?"

"Manny Santana is looking for someone to run the Mexican Heritage Center in Watsonville," he urged, "and with your experience, you could do it!"

Hesitating a moment, I faltered, "Oh, I don't know if I am ready for that."

"Go talk to him," Paul insisted.

George drove me out to Manuel's Mexican Restaurant in Seacliff Beach, a cozy, joyful place. Manny, a jovial, good-hearted, massive hunk of a man, was in the kitchen sweating as he cooked. He wore a large, brightly flowered, printed apron, his bald head shining like it had been polished.

"What's up, Catalina?" he said, picking me up and setting me on the worktable next to the stove like a ragdoll.

"Paul mentioned that you might have a job for me at the Mexican Heritage Center. I did run a teen center in Fresno while I was there," I replied.

Manny wiped his head with a towel, reached into a drawer, and pulled out a pint of Jack Daniel's. Opening it, he took a swig and offered it to me.

"No thanks, it's too early," I lied politely.

After taking another long swill, Manny put it back into the drawer, and said, "We got this fellow Fernando who is supposed to be running it, but he's not experienced. We need a go-getter, someone who can do fundraising and plan events."

"I can do that," I said confidently.

Manny continued, "To start, get us some donations of furniture, plants, and stuff for the walls."

"Sure, I can do that," I assured him.

Manny said, "Okay, you are hired. You start tomorrow. The pay is $500 a week—and if you got any problems, come to me. And while you are here, why not have some dinner? It is on the house."

I thanked Manny and gave him a big hug. Before I got out the door, he spoke to me with authority, "No company car," and we both laughed.

Manuel's was painted in bright colors by Manny himself. A talented painter and creative cook, he was also a benevolent, generous human being. Weekends at Manuel's had long lines of people waiting outside the door to get in. Sometimes the wait was an hour, but people waited cheerfully, amusing themselves with conversation and a glass of wine. The bar was stacked two rows deep, and you had to squeeze between friendly people to get a drink.

Dinner at Manny's was always a happy, festive occasion. There was no dress code, the accepted attire was a ready smile, and the food was excellent. George would go from table to table, joining in conversations and waiting until someone pushed their plate away. He would ask, "Are you going to finish that?" If the reply were no, he would pounce on the half-empty plate, eating the remainder of the dinner. No one seemed to mind. George was sincere about not wasting food—and I pretended like he was not with me.

George always acted uncomfortable in public places, but Manny's was one place on the beach where he felt at home. We talked of other times we had eaten there. One time we ate there, Peyote came for dinner and we could not eat anything. Manny sat with us wearing a knowing, amused smile.

Every year Manny gave a party to his friends just before he closed for vacation and went to Mexico. Everyone came to the restaurant late, around eleven. Manny closed the doors when his last paying customers were gone and began to cook in earnest for his friends. This was not your typical Mexican food, but gourmet Mexican cuisine was on the menu. Seafood, shrimp, and special mole were some of the entrees, and the main event was a stuffed hog's head. Guests were to pace themselves, eating only a small amount of each dish as the courses kept coming late into the night. Manny knew how to throw a party. First-timers burnt out long before they got to the good stuff. Of course, if you did not consider the hog's head "good stuff," it was better to fill up on the shrimp. Manny's reminded me of Hemingway's book "A Movable Feast." There was always good conversation and great food there.

The Mexican Heritage Center was located on the main street in an old office building. Parking in the back, I found Fernando lounging on a faded, wine-colored, corduroy couch. I approached him and introduced myself. He looked stunned as he hadn't expected me.

"Habla Espanol?" he asked me.

"Si, poco entender mucho!" I responded.

He shrugged. This became our pattern. I dutifully practiced my Spanish.

Fernando was a part-time student at San Jose State. He was into La Raza: if you were not brown, you were unacceptable. I busied myself calling on merchants soliciting whatever they had to donate to the center—plants from the florist and apples from the grocer. I was looking for things to hang on the walls that were not serapes, but pictures of first-generation immigrants or Mexican historical prints. None seemed available, so I gave that up and decided to do something I knew how to do, organize a dance for teens. Locating a Mexican band and a hall, I had posters made for Saturday night.

On Thursday, Manny asked me to drive a group of students to San Jose State to enroll, and he even allowed me to rent a car. I picked up my charges at the center Friday morning at five in the morning: two guys and a girl. The conversation was spoken in rapid Spanish. I was excluded.

Okay, I thought, I'm here to drive, and that is what I did.

In San Jose, I found the registration office and explained the process in careful, slow Spanish (though they all spoke English) and said that I would pick them up at four o'clock. They agreed, and I spent the rest of the day at the library. At four, I returned to the registration office. One guy and one girl showed up. We were missing one of the guys. We waited an hour, and then I began hunting for him on the campus, starting with the building that sported a La Raza banner. Finding him engaged in a heated political discussion, I waited a few minutes for him to notice me and to realize that he was late. He ignored me, and finally I interrupted him, stating that we were ready to go. He said he was not ready, so I asked him how much longer he would be, and he retorted, "When I'm ready."

Explaining to him that I was leaving at six-thirty, I exited the building and waited for him at the registration office. At six-thirty, I herded my charges back to the car and into the rush hour traffic, back over the hill. It was almost eight o'clock when I reached the center. The girl's parents were waiting and very distressed. I let her explain. They eyed me as if I were untrustworthy, then nodded and took her by the arm, leading her away. I stopped by Manuel's restaurant and found Manny. As I explained what happened, I expected to be blamed for not handling the situation right. Manny received a phone call from the other boy demanding I return to San Jose and pick him up. Manny informed him that he needed to find his way home. He won my heart for his fairness.

That Saturday night rolled around, and the scene at Manuel's was familiar shades of Damhara. Kids were having a good time. We were merely there as chaperones. Listening to the music for a while, I absently wondered if I asked Fernando to dance with me, would he? Noticing a group of boys against the wall, I saw a bottle being passed around, so I ambled over and got a closer look. Yep, it was tequila. I knew what I had to do, so I stepped into the middle of the group. Before I could say anything, I was grabbed by my blouse and thrown against the wall. A knife appeared out of nowhere and was held against my throat. My eyes bugged out of my head. I was speechless. The boy holding me spewed, "This is not your business, gringa. You don't belong here!" The other boys had crowded around, concealing me from anybody that could help me.

Where was Fernando? My mind raced. These were not the stoned peaceniks I was used to dealing with, these were hostile angry kids, and the one with the knife at my throat was drunk. My mind searched for words. Finally, I said, "Okay, but may I have some tequila?"

It took a minute for my request to sink into the alcohol-addled brain of my captor. Slowly a twisted smile spread across his young face, and he released me, wiped the mouth of the bottle with his hand, and handed it to me, "No limes," he quipped. Trying not to show the fear that had gripped my heart, I smiled, took a long pull at the tequila, and handed it back to the young man.

"Thanks," I said, deciding not to use my broken Spanish, as I would not want to offend him with my accent. "See you around," I said, and on wooden legs stumbled off to look for Fernando. The next day I went to see Manny.

"I quit!" I said and told him the story of the knife at my throat, leaving out the part of how I got out of it. Manny laughed long and hard, putting his hands under his armpits to make wings. He flapped his wings and made chicken sounds.

"Hey, the kids are showing some spirit! Don't take it personally."

I was getting irritated quickly.

"Okay. I am a chicken, but the knife was not at your throat. I cannot handle it, Manny. Sorry, I am still not over Fresno."

My job at the Mexican heritage center lasted two weeks.

★★★Christmas Money★★★

Christmas was approaching—and I was out of work. As I stood in front of the mirror in the bathroom curling my hair, there was no heat in the bathroom—you could hang beef in there, it was so cold!

With a little luck, I convinced myself as I applied lipstick and smiled, I'll have a job tonight. I had not worn lipstick in over a year but tonight, in my magenta jumper and white sweater, I looked nice. Leaving the cold room, outside, the temperature was warmer than the house, but I could still see my breath. It was dry. Still shivering, I did not have a coat. Walking around the block to Oceanside Street and two blocks to the Oceanside Inn, I entered a large, cavernous building that housed a bar and Chinese restaurant with banquet facilities and applied for a job.

That night I was serving cocktails in a miniskirt and go-go boots. I had a job, and Christmas would not be so bad. I thought to myself, This one is not like the one in San Francisco, where I had decorated the donated tree with jewelry from my jewelry box and sent Beau to his grandmothers because I did not have money for dinner, certainly not a turkey dinner. That was an extremely sad, lonely Christmas. I would never go through that again.

Good at cocktail waiting, I remember carrying as many as ten to twenty drinks at one time. Serving swiftly, I made good tips. That night when I fell into bed, my whole body quivered with a tiring vibration. After several nights of working banquets, the boss asked me if I would like to work the Christmas banquet at the Coconut Grove on the twenty-third.

That night I picked out my best dress, a little black number with a sailor collar, trimmed in white and a waist that nipped in, making the best of what I had. Everyone was in the Christmas mood, and there were plenty of spirits enjoyed. I saw to it, that was my job. I recognized Bud and Vinny from Shopper's Corner grocery store. I had shopped there often. Some of the other merchants sitting around with Bud insisted that I sit with them for dinner. I was a bit uncomfortable feeling as though I should be serving, but he insisted, and no one seemed to mind. Prime rib was a great treat for me, something I had not had in a long time. Their table was a warm and friendly group of people, and I was grateful.

Immediately after dinner, I jumped up and started making my rounds again. A tall, older man watched me and seemed to have more on his mind than just drinks. He paid me several compliments and tipped very well. Finally, he slipped me a phone number, bent over, and whispered in my ear, "I would pay a lot to get you into bed." I smiled shyly and backed away. I did not think much about it until later that night when I counted my tips and came across the phone number again. I put it on the dresser and forgot about it.

The next day was the twenty-fourth of December. Once again, I counted my tips and tried to figure out how I would afford a turkey dinner and gifts for the kids. I could not have another depressing Christmas. That phone number was staring at me. I started thinking: He said that he would pay me a lot of money. What did that mean? "Come on, Carol," I said to myself, "the man thinks he can buy you."

"Can he?" I asked myself. "How bad could it be? How much would he pay me? Could I really do it?" Reasoning that it could make a difference for the kids on Christmas, I decided to make the call.

First, I phoned Paul and said, "I'm thinking of going to bed with someone for money. What do you think?" He laughed. "I'm serious, Paul. I do not have enough money for dinner or gifts, and it could make a big difference for the kids on Christmas. I think I could do it if I put myself in the right frame of mind." Reasoning with myself, I thought, Yeah, with a fifth of Jack Daniel's. No, I will pretend to be an actress playing a part. I'm going to call him.

With a deep breath and shaking hands that had turned cold, I dialed the number from the small piece of paper. When the man answered, I told him I was the waitress from the previous night, and he remembered me.

"Oh yes," he said.

I got right to the point and asked, "Did you mean what you said?"

"Yes," he said.

"Okay. I want $500," I blurted out and held my breath,

"Alright," he said without hesitation. "When?"

"Today," I answered.

"Okay, where?" he asked.

"The Dream Inn would be fine," I said, thinking quickly.

We decided to meet at three o'clock, and I hung up quietly, realizing that I had just made a date for sex, for money. Was I going to do this? Like a child playing dress-up, I chose to pretend I was Elizabeth Taylor in "Butterfield 8."

The rest of the morning was spent doing busy things and trying not to think about what was about to happen. Determined to go through with it, I reasoned that he was a horny, local businessman with too much money and that my kids deserved a Christmas that I could give them from tolerating just an hour.

At one o'clock, I began to prepare myself: bathing, shaving my legs, carefully applying makeup, and choosing the right clothing to wear. My outfit needed to be easy to step out of, a skirt, buttoned blouse, a lace bra, and panties, something I usually never wear. I tried out different seductive looks in the bathroom mirror. At two o'clock I called Paul and asked him to drive me to the Dream Inn.

"What if he's a pervert or a murderer? Come with me and wait an hour," I pleaded, "if I don't come out, bust in and get me."

"You want me to pimp for you?" Paul questioned me.

"No," I said, "I got the job myself, and I just need a friend. I will pay you fifty dollars."

Paul agreed, shaking his head with a sly smile on his face. The kids would come home from school, so I left a note saying I would be back shortly and was out the door.

Paul was there to meet me in his little black psychedelic painted Volkswagen. "Make love, not war" was painted on the side with a peace sign on the rear, surrounded by purple flowers. I got in, and we buzzed down to the beach.

The Dream Inn was located on a cliff overlooking the bay at the surf spot known as Steamers Lane. It was well lit with afternoon sunshine, not a likely place for a shady rendezvous. The lobby was empty except for the bartender. I seated myself at the bar and ordered a Jack on ice, waiting patiently. It was not long before he was there beside me, a tall, kindly man who looked like someone's grandfather. He ordered a whiskey and apologized for being late. We talked about the weather, and then he downed his drink and stood up, slipping a key in my hand, whispering a room number. I finished my drink and followed. The room was on the 2nd floor, and I put the key in the lock, taking a deep breath. Here I go, I told myself, and I entered the room. He was in bed under the covers. I walked to the dresser in the center of the room, in front of the bed (center stage), and began slowly to unbutton my blouse. Wishing I had music, I said in what I hoped was a casual voice, "Did you bring the money?" I had learned this from a movie: always see the money first.

"Yes," he answered, "it's right there," pointing to the dresser and sure enough, fanned on the dresser under a brown bag containing a liquor bottle were five, crisp, hundred-dollar bills.

"I thought you might want a drink," he offered.

"I'm fine," I lied, stepping out of my skirt, sucking in my stomach, and trying to look seductive all at the same time. I undid my bra and put it with my blouse. Everything went into one pile just in case I had to grab my clothes and run naked to the waiting car. Imagining Paul's face if I did have to run naked through the parking lot, I smiled to myself, and walking across the room to the bed, slid in beside the gentleman. He pulled me closer to him and kissed me, and I wondered if he had false teeth. He was still wearing his t-shirt.

He asked, "Do you mind? I do not want to take it off."

"No, I don't mind," I said, wondering what he was hiding under his shirt. I did not want to see anyway. It was over in five minutes, and he apologized for being so quick.

"Oh, that's alright," I assured him as I slipped out of bed and into my clothes, sliding the money into my pocket. I had not brought a purse with me.

"Thank you," I said sincerely and was out the door before you could say "Jack be nimble," walking just short of a run.

Paul was sitting on the hood of the car gazing out to sea. He looked at me and said, "no show, huh?"

I replied, "Drive quick and get me out of here and home. I need a shower. I feel dirty!"

Back at the house, I showered, scrubbed myself pink and brushed my teeth twice. When I had gotten clean, I burned the clothes I had worn and changed into jeans and a t-shirt. I gave the kids their snacks and informed them that I had more shopping to do and would return in a couple of hours. As I left the house feeling like I had just wakened from a bad dream, I comforted myself with the thought, It is over. Fingering the $500 in my pocket as I walked down the street to Paul's, I said to myself, "Let's go shopping."

CHAPTER 29

The Pebble: my first restaurant

One day while pulling weeds in the driveway, I had a great idea. Extremely excited, I wanted to share it with someone, so I ventured into the basement where George was glassing a surfboard. He did not like to be disturbed when he was working on a board unless, of course, it was a call for "surf's up." He had started making boards for friends, and now he had orders to fill for actual pay. His boards were short and fast, not for beginners. I poked my head into the gloom of the basement where he was working under a single light bulb that cast a halo around his blonde hair, his face set in a "do not bother me I'm concentrating" mode.

"I've got an idea," I said. "How about we turn the front room into a restaurant? We could close off the big doors and still have the second room for the family. We have a couple tables, and I could find a few more secondhand, and I could make tablecloths. You and Beau could be waiters, and I could cook. We would never be hungry because we would always have food. We could advertise very quietly on the beach. Surfers like to eat, and I could do an entire dinner for say two dollars and fifty cents, including soup, salad, and bread, maybe even dessert. No—desserts would cost extra. Six tables, seating twenty people that would be about fifty to sixty dollars a night. What do you think?" I asked breathlessly.

"Sure," he replied without looking up from his work.

Dashing on my bike, I set out for the secondhand store on Ocean Street. There, I found a couple of tables for five dollars and called Paul to help haul them home. We stacked them in the back of his Volkswagen, and he gave me another table from his house. Now I had four tables, enough for a start. I arranged them in the front parlor of the Victorian bay windows and decided I needed to make curtains and tablecloths to match.

"This is going to take some doing, Miss Scarlet," I said to myself. Could I turn my clothes into curtains? No, that would not work. I would have to buy some fabric, maybe another secondhand store would have some, and I still needed candles. My next thought was for a sign, and I ventured back to the basement. George was still bent over the surfboard that was beginning to take shape.

"Do you suppose you could make me a sign for the restaurant?" I asked.

"Sure," he replied once again without looking up at me. "What's its name?"

I had no idea. I told him that I would have to put some thought into it, and then left to go in search of fabric for the tablecloths. Now my sewing lessons will pay off, I thought, And I won't have to wear a wig.

My next thought was even more inspiring: I won't have to go to work. I can stay home and cook. What fun—I can make soup and bread and maybe stuffed game hens. Yeah, that is what I will serve: stuffed game hens in an orange sauce with wild rice, followed by a brandy cream pie for dessert—or brownies. No menu, just dinner and maybe wine for an extra dollar. Surfers love brownies. I could make up little fliers to pass out on the beach. "Beach dinner—$2.50—Bixby street."

"What's the name of the place," George asked again. "No name Cafe?"

"No," I replied, "that's been used already." We still had no name.

My head was buzzing with plans, and by sunset that night, I had a small restaurant set up in the front room, and George was on the beach recruiting customers. In the window was a small sign proclaiming, "The Pebble: A Restaurant."

George had chosen the name, made a small sign carved out of wood and placed it in the window facing the street. We agreed when the candles were lit and the sign was in the window, we were open.

Cooking my heart out since early morning when I had ridden my bicycle to Shopper's Corner and bought fresh vegetables and game hens, I had made soup, baked bread, put fresh flowers on the tables gathered from the neighborhood, and added candles. We were in business. Not long after, we had our first customer.

Capper showed up practically salivating and of course, still wet from surfing. Two other surfers, both lean and hungry, joined him. George played waiter and wrote their orders on a spiral tablet very carefully, repeating their orders with his tongue hanging out of the side of his mouth. Heavy in concentration, he carefully scrawled "two dinners." I dished up the soup, wrapped the warm bread in a napkin in a basket, and sent Beau in with the food. He was so excited to help and was eyeing the game hens coming out of the oven as I spooned orange juice over them, basting until golden brown.

"Oh boy," he said, "we eat tonight! I could eat two of those babies."

Just then, Crazy Ted popped into the kitchen. "Smells mighty fine," he grinned. Ted's hair was also damp, and he beamed with an afterglow from both sun and surf, or was it the pot?

"Out of the kitchen," I demanded, "Out! Out! Out!" He retreated to the dining room.

"We've got six more," George announced, and I had a moment of panic.

"Just take their orders," I said, cutting three of the game hens in half and adding more rice.

"Take them soup, Beau," I instructed.

We served fourteen dinners that first night. George smoked the pot that Capper and Ted had brought for a tip, and Beau pretty much took over the tables' waiting. George ate from his buddy's plates. Capper did not have any money and asked to establish a tab. Ted just exchanged pot with George for his food. George made a mistake and only charged four of the six surfers for their dinner. They certainly did not notice, because they were stoned from the joint that Ted had rolled at the table and shared with them. When everything was said and done, I had a pile of dirty dishes, a tired kid, a stoned husband, and no food left. They had eaten everything.

Beau looked at me with a most forlorn, tired but somehow happy expression, probably a contact high. "I guess they liked everything. Can I have a bowl of cereal, Mom?" he asked. "I'm tired."

The next day I started the soup and bread, then rode my bike to Shopper's Corner and bought more game hens and vegetables. Today I would make a brandy cream pie and sell it for two dollars and fifty cents. It was worth it, and with stoned surfers, the munchies would make the pie a sellout. This is what I was thinking as I peddled my bicycle back from the store. I spent the afternoon preparing the night's dinner. It was a lot of work, but by sunset, I was ready when the candles were lit.

George was looking forward to another night of getting stoned with his buddies. Beau was looking a little tired, and I suggested that he eat before we started to serve. His eyes lit up with a *thanks Mom* as I pulled a plump game hen from the oven. He tucked a napkin in his shirt and began to eat like someone was going to take it away from him, like a wolf holding down his prey with his foot as he tore the flesh off for his meal. I looked away.

That night Manuel's son, Louis, came in with a group of four. He had heard through the grapevine what I was doing. He asked for wine, and I was delighted that I had the foresight to buy a bottle.

Ah, big spenders, not surf bums, I thought to myself. One dollar a glass extra revenue, and I won a bet that they would love my brandy cream pie. Ted and Capper got to it first and, in food frenzy, ate the whole thing. George should not have taken the whole pie out to them. What was he thinking? They did not have any money either. Ted offered to do the dishes, and Capper slipped out the back door, muttering something about paying when he got a check from his grandmother.

We sold sixteen dinners that night, and when the dishes were done, I sat down to count the money. After paying for the food that I had bought that day, we had six dollars. Split three ways, that was a mere two dollars each for Beau and George, and I did not get any dinner. George ate from the plates going and coming. The girls were with their grandmothers, so I did not have to worry about feeding them. Maybe the next night I would get to sell my pie.

The next day was the same as before. I baked, shopped, and cooked, setting the tables with flowers and candles, lighting them at sunset. I thought that maybe we should have named our restaurant "The Sunset." But, George had already given his creative input in naming the restaurant and in carving the sign, so "The Pebble" would stay.

That night Louis returned with seven people proclaiming, "This is the best restaurant in Santa Cruz." He proceeded to roll a joint at the table.

Well, at least they have good appetites, I thought to myself, stoners can always eat. Louis became my favorite regular customer, and he always brought several friends and paid, not like Capper and Ted who never had any money.

The Pebble restaurant lasted a couple of months with Capper and Ted not paying and George not charging people or making mistakes on the tabs. We were often without food at the end of the night and had just enough money to buy supplies for the next night. Finally, when Capper complained about not getting enough bread, I said, "That's it. I am closing the restaurant." And another chapter ended.

When I first met Ted, I had picked him up hitchhiking on Highway 17. It was night, and he was carrying a long surfboard and wearing a white sweater with a high school block letter. He was the picture of boyish good health, short hair, white teeth, and an innocence about him that only comes with youth. He lived in Stockton and was going to the beach to catch some waves. I took him home with me, and he spent the night and went surfing with the boys the next morning. He became a regular visitor on weekends. One Saturday morning as we were having breakfast, Ted arrived from the valley to surf and, without asking, reached over George, and helped himself to a large glass of orange juice from the blue Fostoria pitcher on the table. He drank it down fast. Before any of us could say anything, he refilled his glass and had a second one. I looked at George, who was grinning from ear to ear. The pitcher was loaded with LSD, enough for four of us. Ted had just swallowed a double, and this clean-cut schoolboy had never even smoked grass.

Two hours later, I was lying in the sand at Castle Beach when Ted came in from riding a wave. He was wet and glistening. He glowed. His smile was radiant, and he beamed. Looking up at the blue sky, he said, "A perfect sky," and looking down at the sand, said, "Wow! Look at the sand," dropping to his knees, staring at the sand. He looked up again and said, "Wow! Think I'll go back out," grabbed his board and was gone without questioning.

He knew where to spend his high. Cool! I thought, turning over to tan my other side and going back to my book. As Ted tells it, his life was my fault.

I ask you: did I tell him to drink that juice? He would have asked if he had any manners before taking the orange juice and would have gotten a warning. But no, Ted, as always, just helped himself. Ted moved to Santa Cruz soon after that and holed up in our basement, where he would crash at night after a day of surfing. He wore red surf trunks, and they became his only attire night or day, and of course, he was barefooted and bare-chested. He did let his hair grow and became a vegetarian. He rode an old bike with a wooden box wired to the handlebars in place of a basket. When he was not on the beach, he was riding around town looking for fruit trees to plunder. When he spied a plum tree on Pine Street, he would go back at night and harvest it. He lived on free fruit from other people's yards until he discovered the bins behind Shopper's Corner.

"You wouldn't believe what people throw away," he said.

Ted was getting way out there. When I was missing the honey bowl, I knew where to find it. Ted would make nightly raids to my kitchen and steal the honey bowl and carry it with him to his snarl of blankets in the basement, and if he could get away with the peanut butter, I would find them both by his bed. He became such a pest that finally we asked him to find his own place, and when George finally yelled at him, he moved in with Paul Martin, another surfer. Every day, we would still see him riding his flyer to check for surf or fruit, Ted's two passions in life. Then, he discovered enemas. Ted would stop by to tell me he had taken an enema that morning and how good he felt.

"It's the best thing to happen to man since peanut butter and honey," he would proclaim, "as a matter of fact, I think I'll go home and have another," and he would leave us as we shook our heads in amazement. Every time we saw him, he talked about enemas and nothing else.

"Yeah, I was feeling stopped up, so I took an enema, and that cleaned me right out. You should try it. It really makes you feel better," he would proclaim.

I was wondering, with all that fruit, he needed enemas, too? What was this boy's problem? Talk about anal-retentive.

Ted moved again to lower Pacific Avenue, a few blocks from the beach. It was a cute little house with shutters and window boxes. He proceeded to grow pot in the window boxes on Pacific Avenue. Was he crazy? Yes, he was. Not too long after, a policeman spotted his garden and knocked on the door. Ted was out surfing or looking for free food. Lieutenant Lewis left his business card. When Ted came home, he found the card and went directly to the police station wearing his red surf trunks and walked right in. At the counter, he asked in an innocent boyish Ted-ism, "Did you want to see me?"

"Why yes," the officer replied, "do you live at 1556 Pacific Avenue?"

Ted answered, "Yes, that would be me." The officer asked Ted if he was growing marijuana plants in the window boxes.

"Yes," Ted replied.

"Then come with me," said Officer Lewis. "You are under arrest."

Ted spent several days in the jail on Front Street in his red surf trunks, freezing his ass off until his parents were notified and came to bail him out. Ted appeared before the judge and was given three choices: join the army, go to jail, or move home with his parents and continue his education. This is how Ted became a college graduate, giving up the vegetarian, enemas, dope-smoking, and the hippie surf life he had made his own.

George was working for Everett and making surfboards on the side for a little cash, and I had discovered public assistance. After what I had been through in Fresno and The Pebble closing, I was ready for some time off. I accepted the free food and the $400 check that came once a month in the mail. It was enough to get by, and I could spend more time on the beaches and in the hills exploring Santa Cruz. I had been there for one year. Pete had moved back home with his parents. I had married George. The kids were happy in the neighborhood. I had new friends; Paul Fuller and Paul Bartko. I was settling into the grove of Santa Cruz.

My daughter, Lisa, became best friends with a sweet, shy, seven-year-old girl with big brown eyes and a pixie face, named Monah. They were inseparable. She lived down the street in a motel with her father and stepmother . . . She spent a lot of time at our house. One morning at about ten o'clock, there was a knock at the door. I opened it to find Monah and her stepmother, whom I had never met. She was wild-eyed and angry—crazy looking. There was a cardboard box in front of them. "Take her," the crazy lady said, "she wants to live with you." And with that, she stomped down the steps and left. As I brought Monah into the house, she did not say a word. She was stifling a sob and looked at the floor. I bent down and hugged her.

"Everything is going to be okay," I said. That afternoon, a welfare worker appeared at my door and asked if I could keep Monah till they could find a placement for her. Of course, I would take care of her, it was not a question in my mind. And that is how I became a foster parent, gaining one of the sweetest people in my life. She is my daughter to this day.

In Fresno, I had been a radical hippie. Here, I was a conservative welfare mother. George got a job for Haut Surfboards glassing surfboards. The Haut brothers, Doug and Dan were two Santa Cruz icons, along with Jack O'Neill. They ruled Steamer Lane. Younger surfers always deferred to them out of respect and admiration. They caught the first wave while younger surfers hung back in the pack. I watched the ritual from the shore and spent a lot of time on the beach with a book.

Marti, my new friend from across the street, lived in an apartment with her redneck husband, Al. Her mother, Mary, was an amazing woman in her sixties: tall, elegant, and soft-spoken, with a twinkle in her eyes and ready laugh. Always finding the lighter side of things and the best in everyone, she had been married to her husband Elwin for thirty years.

Hand in hand, I would often see them strolling about town in the evening. Theirs was a remarkably enduring love story.

Photo 16 - Me and Marti

Marti was her mother's daughter; tall, willowy, with a positive attitude and a fun-loving nature. We would take the kids to the river mouth beach together, letting them play in the surf while we tanned and talked. Her husband always had a six-pack under his arm, and mine held surf above everything, including me. Neither of us were particularly happy in our marriages but made the best of it.

George had a quick temper. One summer night Marti and I decided to go for a bike ride. I had a bike, she did not. We slipped down to the restaurant where the guys were hanging out playing pool and took George's bike. George saw us as we were riding up the hill by the trestle, and at that distance, he could not tell it was us. He thought we were some kids stealing his bike, so he chased us, cursing, threatening, and generally working himself into an angered frenzy, pumping his arms, running as hard as he could. Feet pounding on the payment, he screamed at the top of his lungs the things he would do to us when he caught us. We were not about to stop, and pedaled as fast as we could up the hill and around the corner, out of sight, laughing breathlessly. Then we stopped and caught our breath. We rode around town for a while, enjoying the summer night and the quiet streets.

When we finally turned onto Bixby Street, George was waiting for us and caught us as we pulled up in front of the apartments across the street. A new couple moving in on the third floor while standing on their balcony were treated to the sight of George ranting and raving. Marti called it "wigging out" as he called us every name in the book—we were "whores and bitches not fit to walk the earth." The baffled couple watched us as we were verbally abused into the ground. Marti and I said goodnight and went to our separate homes.

George was so mad at me that he went to work at the Haut shop. In a fit of anger, he kicked over a can of resin into a small heater and set the place on fire. The Haut shop burned to the ground that night.

George's temper, when it flared, as it often did, things were thrown through the air. Once, he grew so enraged (funny, I don't remember why, but the results I do remember), he picked up a cast iron Dutch oven and hurled it at me. I whirled (a move remembered from fourth-grade dodge ball) and missed being hit by the pot and its contents, the previous night's beef stew. It smashed into the kitchen wall behind me with such force that the handle came off, and stew splattered all over the surf collage on the wall. I refused to cook for him again until he welded the handle back on. My grandmother had given me that Dutch oven.

George and I fought like a couple of puppies wrestling—biting, pulling hair, spitting—all while cursing. The smallest things set us off. It really bugged me when I cooked a meal and was just putting it on the table when a head would pop in the door yelling, "Surf's up!" and he'd take off, never thinking about the effort I'd put into dinner. Be it my birthday, Christmas, or Easter, no matter what he'd promised me earlier he'd do—take out the garbage, clean up, whatever—if the surf was up, George was gone.

CHAPTER 30

Bill, a love story

Usually, a thick summer fog rolled in on the Fourth of July, but that day it was unusually clear and hot. George and I decided to go camping with Marti and her husband, Big Al.

Usually, Marti wore short miniskirts with her hair pulled up in a ponytail, but today she was dressed in cutoffs and a tie-dyed t-shirt. I was wearing a similar red, white, and blue tie-dyed t-shirt, which Marti had made for me the previous day.

Having planned our meals, we gathered apple turnovers and bread from Maddox Bakery, to which we added to our cheese, apples, eggs, and beer. Packing it all into our backpacks, we evenly distributed the weight, envisioning how it would be carried on our husband's backs. That is when George came bursting into the living room with a wild grin in his face.

"Surf's up," he announced, grabbing his long board, and heading towards the door. Marti and I exchanged glances, thinking, What about our camping trip? The door swung open and Big Al, the "Lodi cowboy," stood there with his usual quizzical expression. He always looked like the world around him was a surprise. He also always had a Budweiser can dangling from his hand. Al had drinking issues.

"Where ya going?" he asked George, as if it wasn't obvious.

"Checking the surf," George announced, pushing passed him.

"Hey, wait—I'll get a six pack," cried Al, rushing across the street to his apartment. They were both gone before Marti and I could voice any objections.

We waited for several hours for their return, and then began to get mad. We waited some more. About four o'clock they came up the stairs stumbling drunk, laughing, and having a good old time. Al carried another six pack under his arm and George cradled his surfboard, hair still wet, nose sunburned under the white goop he put on for protection.

"You're drunk!" Marti exclaimed, hands on hips.

George found this very funny and laughed out loud while he stood his board against the wall. Marti and I went into the house for a conference. At that point, we decided to go camping without them, it would serve them right! We shouldered the backpacks and set off, ignoring their laughter.

We walked down Bixby Street and turned the corner on Seacliff Drive, which was bumper to bumper with traffic heading for the beach and the fireworks. Our packs were heavy—we adjusted them and kept going. We hadn't trudged a block when we began to hear catcalls, hoots and hollers. The boys, our husbands, drove alongside, hanging out the window, pounding on the door.

"Hey baby, want a ride?"

"No thanks," we said in unison.

They passed us, circled the block and we continued up the street. Boy, I wish someone would come along and pick us up, I thought, and then looked up.

"Yeah!" I exclaimed, "Motorcycles!"

Marti chimed in, "Two motorcycles!"

Riding them—two Hondas: one red and one blue—were two great looking guys. As they zoomed passed us with their long hair flying and one with a bared bronze chest, I let out a surf *whoop*—the call of the wild.

The two bikes turned around in the middle of the street and pulled up beside us. Boy, were they cute!

"Hi ladies, want to go to a barbeque with us?" one asked.

Marti and I looked at each other. There was a moment of hesitation as we sized them up.

"I will if you will," said Marti.

"Yes! We do," I said, and quickly made a choice that would change my life. I climbed on the back of the one with the bare, tanned, and muscular chest, and wrapped my arms around him, grinning at Marti. We were escaping—our wish had come true.

Stopping at a food market, the guys picked up some steaks and a bottle of wine. We were back on the bikes and heading out of town, turning at the University of California Santa Cruz. Up the hill we flew, wind in our hair, sun on my back and arms tight around a bare chest. Oh, yeah, I thought.

We pulled into the field house parking lot and dismounted. We found out that their names were Bill and Howard, they were university students, and the barbeque was a private one, just them and us. We walked out over the green lawn to a picnic table on the edge of the grass near the swimming pool. No one else was there, as everyone was off campus for the holiday.

We produced the beer, still cold, and apple turnovers. While Howard built a fire, we drank beer and got to know each other. Of course, neither Marti nor I mentioned that we were married. Why open that can of worms? We talked and laughed and ate and drank as the sun set. Bill suggested that we go for a swim. Neither Marti or I had brought bathing suits and we gave each other a look: *I will if you will.* I smiled shyly as I pulled my t-shirt over my head and headed for the pool where I dropped my shorts and jumped in. We all skinny dipped in the university pool.

We were having a great time. After our swim, we dressed and went out to the edge of the lawn overlooking Monterey Bay, and watched the fireworks. The fog had started to roll in, so our view was obstructed a bit, but the fireworks that flashed through the fog drew "ohs" and "awes" from the four of us.

After the fireworks, the guys asked us if we wanted to come home with them. We asked where they lived and they replied, "In a tree house." I didn't believe them, but I gave Marti that look again—*I will if you will.*

We set off in the gathering darkness, holding hands and stumbling along. We had walked quite a while, leaving the student housing area behind and hiking through a meadow and then trees, laughing and joking the whole way. We stopped in the middle of the forest and Bill announced that we were there.

Where is there? I thought. He read my mind and pointed straight up into a redwood tree. Though I saw nothing, Howard said that he would go up and light a lantern. He put his pack down and jumped for a limb of the tree, pulling himself up and then standing on the limb. He started to climb. After a couple minutes a light appeared about fifty feet up. Looking straight up, I had to crane my neck and tip my head all the way back to see it.

"You're kidding," I exclaimed.

"Nope," Bill replied, laughing. "We built it high enough so it wouldn't be seen. It is three platforms strung between three trees with rope, so it sways with the wind. It is kinda nice, like sleeping in a cradle. Come on, I'll give you a shoulder up."

"Oh, no, not me, I'm afraid of heights," I said, backing away, still looking up. Marti was already at the tree trunk. Howard had climbed down to give her a hand up. With her long body she didn't have far to reach, and he pulled her up easily. There she was, balanced on the first limb, laughing out loud.

"Come on Carol, it's fun!" she exclaimed.

There was no time for the *I will if you will*; Marti was going up the tree. I watched in amazement as she climbed, talking and laughing with Howard the whole time. He was holding the lantern above her head and showing her where to put her hands and feet. The tree was taller than two telephone poles, and I was not going up there; this was not fun anymore.

Bill said, "Let's sit down for a few minutes and talk."

Telling me how they built the tree house, he said that there was another roommate. The three of them had decided to save money and not pay for student housing, and therefore, built the tree house on the back of the university property. It had taken them three days of hauling the wood up the tree with ropes: first, was the observation deck, the smallest on top; next was the sleeping deck below it; and then the living room and kitchen on the first floor. No nails were used so as not to hurt the tree. Each night they climbed the tree and rolled into their sleeping bags in the top of the trees, under the stars.

"What about rain?" I inquired.

"Oh, we have tarps. We study at the library and shower at the gym. My mom wanted me to get a college education and I didn't want to disappoint her . . . but I'm not really sure what I want to study. Right now, I am a history major, but I'm thinking of changing that, but I don't really know what to change it to."

Bill shrugged his shoulders and said, "Ready to go up?"

Then he jutted his chin towards the tree and as he stood up, took my hand and pulled me toward the tree, saying, "How about we go to the first branch and you see how it feels?"

Trees are strong, this one is my friend, I kept telling myself.

The first branch was eight feet off the ground. Bill lifted me onto his shoulders and suggested that I grab hold and pull myself onto the limb and just sit there, and I did.

As he swung his six-foot frame up beside me with ease, he said gently, "There, feel safe? The trick about climbing a tree is to stay close into the trunk, hugging the tree."

Sitting down beside me, we continued our conversation. "Scott and Howard, my partners in the tree house and school, both know what they want to do with their lives. I don't. I'm only in school because of my mother. I feel guilty taking her money for school, so I try to save money by living as cheaply as possible, and by not paying for a dorm or buying much food. I'll get a job this summer and try to pay some of the expenses myself. Meanwhile, the best I can do is get good grades and not let her down."

Pausing for a moment to study my face, he said, "Can you reach up and touch that branch over your head? Now with both hands pull yourself up, standing close to the trunk. There you go . . . now, pull yourself up to the next branch and let's sit there awhile."

Now we were ten feet off the ground.

Bill continued, "How about we try for the next limb, just stay close to the trunk. You're safe, I won't let anything happen to you—want to go higher?"

"Okay," I said, feeling a little schoolgirl-silly. "Sure, let's climb higher."

The branches were closer together now, about two to three feet apart, so it was easier to get from one to another. The smell of cedar surrounded us. After a few minutes we were halfway up the tree, and I began to feel queasy in my stomach and had that vertigo feeling of *oh my God, I'm going to lose it*. I could hear Marti and Howard above us, talking and laughing. Marti had made it to the top and was standing on the platform. This was one time she had shown me up.

Bill could tell I was scared and put his arms around me. "All right?" he asked.

"Yeah, just a little shaky. Can we sit down some more?" I asked.

"Sure," he said, smiling at me with his big brown eyes. We sat in the tree in silence. Reassuring me, he stroked my back. "We won't climb higher than you want to. I promise I won't let you fall, I'm right here beside you. I've climbed this tree a million times and I haven't fallen yet— and I don't intend to! It sounds like Marti and Howard have hit it off. I haven't heard Howard laugh that much in a long time. Actually, never. Howard's a little shy with girls."

"Hey, Marti," I called up, "How's it up there?"

"Fabulous!" she answered, "Carol, come on up, the view is awesome!"

"Okay," I shouted as I looked at Bill, "I'm ready to go further now," I told him.

We climbed up, with me hugging the trunk, reaching up for the next limb, and then the next, with my feet following. We climbed towards the light and the laughter. I could see that we were almost there when my heart sank. Just before the platform there was a space of about four or five feet with no limbs—a bare, open space in the tree. I would have to stand on a branch and pull myself up with my arms onto the platform.

No way, I thought. So close and yet so far. I could not do it. I looked at Bill in wide-eyed fear, with a trembling lip and told him that I couldn't go any further.

"Yes, you can," he reassured me. "I'm here and you're not going to fall, and Howard's going to help you up from there." Howard's face beamed a wide smile down to me with Marti leaning over his shoulder.

"Come on up, it's fun," he cheered.

Looking at Bill again, he smiled down at me from his position curled around me and waited for me to make the call. I stood on a limb and Marti said, "It's easy."

"Yeah, but you have long arms and legs," I complained to Marti.

"You have me," said Bill. "Just try to reach up and see if you can touch the last limb while I hold onto you. Okay . . . ready Howard, grab her hands."

The next thing I knew I was being pulled and pushed through the opening to the platform, then lay on the floor panting and shaking like I had just run a marathon. Marti was sitting beside me saying, "Oh, Carol, it's all right. We're just having fun."

Bill took me into his lap, cuddled me like a baby, and with his big eyes smiling down at me, kissed my brow. There was nothing to be afraid of—I made it!

"Congratulations! You're on top of the world," Bill exclaimed.

As Marti and Howard climbed up to the next platform, I had a fleeting thought about how I was going to get down. I looked at Bill, at the man who had talked me up the tree. He was big, six foot two, with broad shoulders. He wore a faded denim jacket, unbuttoned, exposing a muscular, golden tanned chest with a well-defined, hardened six pack. He really took my breath away. His face was gentle, sweet, honest, and kind. Young, but wise. This was a good man. His hair was light brown and hung straight down to his shoulders. He looked like Cochise, an Indian warrior—Brave Heart! His nose had his only flaw, a light bump like his mother had dropped him when he was a baby, yet it lent character to his face. His eyes shone with a bright light that came from a genuinely good soul. Oh boy, just like that, I was in love. He leaned forward and kissed me—a long, slow, gentle kiss. "Cold?" he asked.

"A little," I replied, as he unrolled his blue down sleeping bag. He told me to climb in as he got up and blew out the light. Now we could see the stars. The next thing I knew, he was beside me and I was in his arms, feeling like I had come home. It felt so right; I was safe and secure. He gently kissed me again, softly and with love. We lay in each other's arms and I felt peace like I had never experienced before. My eyes were adjusting to the dark and I could see the star-filled night sky. The moon had now risen and was shining on us through the trees. We looked at each other for a long time. Feeling as though I could get lost, no, found, in those eyes, I said, "I know you."

"Really?" he said, smiling.

"Yes, I don't know where from, but I know you." He kissed me again, but this time longer.

In the morning Howard made breakfast of nettle tea and oatmeal, cooking over a Bunsen burner. Marti and I finally asked them where the bathroom was.

"Oh, you just crawl out onto a limb," Howard said, pointing over his shoulder.

"I think I'll wait. You go ahead, Marti," I said as I knew this would be incentive for me to get my feet back on the ground.

"Ladies, would you like showers?" Bill asked.

"Oh, yes please."

They suggested the field house as no one was there that morning.

"There is water, and we have towels," they told us.

The trip down the tree wasn't as difficult as getting up, and, of course, there was light outside now. Bill went first, guiding me. In fact, it was hardly any time at all before I was on the ground again. Thank God! I felt almost giddy.

We trucked up the hill through ferns, rhododendrons, and azaleas growing in the soft soil. An early morning light filtered through the redwoods and cedars, casting an iridescent glow on Bill's hair, looking to me like a halo on a renaissance figure in a stained-glass window. Lord! He is handsome, I thought. Retracing our steps from the night before, we returned to the field house and Bill gave us both towels.

At this point, Marti and I were free to discuss the night's events.

"I think I'm in love. He's the kindest, gentlest man I have ever known." I said as I looked in the mirror and discovered that I had a hickey on my neck. "Oh, now what am I going to do? What are we going to tell Al and George?"

"Well," said Marti, drawling out the word, "we don't have to tell them anything. At least not today. Let's not go back right away. For today," Marti explained, "let's just enjoy the day. We'll worry about everything later."

"You mean not go home now?" I asked.

"Right, that's exactly what I mean," Marti said, grinning.

After our showers we met up with the guys for a stroll around campus. It was my first time there and I was overwhelmed with the beauty and serenity of the colleges. Crown College was Bill's, Merrill was home for Howard, and Cowell had a sunny plaza with a view of the bay. Cowell was located in a white building circling the plaza and it gave me the feeling that I wanted to be there. I wanted to go to school there. A dream was starting to play in my head as we sat on the lawn and talked. Bill told us about a friend of his whose girlfriend took off her clothes and sat on the lawn in protest. Pretty radical: "Bezerkley" by the Sea, I thought. This campus was for me.

That afternoon it was time to go home. Marti and I had prolonged the inevitable for as long as we could. I had fallen head-over-heals in love with Bill, and as Marti pointed out later, we had connected. Feeling that I had known him all my life, I was sure that I knew him! But from where? I could not remember. Not in this lifetime, anyway.

Photo 17 – Bill

CHAPTER 31

Bill (continued)

"Oh what tangled webs we weave when first we practice to deceive."

The famous quote from Scottish poet Sir Walter Scott's, *Marmion: A Tale of Flodden Field* sometimes attributed to Shakespeare, rumbled through my mind as Marti and I returned the next week to climb the tree in bold daylight and leave cookies for Howard and Bill. We started to see them, sneaking away from the Bixby Street house to the "Mecca of Higher Learning"—actually, to the tree house in the redwoods.

Bill had told me that I could audit classes by just showing up, talking to the professor, and asking to join the class. No money, no credits, but the education was there for the taking.

Wow! What an opportunity! In September I would plan to do just that.

Meanwhile, we had the summer on their motorcycles. There we were, Marti and I, clinging to the boys' backs, hair whipping us in our faces. We toured the mountains, picnicked in the woods, and swam in the rivers. The four of us became a group. None of us had any money, but fifty cents worth of gas could go a long way in a Honda bike. Marti and I would usually pack lunches. We snuck away from our other lives every chance we had—and it was easy because our husbands were involved in surfing and drinking, and didn't miss us, except when they wanted food. As long as we left food out, we weren't missed at all.

I finally told Bill I was married and explained that I had married George to keep him out of the draft, and that it wasn't a real marriage. I was beginning to believe that myself, although I had real affection for George, and yes, I loved him. But, Bill was my soulmate; everything and everyone before him were just stepping-stones on the path of getting to Bill. I had helped George and he had helped me, and we'd had a fun adventure, but now it was time to move on. I had found Bill.

Bill was not sure about me. He had a girlfriend from school who had been with several of his friends. He had found a list she had kept of men she had slept with and it included everyone he knew. He had been hurt and said that he did not think he had ever been in love, not with her or anyone else. He told me that he wished he could feel deep emotion, even pain, but especially love, yet he feared this was something missing from his personality. I listened quietly, thinking how glad I was that he did not love her. What a nymphomaniac, God, she slept with thirty-six guys in one school year. That was more than I had slept with in my entire life. But for now, Bill wanted to be with me, and I wanted to be with him.

One day we met on the field house lawn and Bill looked unhappy and Howard, even more unhappy.

"What's wrong," I questioned, touching Bill's arm.

Bill looked at Howard to explain. Howard cleared his throat. "They found our tree house."

"Who's they?" I asked.

"The dean of students," Howard replied. "We have to tear it down and now we have nowhere to live. The man we borrowed the wood from wants to talk to us and we might get kicked out of school."

"Oh, I'm so sorry," I said, as Marti remarked that something good would come of it.

Bill and Howard weren't so sure. They had an appointment at the dean's office the next morning and were spending the night at a friend's house on Pine Street. The next time we saw them was about a week later and Howard was all smiles. Bill was grinning from ear to ear as they pulled up their motorcycles in front of us sitting on the curb on Bixby Street.

"What happened," Marti and I both asked in unison.

"Well, we're living on Pine Street with Charlie and Charlie, who invited us to move in with them at least temporarily." Bill said, exuberantly.

"Yes, but what about the dean and the man you borrowed the wood from?" we asked.

"He took us to lunch," beamed Howard, "at the Nut Tree."

"In Vacaville?" we quizzed.

"Yep!" said Bill, "He flew us there."

"You're kidding!" we shrieked in laughter.

Bill raised his eyebrows, and his voice went up an octave, "Nope, we're not. He is a nice guy and a contractor. He builds houses, and he even climbed our tree. He liked what we did. 'Very creative' were his words. But he said that the only problem was that we borrowed the wood without asking him, and that was wrong. He has this neat little yellow Cessna, and we flew to lunch, where he talked to us in a fatherly fashion. We agreed to pay for the wood and promised never to do it again, and he bought us lunch, and it was great, and my mother doesn't have to know," Bill finished breathlessly.

"Boy! Are you guys lucky," I said.

"See," Marti said, "Good things happen to good people. And now you are living in town?"

"Yeah, but we'll miss the tree house," Howard mused, towing the ground.

"So will we," giggled Marti.

"And I will never forget my first climb," I said, looking into Bill's gentle eyes.

"Want to meet the Charlies?" Bill asked.

"Sure," we replied, "we probably better get out of here."

"Go time," said Marti, sliding on behind Howard who was revving up his engine.

The house on Pine Street sat on a corner with a small garden and a white picket fence. It had probably belonged to someone's grandmother, but like so many houses in Santa Cruz, it was now student housing. It was untidy. Typical, I thought. Dishes were in the sink, and clothes were thrown about a floor that hadn't seen a mop since inhabited by the two Charlies.

Charlie Greir was tall and gangly with long, tangled strawberry hair that would have been the envy of any girl. But his face was not the least bit feminine, nor was the voice that said hello when introduced. Charlie G. looked at us with interest as if he had heard a lot about us and was trying to decide whether he liked us.

"Hello," he said with a laugh. "Finally we meet. You must be Carol and you must be Marti," he said with a smile that turned into a snicker. I then wondered what he had been told.

"Does your husband know you're here?" he said with another snicker.

Oh, he knows that, I thought, then he excused himself, saying he had something else to do as he walked away in his bare feet. My, what big feet, I thought!

Charlie Daniels was standing at the sink shelling peas from the garden. He nodded in our direction, and when introduced he said hi without looking up. His shaggy, dirty-blonde hair hung over his thick-lensed glasses. He was short, stocky and wore overalls, dirty from the garden. His feet were encased in work boots, covered with dry mud, flaking off on the mat he stood on. Earthman, I silently named him—shy, bookish, a hobbit.

Marti, taking interest in the peas, asked Charlie D. what else grew in his garden, and drew him into a conversation.

"Where do you sleep?" I asked Bill.

He laughed, pointing at a sleeping bag on the floor. "Oh, here, or there, depending on what spaces is not taken when I decide to crash. Howard sleeps there," pointing to another sleeping bag rolled up near a fish tank. "He likes the ocean view."

Now that Bill and Howard were living so close, only blocks away and accessible, and no tree to climb, Marti and I could ride our bicycles and drop in whenever we liked—and we liked to a lot. We baked cookies and cakes. Once I brought a Bisquick coffeecake and met Scott for the first time. He was standing at the kitchen sink when I knocked on the open door, cake in hand.

"Ah, you must be Carol," he said, smiling, showing a mouth full of pearly whites that were obviously well-tended. Tanned and wearing only shorts, his long blond hair was tied neatly under a red bandana. A healthy specimen, I thought, and cute—almost too cute. His blue eyes looked at me with amusement.

"Whatcha got there?" as he pointed to the cake. "Something for Billy Boy?"

I flushed; he made me feel uncomfortable. He stepped closer.

"Ah," he said, "bet you made it with Bisquick. Easy, huh?"

I was busted. Guess I should have made something from scratch. Not good enough, was the impression I got from Scott.

"Oh, well," I said, "I was in a hurry."

Scott gave me a look like, *why bother?* Just then a shadow fell on me and I turned around to find Bill standing on the doorstep behind me. I held out the cake to him.

"For me?" he said smiling his sincere delight, which made everything all right. He didn't mind a Bisquick coffee cake. He was happy to see me, and Scott was forgotten.

I learned later that Scott was a baker. All the guys baked, especially Bill. But this was to come later. Next time I would make a better effort. Scott, I was to discover, came from a family with money and was a bit of a snob, a ladies' man, and charming, when he chose to be.

CHAPTER 32

The Grand Canyon

The summer we spent with Bill and Howard was the most fun I have ever had. It was a whirl of music, motorcycles, and MDA. MDA was a cream-colored substance that looked like a sugar substitute. We mixed it in our Mickey Big Mouths (malt liquor) or smoothies and waited for the world to adjust. It was euphoric. High on MDA, you simply loved everything and everybody. The roses were sweeter, and you really noticed them. I wished the whole planet could be on MDA all the time. I remember riding through the mountains on the back of Bill's bike, arms wrapped around him, listening to the music playing inside my head and the hills of Renoir's blue conatus and wild lilac. This was the summer of dreams, laughter, lovemaking, simple foods shared with good friends, and adventures into the hills and deserts.

Bill invited me on a trip to the Grand Canyon. The kids were with their grandparents for the summer, and I was free to go. I packed light: jeans, t-shirts, and my cosmetics bag. Although I didn't wear makeup, I still needed clean hair and shaved legs. I was not a UCSC student yet. None of the girls on campus shaved their legs—yuck! Bill supplying me with a helmet and straddling the bike with my arms wrapped around him, I felt safe. The world was ours to share. We rode from sunrise to sunset, the wind in our faces, the sun on our backs. After we got out of California traffic and the roads became less traveled, the horizon could be seen for miles. Taking off my shirt, I let the sun hit my bare back. We camped in the desert among the tall cacti, making our bed on the sand, with star-filled skies above us.

Being held in Bill's arms was the safest place in the world. When I looked into his eyes, they swam with love and happiness. I had never felt such unconditional love, so cared for, or so fully accepted for what I was. He was the most gentle, loving person I had ever met. There was a sweetness about him, a spiritual kindness that radiated from his very soul. Being in such a state of blissful excitement, I had a hard time falling asleep, but when I did, I woke with a smile on my face. When I turned in his arms, I would see his warm brown eyes smiling down on me with complete, accepting love. A new day would begin.

Lying in Bill's blue down sleeping bag, waiting for the morning chill to subside, I told him about my life before I met him: the disappointments, the hurt, the beatings, the rape, and the mistakes I had made. Had I known he was on the planet I would have waited for him like Siddhartha sitting beside the river. With complete acceptance, he told me that everything I had been through, made me who I was. He said I had depth and compassion because of it, and that he loved me for it. God! He was wonderful. My eyes filled with tears of gratitude. He held me while I cried, cleansing myself from the past.

"There, there," he said stroking my hair and kissing my cheek. "Everything is all right now. We have found each other."

We made tea on the Bunsen burner and shared some dried fruit. After that, we packed up, mounted the bike, and headed east towards Williams, Arizona, and the Grand Canyon. The sun was rising and cranking up the heat. By noon we reached Williams and stopped to buy provisions for a picnic. We got some potato salad from a grocery deli, and sliced smoked turkey and cheese for sandwiches.

"A cold beer would be nice," I said, wistfully

"Shall we?" raising his eyebrows at me.

"Yes, please," I replied. "It's noon and it's summer and we're on vacation."

We selected a couple of Heineken Darks in frosty cool-green bottles and got back on the bike to look for a picnic place on the edge of town. We found a secluded place with a few trees and settled down for lunch in the shade.

"Oh, no," I cried, "we can't eat the potato salad."

"Why?" Bill said, looking surprised when I reminded him that we didn't have any eating utensils. No forks, not even a spoon. Then his face brightened with an idea. "Let's use what they used before they invented forks."

"What's that?" I asked, really confused.

"Our fingers!" he exclaimed.

Feeling quite silly that I was ready to give up the potato salad, I laughed and said, "I never would have thought of that. Boy, am I dumb!"

"No, you're not," he said smiling at me. "You have me to take care of you."

We both laughed and opened the potato salad. After lunch, we lay in the grass and talked some more. Bill told me about his family. He adored his mother; she was strong and smart and his best friend. She had taught him to cook and sew. He said she would like me, and he wanted me to meet her. He promised he would cook for me when we returned, and that he particularly liked to bake bread and was trying his hand at mixed grain bread. He said they did not rise as well as white breads and there must be a secret that he had not found yet. Scott did most of the baking at the Pine Street house, but it was mostly white bread and Bill thought whole grains were healthier.

Bill looked up at the sun in full heaven and as he stood up and pulled me to my feet, said, "Ready to ride?" Holding me for a moment, he then picked up our helmets, handing me mine. We set off into the afternoon sun climbing into the high desert. It was late afternoon when we turned off the main highway onto one marked "Grand Canyon South Entrance." Bill called something to me that got carried away in the wind as he slowed the bike and pulled off the road.

"We should probably look for a place to spend the night," I called out to him.

"What about here?" He said, pointing to a gate with a sign that said, "Please Close the Gate." Behind the gate was an open meadow of grass turned to gold and further back in the meadow was an old grove of sequoias, pine, and cedars—majestic shelter.

"It looks friendly, and it doesn't say keep out," I said. "So, I guess we're welcome if we close the gate."

Bill pushed the bike in as I held the gate open, and we went back to the grove of trees. It was so quiet as the late afternoon sun filtered through the trees casting shadows. I took a deep breath, "It's so peaceful," I said quietly.

"Pick out your bedroom," Bill replied.

After I picked a place under the cedars, Bill began to gather pine needles to make our bed. When he had enough for a double size bed, he spread the sleeping bag on top and then turned his attention to setting up the Bunsen burner for dinner as I sat in the grass and watched. It was strange to have someone doing for me, as usually I did everything for everybody around me. He sat on his haunches Indian style, his long brown hair almost to his shoulders, his face bronzed by the sun. He looks like an Indian, I thought. Cochise, that's who he is, and I thought of my own Indian life.

It seemed to me that Bill and I meshed when it came to being outdoors. As I sat looking at him, I reflected on the way I had felt about him when we first met, as if I already knew him somehow, and that we had been together before. Bill interrupted my thoughts when he turned to me and asked if I was hungry.

"Yes," I replied, coming back to the here and now.

"How about beef stew tonight? Of course, it's freeze-dried rations, but actually pretty good. Shall we?"

"Oh, yes, that sounds wonderful," I replied.

We ate before dark, put away the food, and just wiped the dishes on the grass, deciding to wash them tomorrow so to conserve our drinking water. At that point I was wondering where the bathroom was. "I think I'll take a walk over there," as I wandered off through the trees.

"Good idea," Bill said smiling, knowingly, "I'll walk in the other direction. Just holler if you need me."

It was a full moon that night and we could not sleep. Instead, we walked in the woods and came across one of those big yellow jobs that scoops earth from the ground.

"Are you my mother?" I asked, remembering a child's book in which a chick is hatched and thinks the first thing it sees is its mother. In the moonlight, the big yellow thing glowed with a friendly light. I climbed up on it and sat in the driver's seat. "Rummmm, rummmm," I said, "Rumble, rumble," while shifting gears, hand on the steering wheel. "Let's start it!" I teased.

"No, we can't!" Bill squeaked. His voice broke whenever I suggested anything preposterous. It was cute, such a big man making a squeaking noise.

"Yes, I can!" I stated emphatically. "And I will."

"No, you won't," he said, this time using his deep, manly voice, as he began to pull me down from the driver's seat, but I held on.

"Gonna start it, go for a ride," I chanted.

"Over my dead body," he argued.

"That can be arranged," I challenged. "Run over you with big yellow thing. Please lie down in front of it," I directed.

"What?" Bill said in his squeaky voice. "You would run over me with your big yellow thing?"

"Only a little," I suggested. With that, he flopped down in front of the big yellow thing, spread eagle.

"Ohhhhh!" I murmured, as I jumped down from the machine and threw myself on him. "I would never, never, run over you with my big yellow thing."

Bill was laughing and his eyes sparkled in the moon light. He smelled good—I kissed him. He pulled me tighter on top on him, hugging me and rocking back and forth. Oh! I loved him so much.

In the morning we laid in our sleeping bag, as we had grown accustomed to doing, and talked about our past. We seemed like old friends that hadn't seen each other in a long time and had so much catching up to do. I could tell him everything. Sometimes he cried for me, his big brown eyes filling with tears.

"I wish I could have been there," he would say.

"So do I, but you're here now, and that's all that matters." I replied.

The morning sun was warming us, and our spirits began to rise. "Let's make tea," I said.

"Okay, but first I'll make water," Bill announced, pulling his lanky frame to a standing position, and stretching. "You know, we're low on water. We're going to have to make some soon."

Yeah, find some, not make some, I thought with a smile as Bill shuffled off to a private spot leaving me to brush my tangled hair. That was about all I could do to make myself presentable for the day. We had been camping now for three days and I needed to find a shower. I started the Bunsen burner and poured enough of the water into the pan for tea for Bill. I decided that I would rather wash my face with my share.

He came rumbling back and plopped cross-legged onto the ground beside me and asked me what I wanted to do that day. "Go into the Grand Canyon?"

"Not really, I love this meadow and don't feel like leaving it yet. It kind of feels like home."

"My sentiments exactly," he replied. "The Grand Canyon has been there a long time, it can wait. But there is the issue of water. Let's go out to the road and flag down a car and ask for water—want to?"

"Okay." I complied.

We went out to the road, sat beside the gate, and waited. Not long after, a Volkswagen Bug appeared on the horizon. We stood up and put on our helpless smiles and stretched out our arms to show we weren't carrying firearms. The Bug slowed to a stop. The driver was a long-haired, bright eyed young man in a white t-shirt and jeans. His face was as open as his windows.

"Got anything to drink? Water?" we queried, in unison.

"Only gasoline," he replied, with a smile.

At that point I noticed that he had a guitar and we invited him to join us in the meadow and play for us. Without hesitation he agreed, and we opened the gate so he could pull his Bug through. "I could use a break from driving," as he got out and stretched.

"Welcome to our meadow," Bill smiled a warm greeting. "Sorry we don't have anything to offer you. We're out of water but we'd love to hear some music," as we walked him to our campsite. "I'm Bill and this is my lady, Carol." I beamed. "And you are?"

"Paul, my name's Paul and I'm on my way to the Grand Canyon."

"Of course, you are!" I exclaimed. "Paul is perfect—my two best friends are named Paul and we are also headed to the Grand Canyon."

We reached the campsite and sprawled on the ground, anticipating our concert, and we were not disappointed. Paul began to strum his guitar as he looked around.

"Nice place you have here."

"Yeah, we like it," Bill said, smiling at me. "It's home."

Paul began to play Neil Young—"Cowgirl in the Sand"—Bill and I locked eyes. "Perfect," I said, as Bill nodded in agreement. Both Bill and I loved Neil Young and played him often. Paul was an accomplished guitarist and surprised us even more with a lovely voice—we were enchanted.

After a couple more Neil Young songs Paul stopped and looked up at the sun, which was now in mid heaven, and said, "No water, huh? Wanna go look for some? We can go in my Bug."

"Sure, sounds good," answered Bill as he stood up, reaching out his hand to pull me to my feet. The three of us walked to his car and climbed in. Paul told us that he was a student at the University of Colorado on a summer adventure, just like me and Bill. We headed towards the Grand Canyon and found a campground with water and showers.

"Do you mind if I indulge in a quick shower?" I asked.

Paul replied that he had a towel and soap in the car and offered them to me. I was extremely grateful. A few minutes later I came out feeling great.

"Heaven," I exclaimed. "Thanks, Paul. How can we repay you?"

Bill offered, "How about dinner? We have some yummy, freeze-dried chicken curry and dried fruit—and now we have water."

"Too bad we don't have a nice bottle of wine to go with it," I teased.

As we were walking back to Paul's car, I spotted something on the curb in the parking lot. We were the only car there, no one else around, and I went to check it out. As I got closer, it looked like a six pack of beer sitting on the ground. It contained three unopened cans of beer. Eureka!

"Look what I found," as I bent over to pick them up. "They are warm, though, but I bet they're wet. A gift from heaven."

I carried my booty to Paul's Bug, and we headed back to our campsite. Life was good—music and a shower, and now this! What more could I ask?

We returned to the meadow and Bill cooked the meal as promised while Paul entertained us with his music. I sat on the ground and felt like a queen. The sun was sinking into the West over the cedars and twilight surrounded us softly. We ate our meal in silence, listening to the sounds of the forest. After, we made our beds and laid down to watch the stars and talked about the Vietnam war. Paul had been drafted and this was his time to think about what to do. He was considering Canada.

"But you're a student," I exclaimed.

"Yeah, but I got my notice," Paul answered woefully.

"They can't take you," I said angrily. "Just don't show up," I suggested.

"Think I'll just avoid the whole thing and go to Canada until it's over. I can go to school there. I have friends there," Paul mused.

"Probably best," I said, sleepily, thinking about my friend Paul shooting his foot. Thank God Bill was in school, I thought as I snuggled into his arms and he pulled me closer and nuzzled my hair and murmured into my ear. Yes, this was a safe place.

The next morning, we decided to approach the Grand Canyon. Paul said good-bye and we wished him a safe journey. We took our time packing. The sun was fully up by the time we climbed onto Bill's bike and headed for the canyon. It was hot and I was wearing a t-shirt and jeans, my usual. I had knotted my hair up under the helmet to keep it out of my face; the breeze was warm and felt good on my face. Twenty minutes later we were at the South Rim of the Grand Canyon. It was impressive, awe-inspiring!

Unprepared for the magnificent grandeur that lay before us, I was stunned by the extraordinary colors: pink to violet, rust to beige to blue, yellow. Nothing had prepared me for this—it was enormous and so beautiful. Spellbound, I could barely believe its vastness. Standing there holding Bill's hand, I stared breathlessly at the view. "This is truly one of the wonders of the world."

"Fucking Big," Bill joked as he grinned down at me.

Walking a little way on the trail away from the other tourists, we found a lookout point where we could be alone with the canyon. I climbed over the bars and walked out onto the ledge and seated myself on the ground to commune with the canyon. Bill came up behind me without saying anything, and seated himself beside me. We sat there for a long while watching the clouds drift over the canyon, casting shadows on the walls. The sky was clear blue and the clouds puffy white. The tourists seemed to have vanished and we were alone with the canyon—time seemed to stand still.

Finally, I spoke, "Want to jump?"

"What?" Bill asked in his squeaky voice. "Why would you want to do that?"

"Isn't that what we came here for?" I asked.

"No!" exclaimed Bill.

"But it's so perfect—it's the end of our journey; we can jump into the canyon together."

It seemed like a perfectly reasonable thing to do to me. I knew if I did, I would not die—at that moment, I knew I could fly. But I didn't want to do it without Bill.

"Come on, we can do it," I pleaded.

"No," he said, more firmly, regaining his normal voice. He stood and pulled me up with him, leading us back behind the barrier. I felt dazed. The canyon had cast a spell on me.

"You've been reading too much Carlos Castaneda," Bill said. But somehow, I just knew we would be okay.

"It's not the end of our journey," Bill offered, pulling me into his arms. "It's the beginning."

The canyon will always be there, I said to myself in reassurance as we headed back to his bike and climbed on, leaving the Grand Canyon behind. Another time, I thought. Maybe it was another time . . . maybe we had been here before in another lifetime and maybe we had jumped then. Maybe.

After the Grand Canyon, we turned the bike around and headed home. On the way, we ran into a thunderstorm that seemed to come out of nowhere. We tried to out-run it, but it caught us. It wasn't cold, but it sure was wet! We were soaked to the bone in a few minutes. Bill looked for shelter and found none. We rode on like a couple of salmon headed upstream. My hair was wrapped on my face and our clothes were clinging to our bodies. Bill must have had a difficult time controlling the bike, even at the reduced speed of thirty miles per hour that we were forced to use. We were headed directly into the storm and to make matters worse, a wind started to blow. The bike was holding steady, but we weren't. I hung on for dear life, plastered to Bill's back. "Sorry," he yelled, as if he had caused the problem. "Maybe we can ride through it."

I nodded an okay against his back, my voice muffled by the wind. We rode on with the rain pelting us. Every once in a while a car would pass us, showering us for a moment. We were completely engulfed in a wave of water, like being in a surf tube, I thought. Bill held the bike steady, and we came out of the tube to see another car coming and Bill yelled, "Hold on," as I braced myself for the drenching. I could not get any wetter, but the shock of the water and the temporary blindness it caused was scary. We saw a truck coming at us and I thought that this could be our undoing. Luckily, the truck driver saw us and slowed and swerved as Bill pulled off to the side of the road, as far as we could go. When we saw the wave coming at us Bill goosed the bike and we rode to safety. Laughing hysterically, we pulled over into a driveway, dismounted and clung to each other. Bill had tears running down his face, or was it rain?

"Thank God," he exclaimed, "I would never have forgiven myself is anything had happened to you. You're shaking, you need to dry off." Bill turned his head to look around and his face lit up in a brilliant smile as he kissed the top of my wet head. "Come on," pulling my hand, "We're getting a room." Turns out we had pulled into a motel driveway. There was a God.

"But can we afford it?" I asked.

"Yep, I have some emergency money, and this is an emergency," he answered.

The innkeeper was a thin man with glasses that made his eyes seem huge as he looked at us with sympathy and asked if we needed a room.

"You could say that" Bill laughed, "and a shower," as he pulled a wad of wet bills out of his pocket. "How much for a room?"

"Usually thirty-two fifty, but for you two, our rainy-day special is twenty-five dollars."

The room was small and clean, and the white tile bathroom glistened an invitation. "You first," Bill said, always the gentleman.

"Oh, no," I laughed. "We're in this together; remember, conservation—save water, shower with a friend. Come on, Bill, get in with me," as I pulled him into the shower, clothes and all.

"This way we can wash your clothes first," I laughed. He pulled me to him and kissed me firmly as the hot water warmed us. Bill pulled off his wet but now warm clothes and wrung them out, dropping them outside the tub. We took turns standing in the warm spray.

"Look, there goes my tan!" I exclaimed watching the reddish-brown water running off my body. The tan I thought I had turned out to be a fine layer of red Arizona dirt built up over the last several days. The cold shower I'd had in the campground had not removed it. I was disappointed—I'd thought I had a great tan, but it turned out I was just dirty.

"Boys like dirty girls," Bill chirped, followed by a throaty laugh as he slapped my butt, playfully. We were both giddy from the adrenaline, the adventure of the storm and our ride, ending, as all adventures should—happy and warm. It was the longest shower I think I have ever taken: soaping, lathering and rinsing, and then doing it all over again. Little bottles of shampoo were so thoughtfully provided by management that it brought a smile to my face as I washed my hair twice.

"Oh, boy, Bill, this feels so good. Thank you, thank you, thank you."

"Gosh, you're easy," he said, teasingly. "Give you a bar of soap and hot water and you're happy as a clam."

"Yep. That's me—happy, happy, happy." After our long, luxurious shared shower we filled the tub with clean water and indulged ourselves in a leisurely soak.

"Mmmmm," I murmured, "This is heaven, but I'm starting to turn into a prune. "Better get out of here before we shrink up to nothing."

Reluctantly, I reached for one of the clean, white fluffy towels, conveniently within reach. I wrapped one around my hair, another around my body and handed the other one to Bill. "Oh, my, that was wonderful. Want to see if the bed is half as nice?"

"Wow, I never thought about that," Bill said, wide-eyed with astonishment. "Clean sheets, oh yeah."

And so, we spent out last day on the road in comfort. The next day, I would be going home and would have to face George, George of the jungle.

CHAPTER 33

The nickel game

The kids were still at their grandparents and George was just heading out the door with his surfboard. "Have a good time?" he asked as he grinned at me, not waiting for a reply. He never looked back, "South swell," he exclaimed as he left the house.

Capper came from the driveway with Ted. Both grinned at me and the three of them loaded their boards into the back of George's truck and they backed out of the driveway. Oh, well, I thought, I would not have to confront him until tonight. I knew it was time for a truth session.

Under a full moon that night, I suggested that we go up to the Mountain of the Moon. The mountain was in Bonny Doon, up the coast towards Davenport, and then into the hills that reminded me of the Sierras with tall pines, cedar, and redwoods. The spot was a mountain with a landscape that looked like the moon—white rock, barren with craters and rock formations, no vegetation. Someone had spent a lot of time carving out steps. It was a steep climb, and you were winded when you reached the top. There was a steep drop on three sides, and a view of Santa Cruz and the ocean. On a clear day you could see Monterey. Otherwise, the fog covered the Cruz like a blanket—Brigadoon, I thought. It was a magical spot and when you met people there, as it was frequented by visitors, they were polite, almost as if the place were holy grounds. It had become our custom to go there on full moons, often taking first timers to climb the mountain, smoke a joint, and be entranced by the extraordinary view— where sky meets ocean, and blue fades to silver-blue.

Miraculously, we were able to slip out of the house alone without any of the rat pack surfers. We drove in silence up the coast. When we turned off on Bonny Doon Road, George turned off the lights, something he liked to do and which I found unnerving, although that night I didn't complain. It seemed the moon was supplying all the light we needed. The road ahead was crisscrossed with shadows of the tall trees. The windows were down in the old truck and the night air smelled pungent, a summer mix of pine and dust.

We made the twenty-minute climb up the steps, reaching the top of the mountain. When we got there, George plopped down cross-legged and began to roll a joint. He was wearing a white t-shirt and ragged jeans, his golden hair falling over one eye. He was totally absorbed in his task, giving me a chance to scrutinize this nonconformist before me. Yes, he was impulsive and reckless and wild. But he was also adventurous, fiery, and passionate. I did love him, but Bill was my soulmate and I wanted to be with him.

It was time. "I need to talk to you," I said to George.

"Am I in trouble," he asked, reverting to childhood, tossing his blonde mane out of his face, and lighting the joint, taking a long hit and passing it to me.

"No, thank you," passing it back to him, "I don't feel like it tonight."

"Suit yourself," he retorted, taking another long pull, his face lit by the red glow. "What's up?"

Taking a deep breath and saying a silent prayer, I said, "I've met someone." Before I could go on, he was up on his feet cursing.

"Fuck. God dammit. I knew it. I knew it. I could feel it in my bones. I kept telling myself no, but it was there all the time this summer," as he paced back and forth in front of me, slapping his forehead with his hand. "I knew it. I knew it."

Sitting there quietly, I asked myself, Why does society make you choose between mates? Why can't I love them both? I was reasoning in my head. I love George, but there is no question I must be with Bill, so this is what I need to do. I let George rant and rave some more. It didn't seem as though he needed any more information or wanted it, for that matter. I just sat quietly, waiting.

"Let's go," George said abruptly, throwing down his roach and stomping on it while he started down the hill. So much for pot being a tranquilizer, I thought as we rode back in the dark with George driving with his chin thrusted out, hands on the wheel with a grip that said it was holding him in his seat, muttering under his breath the whole time, "I knew it, I knew it!"

George "Scooter" Kinnear moved out the next morning. He and the whole surf pack, that is; Capper Daw the Third and Ted the Tripper. Art the Gimp's ghost stayed with me. After all, we were Virgos. They ended up moving down the street to my friend Paul Fuller's house. Every time I walked passed his house there were offensive and degrading remarks hurled in my direction from the front porch, which was now cluttered with surfboards, beer cans and surfers.

"Whose friend are you," I demanded of Paul.

"Yours," he declared with a wise all-knowing look. "If they weren't here, they would be at your place. I'm doing you a favor. Besides, they're paying me rent."

"Wow, how'd you manage that? They never paid me anything." I queried.

"Brains," Paul replied, tapping a finger to the side of his head. "Your problem is there," pointing his finger at my left chest. "Too much heart, not enough smarts."

"Well, not to hear them tell it," I said, jerking my head towards his front porch where the group was making themselves at home.

"Oh, they'll get over it. It's the old nickel game," he replied.

"And what's the nickel game?" I asked.

"Well, it goes like this: A professor stood at the door of his classroom and as each student came in, he gave them a nickel. He did this for a week, and at first there was surprise and pleasure. Then, after a few days there was acceptance. Then the students began to expect payment, so they would hold out their hand for the nickel. After a week, he stopped giving out nickels and just stood by the door. The first student in looked surprised and passed through the door, while the second student stopped and demanded, 'Hey, where's my nickel?' So, you see, there are no thanks for the nickels. Only when you take them away, they become angry. It's human nature," he said as he shrugged.

I didn't miss George—I felt sorry for him in a way, but he had his ocean. It would have been much worse if there was no swell to ride. I had done my thing, saved him from the draft, and it had been a good adventure. Now I wanted one for me.

It was nearing September and I wanted to go back to school—I had decided to audit classes. If the professor agreed, you could attend their class for free and even get credits if they approved. It was pretty much a one-to-one thing. I chose Spanish as a language and a teacher that would accept me in English Literature. I got into Greek Mythology with Norman O'Brown and philosophy with Paul Lee, one of Bill's favorite teachers. Then, on a lark, I signed up for a fencing class, one that would leave a lasting impression with me and teach me humility—something for which I had not bargained.

Summer was coming to an end and I needed a job. I heard there was a new restaurant opening at the marina. I dressed in my best outfit, a two-piece aqua knit that had a sailor tie which I thought appropriate for the job and showed enough leg to be interesting; not demure, but not lewd. I did my makeup with care and even curled my hair. I had made an appointment and went in for an interview.

The Crow's Nest was a nice place with a view of the beach and ocean on one side, and the levy and marina on the other. They catered to businessmen and tourists. They served sandwiches with a salad bar and a free carafe of wine with each meal. Free booze, I thought to myself—this place should be a hit. The interviewer introduced himself as Steve and offered me a chair. He was in his late twenties or early thirties with a pleasant face and penetrating brown eyes. "Tell me about yourself," he questioned. He told me that this was not going to be a typical interview, but I launched into what I thought he wanted to hear about my experience in the past waiting tables.

"No," he said. "I read your resume, what do you want to do with the rest of your life?"

Surprised at that, I stammered, "Well, I want to go to school. In fact, I have signed up for classes, but I can still work dinner and even lunch because my classes are in the morning and late afternoon. Also, I have children, but they are in school and pretty much taking care of themselves. I really need a job."

We talked some more, mostly about school. Steve had just graduated in restaurant management and this was his first job. After a while longer he stood up and let me know my interview was over and we shook hands formally.

"Do you want to work here," he asked, still holding my hand.

"Yes, very much," I said sincerely.

"Then be here Friday at noon, and wear something like you're wearing now."

Oh boy, I grinned ear to ear and said "Thank you, thank you. You won't be sorry!" and I turned and walked out the door, feeling high on a cloud. I was in! My life was changing, with school and a job.

My day began at four in the morning, as I made my study time from four until six, reading in bed. At six in the morning, I got up, put in a load of laundry, and started breakfast for the kids and myself. By seven we were all on our way to school, them going to the corner to catch the bus, and me riding a bicycle across town, over the river and up Laurel Street. Though the weather had turned brisk, my bicycle rides kept me warm. Leaving my bike at Bay Street, I hitched a ride up to campus.

My first class was at Crown. Spanish started at eight o'clock, and afterwards I had a lab for an hour. When that was finished, I hitched back down the hill, jumped on my bike, and rode home. When I arrived, I did a quick change of clothes into something suitable, popped out of the house and rode the short distance to the Crow's Nest: up the hill by the trestle, over the bridge passed the marina and through the back door, punching in the time clock by eleven-thirty. The restaurant opened at noon.

I tied a blue and white apron over my miniskirt and began to clear the tables from the night before and reset them. I was aided by four of the most personable girls I had ever met. I was never much of a girl's girl—you know, like a man's man. In fact, I did not trust most women. But these ladies renewed my faith in womanhood. Steve had chosen well. Not only were they beautiful, they were also bright and compassionate. Rosemary was tall and statuesque, almost stately, with a warm, ready smile for everyone and a gentleness about her that suggested she could not harm a fly. Jan Penny was as bright as a new penny, blonde and perky with a ready laugh and a quick wit. Rachel was dark with long black hair and flashing eyes. She was so beautiful that every man fell in love at first sight, and just so darned nice that women had to like her too. She had a dumb-act down pat and reminded me of Gracie Allen—she was the perfect "straight man" for any of us. The last was Terry, who also went to university and was studying to be a teacher. She had a cute figure, wore her hair in a ponytail and had a husky voice and an even louder laugh, with a habit of elbowing you in the side expecting you to laugh with her. You always knew where Terry was because of the laughter. They were a great bunch of girls and it was a joy to work with them. Whenever one of us was down or a little slow, or at that time of the month, everyone else just took up the slack. Never had I had working conditions like this before. This job was heaven.

At two o'clock we closed for lunch and I hustled out the door and rode my bicycle again, stopping at home to put the clothes in the dryer, changing into jeans, and back to Bay Street to hitch up the hill to school. I never had a problem getting a ride and always made it to class on time. Philosophy was on Tuesdays and Thursdays and Greek Mythology was on Wednesdays and Fridays. I would leave campus and make it home by five, in time to give directions to Beau for dinner, check in with the kids and change for work. My dinner shift was from six to ten at night. Exhausted, but hyped from the hustle, I would return home to tuck my children in and fall into a deep sleep until the alarm went off and it was time to do it all over again.

Ground Hog Day. Boy, did I love it! I had two classes with Bill: mythology and fencing. Norman O'Brown, who taught Greek Mythology, was addicted to Coca-Cola. He would lecture with one in his hand. Once the Coke machine outside the auditorium broke, our class of several hundred—it was a popular class—sat and waited twenty minutes while a student ran across campus to get Professor O'Brown his Coke. I liked him because he addressed the class as senseless lumps of clay. He told us the first day that it was a pass or fail class and all you had to do was show up at the orgy at the end of the semester.

Fencing was another story. It was taught by Charles Selberg, a commanding figure of a man who demanded your full attention and got it. The first day he told his students to leave their egos outside the door, and I felt like he was looking at me. I found out later that almost everyone in the class felt he was singling them out. No one dared to speak in his class. He was one of the most high-powered, energetic, charismatic people I ever chanced to meet. It felt like an honor to be taught by him. In 1970, Selberg and his foil team had won the Fencing Masters World Championship gold medal for the United States, the first time the US had taken a medal in fencing. He told great stories while working with us, shaping our intellect, and honing our physical agility. Everyone gained humility while our posture improved. He was electric and charged our batteries. I was thrilled and never missed a class. Bill and I drove to San Francisco to buy our own fencing masks after having used the school's supply for a while.

Charlie Grier was also in the same class. He and Bill would practice together in the street. Both being over six feet tall, they were a perfect match. However, being five foot two, I practiced on a board on the back door. Lunging across the kitchen, lunge, lunge, thrust, thrust, parry left. Being left-handed was an advantage. So was being a woman. When a male opponent stabbed at my breast, I let out a shriek, unnerving and embarrassing him. Then when I had him off guard, I went in for the kill. Selberg loved it—physiological advantage. However, this technique did not work with either Charlie or Bill; they saw through me the first time. Charlie tossed his strawberry blond mane and laughed hysterically, "Oh no you don't, Flemming," as he came after me, finishing me in one direct hit to the heart. His arms were extremely long. As a result, I did not fence with the big guys. Too bad Howard did not take the class. He and Scott were into the garden, taking gardening classes from the master himself—Alan Chadwick—and learning to milk goats on the farm. UCSC—University of California, Santa Cruz—was a liberal arts college. Where else could you get credits for milking a goat?

One day Bill met me before class with a frown on his handsome face. "What's wrong," I queried.

"Gotta move," he muttered. "Landlord's selling the house and wants the students out."

My face lit up. "Come live with me."

It was settled. Scott, Howard, Bill, and the Charlies moved in that weekend. I had five male roommates. Of course, Bill slept with me, which was wonderful. Scott and Howard baked bread and Bill cooked. Howard also provided us with produce from the garden. And Charlie, well, he was the resident sage, given to thought. I sometimes thought that Charlie was not of this earth. His fields of philosophy included metaphysics, psychology, idealism, and existentialism—and perhaps a little transcendentalism.

Charlie made his bed in front of the fireplace every night. It was like having a house troll, only he was too big for a troll. He had huge feet and was normally barefoot which was a blessing for me because when he wore his huge dirty work boots—his only shoes—they were caked with mud. When he gardened, he always managed to find water and make mud. I could always tell when Charlie was home as there was mud on the kitchen floor. I would joke about him being a Pisces; there was always water when he was around, and me being mother earth Virgo, the mixture was mud.

Living with five men came easy for me. Although, one night at dinner when we all sat down together—five men, three children, and me—Howard looked across the table and blinked his big blue eyes and said, "I feel like we're all married to Carol."

Bill and I fell into a routine. He got up with me in the morning at four to study, and then started taking over my kitchen duties in the morning, fixing the kids' breakfast. He made homemade granola: fresh, crunchy, and delightfully tasty. The kids loved it. We bought collectively from the food co-op and had large stores of wheat germ, whole grain flour, and honey. We split the rent, each paying twenty-five dollars a month, and lived very comfortably. The children also had live-in mentors, tutors, and cooks. They thrived.

There was also much laughter in the house, especially after finals were done, and chaotic food fights broke out. Howard started it with a pie in the face, and for days no one could come around a corner without getting hit in the face with a pie. Maddox Bakery sold day-old pies for a dollar, so we had a never-ending supply of pies. Of course, cream pies were the best, but Howard looked quite good in blackberry when I managed to surprise him by standing behind the kitchen door, scoring a direct hit. It left him looking like a minstrel player with just his big eyes looking out at me from behind all that pie. "Mmmmmm," he declared, licking his face, "my favorite!"

Bill got smashed with a lemon meringue pie that afternoon. I had to stand on a chair to reach him, but I suspected he was anticipating it because he caught my arm and managed to redirect it at me, and we both ended up getting covered with gooey, sweet stuff.

Charlie was hard to catch. He would slip into the house through the back door or a window, laughing his hysterical laughter. He sounded like a horse with hiccups. Howard served him breakfast in bed one morning before anyone else was up. Charlie awoke to chocolate cream coming at him at a hundred miles per hour. Direct hit—*wham!*—right in the face. The gooey stuff proved difficult to get out of his sleeping bag, and he bitched about it for days.

The year passed quickly. Working at the Crow's Nest, going to school, and having a home filled with joy and laughter was now my life. Summer came and Bill announced he would have to go home to Concord unless he could get a job in Santa Cruz. Losing Bill for even a summer was not an option for me. I had a conversation with my manager, Steve, and suggested that he hire Bill at the Crow's Nest. I proposed he try him for a week and that I would pay his salary. If he like him, he could keep him on—what did he have to lose? I told him that Bill was a good cook and a fast learner. I said he was honest and that I knew he would like him.

"Please," I begged him. "You need backup in the kitchen. He will wash dishes or do food prep."

Steve squinted his eyes at me in a friendly scowl. "You'd better be right, Flemming."

"I am. You won't be sorry," I assured him.

That's how Bill came to work at the Crow's Nest as a cook—and a damn good one, I might add. I rode to work on the back of his motorcycle instead of my bicycle—that was, until I got the Porsche.

One day, Bill looked at me and said, "I want to make an honest woman of you and my mom would feel better if we were married." It was decided. We set the date for September and planned a wedding on the grass at historic old mission on a hill overlooking Santa Cruz. I commissioned my favorite gown maker and gave her free rein to make my gown. But, to my dismay, the gown was pink with layers of lace, and very foo foo—ingenue, I was not. However, I could not hurt her feelings and wore it anyways. I decided to wear a pink chicken head down the aisle and Bill would lift the head off my shoulders and voila, there I was. Paul Fuller gave me away, and unbeknown to me, he found out what I was planning and had a plan of his own. He made himself a duck head and wore it with a black cape. Now Bill's side of the family wondered what strange meaning this had while my side just knew it was crazy fun. After the wedding, we had the reception at John Tuck's house. Bill made the wedding cake, a delicious apple cake. We made it a potluck, and splurged on a case of champagne. A good time was had by all. Marrying my soulmate, life was just getting better and better.

Photo 18 - Wedding with Bill

CHAPTER 34

The Porsche

One afternoon at the end of my shift, Steve came over to me and said, "I hear you like Porsches," grinning, like it was a secret joke. "There's a man at the bar that wants to talk to you about one."

"What?" I stammered. "Who?"

"Go," he pushed me, propelling me towards the bar to a man who looked like Omar Sharif. He was drop-dead handsome, tall, and dark, with flashing eyes and a dazzling white smile. Next to him sat my friend Jim, one of my regular customers who had become my insurance man. He smiled encouragingly at me.

"This is Tom Black, he's got a deal for you," as Tom smiled and held up a set of car keys.

"It's in the parking lot," he said. "Take it for a spin. See if you like it," as he dangled the keys in front of me, Steve and Jim watched on in a conspiring manner.

What was up? I wondered. What was the plot?

"Okay, I'll take the bait."

I snatched the keys from his hand, turned on my heels and headed for the parking lot, not looking back. Outside, I found a shiny new 1972 silver Targa 911T. It was beautiful. The key fit and I climbed into the soft silver-gray leather bucket seat, put the key in the ignition, and adjusted the seat and mirrors. My heart was racing with excitement. I could not afford this car, but a drive would be nice. I cautiously pulled out of the parking space and headed down the beach.

Of course, it drove like a dream. I cruised around Twin Lakes and out to 17th Avenue where I reluctantly turned it around and headed back to the harbor parking lot. It was a fine automobile, and I was thrilled to drive it. I had felt like a kid at a carnival, on a ride that ended too soon. I parked it carefully and brought the keys back to the owner. All three men were still clustered at the bar.

"What do you think of it? Do you like it?" Tom asked, accepting the keys, while Steve just beamed at me, looking like the cat that ate the mouse.

"It's beautiful," I replied, "but I can't afford a Porsche."

"It's not for sale," he said. "Sit down, Jim will tell you all about it, and me," he said as he got up and sauntered towards the men's room.

As I took Steve's place at the bar, Jim asked if he could buy me a drink, to which I declined. Instead, I asked, "What's up?" as I watched Tom walk away.

"Oh, Tom's a nice guy. He is my best friend. He flies for TWA, European trips. He's gone for two weeks at a time, needs someone to drive him to the airport and then take care of his car until he returns. I suggested you. All you need to do is drive him to the airport and then pick him up two weeks later. Then you get to drive the car for two weeks out of every month. I told him that you loved Porsches and were a responsible person and would take good care of his car."

"Are you kidding?" I blurted.

"Not in the least. He leaves in an hour. Can you drive him today?"

"Can I? Are you kidding?" I stuttered.

Jim replied that he certainly wasn't kidding as Steve grinned at me and wandered off to take care of his restaurant. Tom came out of the men's room, smiled at Jim, and nodded at me, "Ready?"

There was never any question in anyone's mind. I jumped off the barstool, exclaiming, "Ready!" while I saluted and clicked my heels. I gave Jim a big hug, waved to Steve who was grinning like the Cheshire Cat, and led the way out the door to the waiting Porsche.

"Want to drive?" Tom asked, holding out the keys to me.

"Do I? Sure!"

On the way to the airport, I found out a little more about Tom Black. He had a wife and five other cars and not enough garage spaces, so his poor Porsche was forced to stay out on the street. His wife had her own Mercedes and was not interested in the Porsche. Jim had told him about me, and they had devised this plan together. Wow. Was I lucky, or what? I could hardly wait to see the look on Bill's face when I drove up in this beautiful automobile—which happened a couple hours later. I dropped Tom off at the terminal and agreed to meet him back there in two weeks when he called. Meanwhile, I promised to keep the car clean, gassed up, and tuned.

"Don't worry," I assured him, "I'll treat it very well."

"I know you will," he replied. "I'll see you in two weeks." With a wave he was off, and I was headed towards home, feeling like I had just stolen the crown jewels. What good fortune!

When I got home, I ran up the stairs two at a time and hollered, "Bill, Bill . . . everybody! Anybody home? Come look, come look and see."

Beau was the first one to the door. I pointed at the Porsche in the driveway and laughed out loud. "Look," I said. Beau's eyes were as big as saucers, and he asked if it was ours.

"Kinda, at least for now."

Bill came out behind him followed by the girls. They all stopped at the top of the stairs. Bill sat down and just stared at the car, then over at me, then back at the car, then at me again.

"Where did you get it," his voice raising and cracking. "Who does it belong to?"

"Well, it's a short story. Come on, I'll take you for a ride and tell you all about it."

Beau and the girls asked eagerly if they could go, too.

"Sure," I exclaimed, "you and the girls can fit in the back seat area."

I took them for a ride and explained everything. I think Bill had a hard time believing it was that simple, but in the end, he accepted my good fortune as his own and just smiled, shaking his head in disbelief, but relieved, I think, that I had not stolen it. We had lots of fine adventures in that car. It gave us a freedom to roam and take people with us.

-COP KARMA-
The Great Escape

Once Marti and I set off for Big Sur on a Friday afternoon. Enjoying the drive down the coast, we stopped at Nepenthe, a bar and restaurant set on the cliffs overlooking the Pacific. It was a truly magical spot—the view was spectacular! People talked in hushed tones, as if in a spiritual place, and the music of Santana came from speakers hidden around the patio. We danced on the flagstone under a late afternoon sun and then watched it set into the ocean, leaving a gold ring around the water. We sipped our drinks and I said, "You know, I think you should change your name to something exotic."

"Like what?" Marti giggled.

"Oh," I said, gazing at the bottles behind the bar, "how about Tawaka?"

Marti giggled again and said, "Maybe you should change yours to Jack." We were having a great time. The charm and ambiance of Nepenthe was working its magic, but something was missing: the guys. They were studying for finals when we left.

"Let's go get them," I said, and Marti agreed without hesitation.

We finished our drinks and left, driving the sixty miles in no time at all—fast car, good conversation. We only stopped once in Moss Landing to pee and buy a bottle of Southern Comfort. Then we decided on a plan. We would kidnap the guys in case they did not want to come willingly. We would simply drive up, run into the house, and say "get in the car!"

If either of them objected, we would tell them we had something to show them. A surprise! Yeah, that was the plan. Once we got them in the car, we would drive off with them to parts unknown on a great adventure. With Big Sur behind us and a bottle of Southern Comfort being passed back and forth, we lost the attraction of the Pacific coastline and instead decided to head to Virginia City in Nevada.

Getting the guys into the car wasn't all that easy. Howard wasn't around. Paul Fuller was, so we switched our plans and in the glint of an eye had Bill and Paul in the car without knowing where they were going or what was happening. We had pulled it off by saying "Quick, come with us. Get in the car, quick." They had done as directed without any questions.

We set off up Highway 17. I had just shifted into fifth gear and Marti lit up a joint. I passed them the bottle over the back seat to the abductees and before you could say "Jack be nimble" there was a red light on us. It didn't take me long to figure out it was a California Highway Patrol car and it wanted me to pull over. My mind flashed on the bottle I had just passed over the back seat, and then onto the smoke in the car.

"Okay, here's the plan. Marti, I will slow down looking for a place to pull over. Roll down the windows and get some air in here. When I stop, I will get out of the car and distract them. When I do, throw the bottle as far as you can, out the window, and the weed with it.

Heart pounding in my chest—*ker-thump-ker-thump*—mouth dry, I put my blinker on and began to slow, looking for a safe place to pull over. As I got out of the car, I remembered the roll of bennies (speed) I had in my pocket. I reached in for them, pulled them out and dropped them in the gravel and stepped on them, grinding them into the dirt, while I put on a big, happy smile for the officer.

"Was I speeding?" I asked, in all innocence. Boy, was I. Marti and I had each dropped a bennie on the way back from Monterey.

"May I see your license, please?" he asked. I already had it in my hand. I was prepared for this. My mind was racing a million miles an hour while I stood well back, hoping he would not smell the liquor or pot on me.

He looked at my license, shining his flashlight on it and said that I was going a little fast.

"Sorry," I replied, "It's easy in that car."

"Try to keep it down," he said with a smile. "You can go."

What? That was it? I was shell shocked. I had been prepared to be searched. He did not even ask me for the registration; he never even approached the car. I was flabbergasted. "Thank you, officer. Have a good night."

"You, too," he said.

Ghost white at that point as I walked back to the car, as three criminals cowered there, I stuck my head in the window and said, "He said have a good evening."

I took a deep breath and opened the car door, strapped myself in cautiously, put on my blinker, and pulled out slowly onto the highway. Bill pointed out to us that we had enough offenses to put us all in jail for a long time: Driving under the influence, open container, not to mention possession of controlled substances. I was still in shock. My entire attention was focused on driving, but I did catch a glimpse of Marti sitting composed with her hands in her lap, smiling like Whistler's Mother. Then she began to laugh. "That didn't really happen, did it?"

"No," I said. "Pass me the bottle." Then we really began to laugh.

"You two are so lucky," Paul said, finding his voice. "Why the hell are we with you? I was studying, just an honest student. Then we get kidnapped and almost spend the night in jail."

"Yeah!" Bill piped in. "What's with you two? Trying to ruin our lives?"

"We just missed you and wanted you to have some fun," we replied.

"Fun, my eye." Paul's voice was getting stronger and louder. "You two girls are both nuts. Where are we going, anyway?"

I swallowed hard and looked at Marti as we both giggled. "Nevada," I said.

"Nevada?" Bill squeaked.

"Nevada?" Paul croaked.

"Yeah, we thought you needed a break. We planned on bringing you back tomorrow." We were already in San Jose and without a lot of protest, they agreed to come along for the ride.

"Well, at least give me some of that stuff you and Marti are on," grumbled Paul.

"Can't," I said. "Ditched it when we got stopped."

"What?" he stormed, "No weed?"

"Nope," I said, "Marti threw it out the window."

"She did what?"

"I told her to. Would you rather be in jail?"

"No, I'd rather be home studying," he complained, snorting as he harrumphed and slunk down into his seat.

Bill turned and looked out the window. "Got anything to drink?"

"Nope, we threw that out the window, too."

"Fine," he said, disgruntled.

Marti and I looked at each other and giggled quietly. I drove in silence trying to think of a way to retrieve this adventure. "We can gamble and make lots of money," I said.

"Oh, sure," Paul snarled. "With what?"

"I have some quarters."

"Oh, sure, we're gonna make a fucking fortune with your quarters. How many you got?" he asked.

"A handful," I replied.

"Good," Paul exclaimed, "Let's stop and get something to eat, I'm hungry."

"Me, too," Bill chimed in.

"Well, we're not," I said, still buzzing from the bennies we had taken earlier.

"Greaaaat!" Paul roared, "More for us then."

I began to look for a fast-food place, but we were out where nothing was happening, and I knew there wouldn't be another stop for at least an hour but didn't want to tell the boys that. I told them to keep an eye out and to tell me if they saw something. Both guys fell asleep and didn't wake up until we pulled into Reno.

This was becoming a soon to be forgotten road trip. We woke them, counted our collective money, and went out to breakfast. Then we wandered around with the guys who were acting like they had been taken against their will, and they had. Not all road trips are fun. But they are all an adventure.

CHAPTER 35

Virginia City and snow fun

During winter break the kids had gone to stay with their grandparents. It was the day after Christmas and Bill packed a box of food with cheese, crackers, sardines, cookies, sandwiches, and bottled water, tied the toboggan on top of the Targa and we set out for an adventure. We ended up in Virginia City in the middle of a blizzard. The town was a ghost town, covered in white. We drove slowly down the main street looking for life. Lights twinkled from a window—a Christmas tree—and the sign said, "The Silver Dollar Hotel."

"Stop!" I yelled, as Bill pulled up front. "I'll go see if they have a room." Pulling my old fur coat from the back seat, I stepped gingerly out onto the snow-covered curb. A small bell tinkled as I came through the doorway. There was a fire in the hearth and a small wire-haired terrier curled up on a braided rug in front of the hearth. An old woman sat in front of the fire, reading.

"Good evening," she said.

"Hello. Do you have a room for a night or two?" I asked.

"Take your pick. They're all empty." She replied, and I inquired about the price.

"For how long? We don't rent by the hour," she cackled, and I laughed. She then went on to explain that in its day this hotel was a brothel and had seen a few somewhat famous ladies of the evening, and each room was named after them.

"Perfect," I said. "Maybe a night, maybe a week."

"Cheaper by the week," she added.

As I looked around at the cozy setting and the old lady with the twinkle in her eye, I asked how much it would be for a week.

"How does a hundred dollars sound?" she replied.

"Sounds great, I'll take it. Let me tell my, uh, husband," as I dashed back to the car. Bending down to the window I poked my head in and said, "Bill, it's great, cozy and charming and the old lady that runs it is a trip. I want to stay, alright?"

"How much," he asked.

"It is cheap, one hundred dollars," I said.

"A night?" he squeaked. For such a big man he sure could squeak.

"No, a week, and we have food."

"Well, in that case, where do we park?" he replied.

"Right here. Come on in, you're going to love this place," I said, as Bill got our bags from the car while I went back in and warmed my hands in front of the fire. I was hoping for more conversation with the old lady, and I got it.

Her name was Florence, and her dog was Hector. Hector was nearly as old as she was. He stretched and rolled over, opened one eye, looked at me and went back to sleep with a doggie moan. She told me she had married at twenty-eight years old, old for her day, to a man of wealth who owned silver mines. However, he had died their first year together, run over by a carriage. She packed her trunks, seven of them, and set sail to see the world. She traveled for fourteen years and saw "sights I would not believe," she said, rolling her eyes. When she tired of traveling, she came back to Virginia City and moved into the hotel and there she remained. There was nothing more she wanted to see, and she never remarried. I wanted to hear more, but Bill had come in and asked if we could see our room.

"Here," she said, taking a ring of keys from her pocket. "Go on upstairs and choose for yourself. I don't go upstairs much more, too difficult."

Taking the keys, I thanked her, said I'd like to change before going out and inquired if there was anything open to get a bite to eat or a drink.

"Not much," she declared. "Not in winter, in this storm, but maybe at The Bucket-of-Blood Saloon. Wear your go-to-hell shoes!"

Bill looked a little shocked, but I laughed and thanked her again as we climbed the dark, narrow wooden staircase. At the top of the staircase there was a bathroom with faded wallpaper and an old-fashioned toilet with an oak cabinet above the commode. The clawfoot tub looked long enough to accommodate Bill's lanky frame. To the left was a window looking out over the snow-covered mountains. The first guestroom was called Lola Montez. I mused that I didn't know that she was a hooker, I thought she was a dancer.

"What?" Bill asked.

"Oh, Florence said these rooms were named after ladies of the evening, and Lola Montez was a dancer. Ah, but she did get around. I remember reading about her."

The room was done in lavender frills and the bed was a four-poster with a canopy. I loved it, but Bill commented that it was "kinda foo-foo" and suggested we look at another room. The next one was called Julie Bulliet.

"Oh, look, Bill! The bed had a beautifully carved oak headboard surrounded by carved vines and flowers with a clock set in the middle. The dresser was equally beautiful, and the room offered a view of the mountains, at least it would once it stopped snowing. On the hardwood floor was a soft rag rug in muted colors. "Let's stay here. Please!" I exclaimed, and Bill agreed.

While thinking about a luxurious hot soak in the bathtub, I looked around the room. There was no closet, but a hook on the back of the door and a small table near the bed with a hobnailed lamp on a lace tablecloth.

"It's perfect!" I said, eyeing the down comforter and fluffy pillows. "Oh, Bill," I murmured as I snuggled into his arms. "Thank you. I love it."

We decided to hold off on our exploration of town until morning, and decided it was time for a soak. We were luxuriating in the mammoth bathtub—I was stretched out between Bill's tree trunk legs. I always thought of him as a tree: big, solid, and friendly. When I was a kid there was a plum tree that I liked to climb. The top branches were so thick that I could lie in them like a cradle and watch the birds as they feasted on the plums, feeling that everything in the universe was as it should be. I felt that way with Bill.

Returning to the room, I snuggled in the magenta-pink fluffy robe that Bill had given me for Christmas and spread a picnic out on the bed. When Bill entered the room, he dropped his towel and started pivoting on his toes, naked as a jaybird, arms raised. He looked like a ballet dancer on a music box as he pirouetted towards me. I was dumbstruck by this fit of fancy. I had never seen this side of the strong, silent man—he was Chaplin, he was a clown, he was a humorist. For me he was a fool—and I found him even more endearing. We both laughed as quietly as possible to not disturb Florence downstairs.

"You big silly," I said. "Oh, I wish I had a camera."

"You wouldn't dare," he said, snatching up his towel and wrapping it around his waist.

"Oh, yes I would, if only I had a camera. I would, indeed!" I teased.

"Well, no one would believe it, anyway," said Bill with authority. I laughed, thinking that was the most ridiculous statement, even more ludicrous than the preposterous act he had just performed. We fell into bed in gales of muffled laughter, crunching the crackers of our picnic.

The next morning, we dressed in our snow togs. Bill had made me an oversized pair of corduroy pants to accommodate the layers of clothing underneath, and I donned a pair of army surplus boots two sizes too big so I could wear two pairs of wool socks, which Bill had water-proofed before leaving home. Bill had army surplus snow pants on and we both wore layers of sweaters. I felt like a little kid, dressed until I walked like a mummy. We walked stiff legged down the stairs and got the toboggan out

from behind the couch where we had left it the night before. Not seeing
Florence around, we let ourselves out and stared at the glittering bright
whiteness that surrounded us.

"Lotta snow," Bill said, wiggling his eyebrows above the scarf that he
added as the final touch to his outfit.

"Yep," I said, wiggling my fingers in my new waterproof gloves, also
a Christmas gift from Bill. "Where should we go?"

"Let's head uphill," Bill said as he took the lead, dragging the toboggan
behind him. I trudged along behind him, trying to keep up. He had much
longer legs than I did, and I found myself looking at his back whenever
we hiked. Not a view I minded, though. His broad shoulders, that fine
ass on top of his tree trunk legs—no, I didn't mind a bit.

We trudged our way up 2nd Street, aptly named as there were only two
streets in town, Main and 2nd. Up there, to our delight, was a mountain
covered with snow: Toboggan Nirvana! Hip deep in soft white fluffiness,
we climbed into this heavenly stratosphere. Sometimes we fell face first—
and other times Bill had to pull me out of a hole. Breathless from the
exhilaration as much as from the exercise, we would stop ever so often to
admire the view of snow-covered buildings, and a cathedral with steeples
shiny bright in the mid-day glow. We climbed for an hour, then sat for a
while, enthralled with the magnificence of it all.

"Kinda like the Grand Canyon," I said.

"Ready to jump?" Bill clucked.

Turning my head, I looked at him grinning at me: so merry, so happy.
"Okay, but only if you come with me."

"You're not getting out of my sight," he replied. "Remember how
to do this?"

"Yeah, sure," I said as I straddled the boards, tucked my feet and knees
in as Bill pushed and jumped on behind me, assuming the same position.
It was a fast, hair raising, stimulating, thrilling ride! There were fire trails
crisscrossing the mountain and we would get airborne every time we'd
hit one, and plunge into the snow again. Still, we were gathering speed
and it was keeping us going with the force of a freight train. We reached
the bottom in ten minutes and fell out of the toboggan laughing.

"Wow, was that a mind-blowing ride, or what? Want to do it again," Bill asked.

"Yep," I replied. "Let's go," and we began to make the climb again, being careful to stay out of the run and stepping in the footprints we had left behind. The climb was easier this time. We made it to the top in less than an hour.

"You want to go higher," Bill asked, looking at me for agreement, his face flushed from the exhaustion, his cheeks rosy, his eyes shining with excitement.

"Sure," I said. "Let's go higher!"

We climbed for another twenty minutes and settled in for the swift descent. This time, yelling with overpowering enthusiasm, "Yeaaaaaaaaaaaa!" and when we hit a bump and shot into the air, only to come crashing back down into the snow and continue our descent, "Ahhhhhhhh!" was all we could utter until we would hit another bump and got airborne again. What a wild ride we had! And we did it again and again, all day. We rode the mountain until we were exhausted, and the sun was setting, shedding a golden glow on all that had been white. We made our heavenly descent from Valhalla. Together, hand in hand, smiles plastered on our face, we didn't feel the chill that was beginning to set in, only the happiness of a day of play with someone you love.

-COP KARMA-
Christmas Day 1972

The weather was clear and sunny. I was driving the Porsche Targa and had just dropped my kids off in Fresno for Christmas with their grandparents. Bill and I were leaving for our annual toboganing trip to Virginia City the next day. Sister Suzie was in the back seat, and we were going to my mother's house for dinner. On Highway Five without a car in sight, I pressed down hard on the accelerator.

"I wonder how fast this thing will go?" I said to myself, as I depressed the pedal some more, then gently eased up, watching the gauge, and feeling the car. Smooth, I thought. The gauge reads ninety miles per hour—now it is a hundred miles per hour!

Holding it steady for a few moments, I gave it a little more gas. At 110 mph, it felt like the speed limit, so I pressed more fuel to reach 120 mph. It felt like sixty miles per hour. I had just hit 125 mph when I saw the "black and white" behind me. Hmmm! I eased up on the pedal.

Damn, I thought. Where did he come from?

Quickly, I lightened my foot and watched the gauge drop. Now he was right on my tail, but no lights, so I thought that maybe he wanted to pass. Putting on my turn signal, I eased over to the slow lane. But he was still on my tail. Now I was doing eighty-five miles per hour, and his lights came on. Guess he did not want to pass. Slowing some more, I waited until there was a nice clear, safe space to pull over.

Getting out of the car, I was wearing my long red Christmas dress, a Victorian jersey that fit me to a T. As the officer approached, I put my hands behind me and, turning toward the Porsche, bent over the hood, in a "ready for handcuffs" position.

He laughed—and then I turned around to see a young, very nice-looking officer. His eyes twinkled when he asked if I knew how fast I was going.

"A hundred and twenty-five miles per hour, if the speedometer is correct" I replied. "I just wanted to let it out once! The road was clear, and the weather good. Boy, you came out of nowhere. What kind of engine do you have in that car?" I asked with real interest.

"A big one," he said, "I was on the overpass when I spotted you. You were hard to catch. Around these parts," he said soberly. "you go to jail for anything over eighty-five."

"What do you think they're they are serving for dinner tonight at the jail?" I quizzed.

"You would not like it," he replied, "so I'm going to write you up for a fast lane change. Have a nice Christmas dinner."

"You too, Officer Lawrence," noting his name badge—and I was on my way. The ticket cost me eighty-five dollars.

CHAPTER 36

Streaking with rambling Jack Elliot

Jack Elliotts manager called me looking for Jack, and I happened to run into him at the cooper house that afternoon having lunch. I introduced myself and gave him the message to call his manager. I also invited him to dinner. He turned to Beau and asked if I was a good cook. Beau gave him a nod. And so it began, we became fast friends. He stayed at my house when he was in town. I also went on tour with him and John Prine later on, when I had my motorhome. He was really a prima donna and would lock himself in the bathroom, picking at a pimple on his face and saying he could not go on. I would have to give him a pep talk and tell him, "no one would notice his blemish," and that "everyone loved him." Jack was born in Brooklyn, New York, but always fancied himself a cowboy; he always wore a cowboy hat. He had a horse, and one of his proudest moments was riding a bull. I still have his yoga pants that he left at my house.

One summer night, while Jack Elliott and I were sitting on the steps of the Bixby Street house sippin' on a Heineken Dark with nothing much to do, I said to Jack, "Tell you what, l think I'll take my clothes off and run around the block."

Jack replied in a drawling country twang, "I'll do it if you do." So, I stood up, pulled off my shirt, dropped my jeans, stepped out of my flip flops, and started to run. Waving to him as I ran from across the vacant lot to where the apple trees grew, I returned five minutes later, and huffing and puffing, sat down beside him, and said, "Feels great—now you do it!"

Jack then slowly rose, pulled off his shirt and boots, stripped out of his jeans, and carefully placed his hat on top of his neatly folded clothes. I watched his white ass until he was on the other side of the block through the apple trees, picked up his neatly folded clothes and hat, went into the house, and locked the door. The end!

Well, no, that was not the end. After he screamed, "That's not fair," and pounded on the door, I let him in.

This whole thing leads to another time weeks later when Jack visited his friend, Hoyt Axton, at his home in Tahoe. Hoyt's neighborhood was nice and peaceful, and as the two were sitting on the porch having a beer, Jack decided to pull off the same trick. It worked out until it was Hoyt's time to streak.

It turns out that Hoyt was not so lucky. A patrol car was in the area, and Hoyt had a lot of explaining to do. All the while, Jack stayed inside as he watched the interrogation from behind the window shutters, choking on laughter as Hoyt tried to cover his privates and explain himself. I thought for certain one of them would write that interrogation into a plucky country western tune. Fortunately, Hoyt was not arrested, but there is no telling who Hoyt got next.

CHAPTER 37

Fishing with Russ

My banker, Russ, managed the Security Pacific Bank on Water Street in Santa Cruz. At sixty-two years old, he was tall and fit, sporting a gray buzz cut. His eyes, a merry blue, always sparked with a *I'm up to something* gleam.

We met every Thursday for lunch, usually at a place I called "Upper Albertson's" because it was located above the market. Occasionally dining at the Cooper House, I would dress for that lunch in fashionable but business-like attire.

Originally built in the late 1800s, the Cooper House, which was destroyed later by the 1989 Loma Prieta earthquake, was a stately brick building in downtown Santa Cruz that housed a variety of shops and a nice restaurant. A Santa Cruz icon, life bustled around its spacious courtyard.

Known for his care in selecting a good wine and for making sure our sand dabs were de-boned properly, Russ enjoyed attention from the headwaiter as he strolled in with me on his arm. He also knew I loved sand dabs and took great pleasure in ordering them for me. Once seated, he would pull out a photo from his wallet of himself with a blue marlin and proudly hand it to me as if I had never seen it before.

"Have I shown you this?" he would ask, as he always did.

"No," I would say, fibbing obligingly. "How big was he?"

Russ loved talking about catching that fish, so I always indulged him.

"One hundred and sixty pounds," he would reply, beaming. "Put up quite a fight, this one did." He would then tuck the photo neatly away in his wallet until the following Thursday when we would have lunch again and repeat the marlin ritual.

On the way back to my office, Russ had another weekly ritual. Driving passed the Holiday Inn on Ocean Street, he would leer at me and ask if I wanted to "stop in for a quickie." I would answer "not today," and without so much as a blink of an eye, Russ would chime in, "I don't think so" and keep driving.

Russ was my financial advisor and always tried to help me with my business. When I was overdrawn, he would cover my checks, sometimes to the tune of $2,000 or more. He would bounce back a check for as little as two dollars if it came from someone he did not like and grumble, "I fixed that son-of-a-bitch." Fortunately, he was fond of me. Once when I called him from a sales trip to Florida and asked him to pay my hotel bill before I got thrown out, he said to put the manager on the phone to assure the man that my check was good. When I got back on the phone, he gently chided me, "Doll, do you know that you are overdrawn by $2,000?"

Shamefully, I said quietly, "Yes, I know, and I'm working on it." He asked if I would be home for lunch on that Thursday. "Yes, see you then," I said, and he hung up. After giving the hotel manager my signed check, I was on my way.

Russ decided that I should apply for a small business loan. With his help, I secured a loan for $75,000. When I went to pay my first installment, I sewed one hundred dollar bills together to make a dress and wore it to the bank under my coat. Russ was at his desk and I walked up to him, opened my coat, and said, "I would like to make a deposit." His eyes bugged out of his head and he jumped up, locked the bank door, and pulled me into the vault, demanding that I take it off. Laughing, I left the bank wearing only my coat, leaving my deposit with Russ in the vault.

"Doll," he said at our Thursday lunch, "these gray hairs are from you." For the next year, our Thursday lunches continued with me talking about my business and Russ sharing stories about his fish and fishing.

Russ had some brank cronies in Southern California that he fished with once a year in a lodge in Northern California on the Oregon border. He asked me to accompany him, and I said I might, and then finally agreed. The trip was still a year away, but as the time slipped by, the proposed fishing trip grew nearer, I began to think, I will have to sleep with the old boy. I had grown fond of him over the years and reasoned that I somehow owed it to him. A few weeks before the trip, we went shopping to buy me some fishing clothes. His plan was to stop in the wine country for dinner and stay at the Benbow Historic Inn, a fine, old bed-and-breakfast in Garberville, California. "You will like it," Russ assured me, as he described the inn with detail.

Resolved that sleeping with him would be part of the package, I packed my bags and met him at the door on that Saturday morning. We were off to the wine country.

Stopping at a few wineries, we had lunch, and arrived at the Benbow Inn just in time for cocktails. Russ was a martini drinker and thirsty. After checking into our room, we went downstairs for dinner. Russ ordered for me, as he always did, "New York steak, medium rare, and a Caesar salad." We each had two martinis and split a bottle of rich Cabernet.

On our way up the stairs after dinner, my mind was racing. Could I do this? Did he have too much to drink and would maybe just fall asleep? That was not bloody likely, I told myself honestly with each step. Russ could down two martinis at lunch and go back to the bank and work all afternoon.

Once in our room, I slipped into the bathroom and slid modestly into my flannel pajamas. When I came out, Russ was propped up in bed watching television. "Look, Doll," he proclaimed joyfully. "Madame

Butterfly! I love Madame Butterfly—it's my favorite opera." Pounding the pillows beside him, he invited, "Let's watch it together." We did.

After two hours of that beautifully somnolent opera, he fell sound asleep. Madame Butterfly? Who would have thought that Russ was an opera buff? Ironically, Puccini's opera of unrequited love had saved me.

The next morning, we had breakfast, which included Bloody Mary's to "get our engines started." Then we were off to meet his conservative banker fishing buddies.

Arriving just in time for cocktails and dinner, Russ checked in and announced that they were all there and eager to meet his "little doll." He asked, "Do you want to go to our room and freshen up first?" I certainly did!

Taking my suitcase into the bathroom with me, I thought out loud, "Now for my surprise." I had always dressed conservatively with Russ, but this time I donned a black leather vest and short miniskirt that laced up the sides, showing skin—and plenty of it. A Fredericks of Hollywood push-up bra showed my cleavage and black, high-heeled thigh-highs complimented my legs. Around my neck, I strapped on a black dog collar with spikes, and around my hips, a belt with spikes. I teased my hair a little and finished off the look with some bright-red lipstick. I was ready to go.

When I walked out of the bathroom in that getup, I do not know what I was expecting from Russ—maybe a shocked look, a "you must be kidding" comment, or a stern directive to "change your clothes, young lady." But he just said casually, "You look terrific," and held out his arm for me. I looped my arm into his and we were off to meet his cronies. All three bankers were sitting in a leather booth sipping their cocktails. They stood to meet me and not one of them blinked an eye. They were polite, even charming. If I had worn a business suit with pearls, would I have been treated any differently? I think not. They clearly trusted Russ and his choice of company regardless of how I was dressed.

Dining on salmon they had caught that day deliciously prepared by the chef, the bankers were interesting and not at all stuffy. I liked Russ' friends and they liked me. Of course, we drank martinis and several bottles of wine. After dinner we retired to the bar for another round of drinks, and then another, and another. These guys could drink with the best of them. No one seemed to be inebriated, however I was a blur. At midnight, when Russ suggested a nightcap, I said "Another drink? Sure. Why not?" He led me to our room and into bed.

Waking at five the next morning, I had a piercing headache and the start of what would be the mother of all hangovers. I was, to put it mildly, a knee-crawling, toilet-hugging drunk. Disoriented, I washed my face and searched for an aspirin, to no avail. Pulling on my jeans and still wearing my flannel nightshirt, I grabbed Russ' keys off the dresser.

Stumbling into the early morning dawn to search for a pharmacy to find some aspirin, I got into Russ' little green sports car and pulled out of the parking lot. Coming at once to a small airport, I parked the car in the lot. Discovering half a dozen people boarding a light plane for San Jose, I got in line and bought a ticket. The next thing I knew, I was in San Jose at six. Phoning my friend, Lonnie, I asked her if she would like to make a quick hundred dollars. She said sure and I told her to come to the airport with an overnight bag and be prepared to travel. She met me within the hour.

"Okay, here's the deal," I began to tell her, "I bought you a ticket to Benbow. When you get there, you will find a little green sports car with the keys still in it parked in the lot. Drive east, take the first right, and when you see the lodge, go to room number eighteen. Tell Russ that you are my replacement."

Using Lonnie's car to drive home, I crawled into bed, pulled the covers up over my head, and didn't come out until nightfall.

When Russ came to lunch that Thursday, I was pokerfaced as usual. He said with a grin, "We missed you doll, but Lonnie sure was a lot of fun."

I could not help but wonder what Russ' friends thought when he showed up the next night with an entirely different woman. How did he explain it? I never did find out because I did not ask. We continued our Thursday lunches every week as usual.

CHAPTER 38

Dinner with Brucie

Bruce "Brucie" Aidells was attending University of California, Santa Cruz, and running a Fat Albert's campus restaurant (which is how we met) while working on a degree to do cancer research. When he graduated and went to Bethesda, Maryland to do research, he discovered he was allergic to white mice. This ended his short-lived science career and brought him back to Santa Cruz.

On Sundays, we would do brunch, either at his house or mine. The competition was stiff. We always tried to outdo each other with a better dish or finer bottle of wine. One brunch at Brucie's in particular, with a Russian theme, lasted until dinner. We consumed a bottle of excellent vodka, along with piroshkis. I fell asleep on his couch.

Crepes were my specialty (or blintzes if you are Jewish), a thin pancake stuffed with sour cream and grape jam, and easy to make once the pan is tempered. The first one goes to the dog, and the second to the children.

When the pan heat was exactly right, they were served perfectly with good champagne.

With other brunches, a gin fizz was a great start. I made mine with vanilla ice cream instead of cream and sugar, a double shot of gin, one egg if it was a golden fizz or only the whites for a silver fizz. Topped with two scoops of ice cream served in a tall glass, it was a meal in-and-of itself.

Then there was my Bloody Mary, considered perfect with a frittata. Adding horseradish, crisp celery, and succulent olives was a must. A Southern California Bloody Mary was topped with a splash of sweet and sour. Try it—you will like it.

Brucie and I cooked together for a while with wild abandon until he moved to DC. Unabashed, he would always say, laughing, "My favorite animal is steak."

When we met again on a humid summer evening in his garden in the city, we shared another fine meal. Brucie said, "Good food ends with good talk! Want to go to New York with me? The food will be great! It is a family get-together, and Erna (Bruce's main squeeze then), does not want to go. You can come and pretend you are Erna. No one has ever met her. Great food!" He rolled his eyes, coaxing.

That is how it happened: my first trip to the Big Apple was with Bruce Aidells by train from Washington DC. We arrived after midnight, and he immediately took me to 42nd Street, which is the equivalent of the Tenderloin in San Francisco, California. Though frequented by pimps, drug dealers, and whores, I felt right at home.

Brucie wanted a Nathan's Famous hot dog, claiming they were the best in the world. After sampling one, I beg to differ. California's Caspers are the best, for which I would drive out of my way for miles. To sink my teeth into a Caspers, which had a warm, soft bun, a dog that popped when you bit into it, fresh tomatoes and onions sliced thin, slathered with relish and mustard, and everything perfectly portioned, was heaven. I guess if you had never had a Caspers hot dog and you were from New York, then maybe Nathans was the best to you, but I was not impressed!

That night to save money, Brucie and I shared a bed. Do you know what it is like to claw the edge of the mattress to keep from rolling downhill into a snoring three-hundred-pound man? American Chef Ruth Reichl wrote about traveling with a sausage maker and trying not to slide into him. I knew that she was talking about Brucie even before she wrote his name.

The next day, being close to the Fourth of July, Brucie and I donned Uncle Sam hats—his tall, mine small—and strolled to the avenues where we were planning to meet his family for dinner. A limo drove passed as we were walking, and the passengers rolled down their windows to shout out "Freaks!" How surprised they were when they discovered that we were part of the dinner party with them—and family to boot.

Dinner was an upscale Italian Caponata: a piquant eggplant mixture with onions, tomatoes, capers, and Spanish style olives. It was very tasty. We also had an insalata di cipolle, which was made basically of marinated onions, but I love onions. Brucie ordered ossobuco, a veal shank stewed in wine with vegetables, for which I have never understood the fuss. I went for the white scaloppini with fresh asparagus, as at that time I was still eating baby cows and it was wonderful.

I was seated across the table from Brucie's cousin, Jason, the one who had shouted "freaks." We spent the entire dinner snarling at each other and arguing West Coast versus East Coast food and culture. Since I was masquerading as Erna, I kept it civil. It also did not hurt that Jason was attractive.

After dinner, we were invited to the village to partake in some after-dinner delights away from the folks. To East Coast and West Coast potheads, a dessert of weed and pot reefers is the same.

That was the first time I had ever seen so many locks on a door: slide locks, bolt locks, and chain locks, altogether. Wow, either Jason was very paranoid, or this was an excessively dangerous neighborhood. Turns out it was just New York. "Neighborhood watch" there means someone is watching you leave so that they can steal your goods.

Jason had some fine weed, and after smoking, we went for a walk in the park. Greenage Village is lovely at night, especially when you are high, and guess what? We were hungry, even after that big dinner. Jason took me to a little place that served steamed clams and an excellent crusty French bread. I did not go back with Brucie.

Instead, I stayed in New York for the next two weeks discovering New York food: stacked Rubin sandwiches dripping with sauerkraut and Thousand Island dressing that were so tall you could not get your mouth around them; crunchy kosher pickles; and pastas with olive oil, garlic, and a slice of good dry cheese. I fell in love with Jason and would have stayed longer. But one day I was on the rooftop of his building, sunbathing, and admiring the view, and suddenly realized there were no trees! I had to leave. My relationship with Jason turned into a "same time next year." For the next seven years, I returned again and again to New York, the village, and his easy swagger and charm.

CHAPTER 39

A trip across the pond: travels with Shan Fred

Why go to Persia? It had to do with the promise I had made to myself: to answer the door the next time opportunity knocked. As it happened, Bill and I had been shopping for hiking boots. Unable to find my size or find a sleeping bag that zipped together, the car also had trouble and the road to our camping site was blocked. Our trip to Salmon River had already been delayed a week. As we exited the last possible store empty-handed where I might have found boots, I said, "Let's go have a beer and talk this over."

We headed to the Catalyst, where we ran into Maggie, a friend I had not seen in years. As we chatted, she reminded me of an opportunity I had passed up and reminded me to not let that happen again. What happened next seemed inevitable. Ten minutes later, Fred showed up at the bar with his friend, Darush (da-rouche). Slight, dark, and young but balding, Fred was warm and kind. I trusted him.

"Hey, Carol," he said, drawing up his chair. "I'm going to Persia next week with Darush—I've asked others to go with me, but no one can get their act together. Would you and Bill like to go?"

"Sure!" I said, enthusiastically.

On our way home, Bill worried, "How are we going to get passports so quickly? What about the kids and the garden?"

Answering quickly, I replied, "Well, we were planning to go to Salmon River. Now we are just going somewhere else. The kids are spending the summer with their grandparents, Howard or Paul will tend the garden, and we will see if we can rush our passports—nothing ventured, nothing gained!"

After a two-hour delay with hundreds of people sitting on the floor waiting, on a cool, gray, July day, we boarded a Capital Airlines DC-8 in Oakland, California, bound for Persia. Capital Airlines was a no-frills chartered flight through the university. Sitting three abreast, I was sandwiched between Bill and Fred. Hot, stale air blew from the cabin's air conditioner.

"I'm sticky already," Bill commented.

"This lousy plane doesn't even have any music," Fred complained.

Fred had taught me two words in Farsi, "salam" which meant "hello" in English and "taavous," which meant peacock. Rest assured, if I met a jaunty peacock in Persia, I was ready to say hello.

During the flight, I met a black British student who, after studying in Los Angeles, was headed home to London for the summer.

"I'm on a PTTS grant," he said, chuckling.

"What's that?" I asked, surprised to hear a black man speaking with a British accent.

"Parents Tired of Their Son grant," he said, shrugging. Motioning toward the flight attendants, he pointed and said, "I fly this route a lot. That flight attendant is a sweetheart." Pointing toward the other, he quipped, "But that one with the long horse face is a bitch and she will give you a look that could kill if you ask her for anything."

Arriving for a quick stop in Philadelphia, it was eighty-eight degrees and high humidity, with a rank yellow-gray, smelly pollution cloying to the air, causing sweat to trickle down my breast. Soaked, my blouse clung to me as I wandered into the bar. Imagining beer would be weak and warm, I ordered a whiskey.

Back on the plane, I enjoyed more cocktails and a nondescript, TV dinner-style meal. Then . . . wonders of wonders . . . the pilot threw open the cockpit door and invited passengers up. Can you imagine this happening today post 9/11? It simply would not. One of the passengers even took command of the cocktail cart and the bar was open. Everyone was in the aisles with drinks in hand. As the sun reddened and started to rise, the horizon became a thin red line. Then . . . holy cow! We got invited to Row 25 to smoke a doobie. Five of us got loaded in the bathroom. I got the last toke and held it in, stumbling back to my seat, blowing residual smoke in Bill's face. He dug it! People were standing in the narrow aisles singing, "Row, row, row your boat, gently down the stream, merrily, merrily, merrily, life is but a dream."

Hot damn! The sun was rising, and I was stoned so far out. Merrily, merrily, merrily, life was but a dream. Never had I seen a sunset equal to this sunrise over the Pacific Ocean. My God, it was glorious; an expanse of shimmering gold tinged with pink as far as my eye could see.

Seated on top of a seat facing backward, I watched as a procession moved passed me into the cockpit. The song changed boisterously to "I'm Looking Over A Four-Leaf Clover," a tune listed as number one on the Billboard Chart in the late '40s. The lady serving the drinks was someone's grandmother, not the flight attendant, and as she handed the pilot a drink, she shouted, "Who's flying this crate?"

The party went on. No one slept on that flight and countless addresses were exchanged. By morning, all the liquor was gone, too. A man perched on the top seat I had relinquished. The alleged "long faced bitch" flight attendant is now smiling so broadly, she is beautiful. The grandmother serving drinks is now affectionately known as "Mama." Fred is pointing his camera at a flight attendant who shrieks, laughing, "No! My mouth is full!" She drops to her knees and wraps her arms around Fred. Roger, a guy sporting light-brown, curly shoulder-length hair, a mustache, golden eyes, and good teeth, grabbed Fred's camera and caught the moment. Roger wears a Levi cowboy shirt, a pocket full of pencils, and wide white and blue striped bell-bottoms. He was cool. With a flourish, Fred jerked the headrest napkin off the seat and announced he was off to pilot the plane, disappearing into the pilot's cabin. I guess someone had to fly the plane—Oh Lord!

In the fracas, one of my black fingernails popped off. Hastily gluing it on, I thought to myself, There is no way I am going to arrive in London without all my parts!

We were a long way from Bixby Street, with the sun shining on billows of white clouds that looked like snowdrifts in December at Virginia City. Mama, the self-appointed bartender, was moving the party to the back of the plane, chuckling as she swept passed her entourage. Behind her, Bill climbed over me to join Fred in the cockpit. A Chinese flight attendant sat with a long-haired youth who worked in a discotheque in San Jose. A hippie with orange hair and black sunglasses wearing a sleeveless black t-shirt with a pink sequin heart emblazoned across the front of it, sat slumped in his seat. People watching, I felt like Dorothy on the yellow brick road.

Below on the right, the Ireland coast stretched beneath us. Everyone began helping the flight attendants clean up. Singing swelled from the rear of the plane as Mama lead the gang in singing "White Christmas." The pilot announced over the loudspeaker, "Fasten your seat belts, ladies and gentlemen, we're on the approach to London," we were all weary but happy travelers.

On landing, a thick London fog encased us. We breezed through customs and took a cab from Victoria Station to an address given to me by the Catalyst's bartender, Pat. The place was dirty, but cheap and friendly. Tired beyond reason, we dragged our luggage up three flights of stairs to a dormitory-style room with five narrow beds. Bill and I stood dazed, looking at each other wistfully. How would we cuddle in one of those narrow beds? We would not.

Located across the hall, the bathtub was filthy with soap scum and hair. A basin was in the same condition. The water closet, closest to the door, was disgusting. In my exhausted, dazed state, I scrubbed the bathtub so I could take a bath, muttering to myself indignantly, "I've just flown three-thousand miles and paid money to get down on my knees and clean someone else's tub!"

Bill knocked on the door. "You okay?" he asked, concerned. "You've been in here a while."

Sighing, I answered, "Yeah, sure. Just give me a few minutes."

Cleaning had always been a sort of meditation for me, though, so by the time I had filled the tub, my head was a bit clearer and more focused. Bathing quickly, I turned the now clean bathroom over to Bill and slipped into one of the narrow beds. It was hard and unyielding.

Fred and Darush lay flat on their backs, with their hands folded across their chests, resembling Egyptian mummies dried and wrapped for burial. I knew though, without a doubt that they were both alive because they were loudly snoring.

Even before Bill inched in next to me, I had fallen into a deep sleep.

Waking hours later, I heard Fred and Darush speaking in Farsi, their own language. Before opening my eyes, I lay there relishing the rise and fall of its melodic sound. Coming off the drone of the plane was like leaving the rink after ice skating for hours. It felt other worldly. When I opened my eyes, Bill was smiling. He had been waiting for me to wake up. Though it was still light outside, we had slept most of the day.

After dressing, we headed out to explore Earl's Court Road, where we discovered American money was not as valued as the US government would have us believe. Traveler's cheques were not accepted in three different restaurants, so we began to think that we would not have money to buy food until the banks opened the next morning. Since Fred and Darush were more interested in looking for a pub to find girls and dope, Bill and I split from them and continued to look for a place that would take traveler's cheques or US dollars. Trying two more restaurants, we finally found a small, quaint French restaurant, called Palio's.

"Might be expensive," Bill said dubiously.

Shrugging, I answered, "We'll find out when we get the bill."

Stout and charming with a pencil thin mustache and napkin draped over his arm, our waiter certainly looked the part. He smiled and gave us menus that listed no prices.

"Uh oh," I said under my breath. "Yep, it's going to be expensive."

Bill shrugged this time, and with a sparkle in his eye, ordered a small carafe of chilled white wine. He expertly ordered cold, marinated trout and vichyssoise, which were excellent, along with a not-so-good duckling in peach sauce. "Ducks are better swimming in water, quacking, and laying eggs than cooked in a sweet sauce," Bill noted. I agreed.

Our next course was chicken with ham and cheese with a half-liter of wine. The dish was no cordon bleu, but more like a sandwich without the bread. Bill poked at it with his fork, as if in a drugged stupor—red-eyed, quiet, and removed. Jet lag was beginning to set in. I was also feeling rundown on the edge of a cold. I ordered fresh fruit for dessert, the biggest fig I have ever seen, and Bill ordered raspberries with cream, equally large.

"They grow humungous fruit here," I said, musing. Bill was unresponsive, staring numbly ahead. Stumbling out of the restaurant, we headed back to our narrow, hard beds. Breakfast the next morning consisted of hard rolls and cold tea.

On the whole, London in the 1970s was horribly polluted. The air quality was fowl, the smog stunk, the streets were dirty, and exhaust fumes funneled the streets causing my nose irritation. It smelled like a water closet. People were friendly though, and called their dirty, old city with its tall buildings and narrow streets, "a bite of alright."

On King's Road, we admired the ironwork on gates and wandered down to Hammersmith to speak to an ironsmith about his work. Young shopkeepers wearing tight trousers with obvious bulges hung out in the doorways. We found it hard to ignore, wondering if a modern-day cod piece was built into their pants. They seemed to be intentionally displaying themselves. Amused, Bill commented, "Must be in style."

One London custom I could not get used to was drinking warm beer. Bill was a sport and indulged our hosts by drinking it, but I drank Jack on ice, much to the dismay of locals. "You Americans drink everything cold, even beer," our hosts chided. "Alcohol should always be served at room temperature."

Londoners start drinking at three in the afternoon and the pubs closed at eleven at night. Since Bill and I did not enjoy large, dirty cities, we walked home while Fred and Darush stayed out. At four in the morning, we were startled awake by Fred and Darush, who brought two English girls home with them. They were all quite pissed (the English slang for drunk) and woke us to offer a drink out of a bottle they were passing around. Since a cold was settling into my head and the congestion was giving me a headache and runny nose, Bill and I got up, dressed, and went for a walk instead. Sharing a room with four noisy drunks was not going to give us any rest.

London is at its best at dawn. People are out sweeping the streets, a custom as old as London. Milkmen and other delivery people are bustling about making their rounds, and each greeted us with a chipper, "Good morning, mates."

But we were anxious to leave London and continue our journey. Though Fred and Darush were nowhere in sight, we headed to Victoria Station in a cab. They showed up not a moment too soon to catch the train. Our fare to Brussels, Germany, was thirty-seven dollars and fifty cents each. Comfortable and clean, the train meandered through the lush green, misty English countryside.

Reaching Dover, we got off the train and boarded a ferry to cross the channel to France on the way to Brussels. Today's trains blast right through the modern Channel Tunnel under the water in a mere thirty-five minutes. But back then, a ferry was the only link between England and France. The trip to France alone took one and a half hours.

On the ferry, Fred endeared us with his clowning which caught the attention of a small boy. Amusing his thankful parents, Fred sat on the deck and entertained the small boy as we passed by the White Cliffs of Dover. With his imperial personality and way of looking at you down his long, straight nose with a regal sniff when annoyed, it was no wonder his friends dubbed him "Shah Fred."

A chilly gray, windy day on the ferry, the crossing was choppy. As the cold air hit my lungs, I began to feel myself getting sicker. The cold had worked its way down into my chest and I had begun to cough. I felt dizzy, and my stomach felt cramped. I was questioning what madness had propelled me to travel halfway around the world at a moment's notice. The musty smell of our dank hotel hall, rank stench of cigarettes, and the drapes behind my bed smelling of mold were finally beginning to take their toll.

Arriving in Brussels hours later, the sun shone brightly through a light fog and the air was fresh and sweet. With its bright-white buildings, cobblestone streets, and every building with window boxes displaying the largest geraniums I had ever seen, Brussels was clean and beautiful. I had started to feel much better.

We had two hours to kill before catching the train, so we headed to a lively pub filled with laughing, jovial people. We were welcomed like old friends. Chairs were pulled up and we were squeezed in and included in conversations. Time passed quickly.

Leaving Brussels, we shared a compartment with a young Englishman from Liverpool, a student on holiday. Tall, dark, and handsome with large, limpid, dark eyes, his name was Tim, but everyone called him Pot. We had chemistry! As his eyes held mine, my mind spun in confusion. I was happily married, and Bill was sitting right next to me, and yet I could not take my eyes off Tim, whose eyes were also locked into mine.

Outside, the Belgium countryside rushed by our window: lush and green, with rolling hills dotted in haystacks, cows, horses, vineyards, red brick houses, corn fields, and wheat. It was beautiful.

Suddenly a throng of people loaded into the train, peering at us on our couch. Pot stood up and left abruptly. The sky was darkening as it began to rain. Fred invited a Japanese lady who was wearing a short, yellow sundress into our car. Her bad manners and nice legs caused Fred to grin. Snuggling into Fred, she fell fast asleep. I did the same with Bill.

Awakened by a train conductor asking for our tickets, Bill and I realized Fred was nowhere to be seen. Searching the length of the train, he had all but vanished. Having not found Fred, I returned to the car and found two sleeping women had taken my seat. Bill had smiled sheepishly at me and shrugged.

"I can't find Fred," I had announced.

Bill rose gingerly, trying not to disturb the sleeping women. "I'll go find him," he had replied with a sigh.

"I'll wait here in case he returns," I said.

Since our compartment had become hot and stuffy, I had stepped outside to wait. Pot appeared out of nowhere and an awkward silence fell between us. Swallowing hard, he looked down at me and quietly asked, "Why don't you come with me to my uncle's place? It is quite lovely there. I'm sure you would like it."

For a moment I had considered it, but then said, "No, I can't."

"Thought you might say that," he answered, pressing a piece of paper in my hand that contained his address.

"Don't want to lose you now that I have found you," he said smiling, gently lifting my chin and planting a soft kiss on my forehead.

Blushing pink, I had stammered, "I'm married."

"I know," he had said softly. "But you came to me and perhaps we will meet again sometime." Then he turned and was gone. I wanted to race after him but said to myself, This is crazy, girl. Get a hold of yourself! But why had I felt this way? Perhaps he was someone from another life, I deduced.

Wishing I could have talked with Pot more and still standing where he had left me, Bill returned with Fred. Two pretty ladies that Fred had pestered were relieved when Bill took him away.

Hamburg was still two hours away when the train stopped in the countryside. I watched as Pot got off the train and met an older gentleman with white hair, tall like Pot, but stooped. The older gentleman put his arm around Pot and led him off, but not before Pot turned to wave at me. Then he was gone.

The pretty-legged lady had stretched out in our car, leaving nowhere for Bill to sit, so he had perched on a small suitcase. Fred had made himself comfortable between the two other sleeping women and Bill had looked at me with a weary smile and shrug. He was a sweet, patient man. How could I have not loved him?

After inspection at the Bulgarian border, we climbed on a bus headed for Turkey. Once in Turkey, we were inspected again, but this time it was accompanied by music and dancers in native costumes. Swirling in long sleeves and heavy pantaloons with intricately embroidered gold brocade thread on red and purple vests, they wore headdresses that must have weighed twenty pounds. Persians are everywhere, jabbering in Farsi with exaggerated hand gestures. Everyone was smiling.

Fred came out of a duty-free shop with a Persian friend from Chicago. In the sweltering sun, they were both, like me, sweating profusely. Bringing him over, Fred's friend says he was driving to Iran, and we were welcome to join him. "I have room," he said, smiling. "I drive fast without stopping!"

This pronouncement did not inspire me. We had already paid for the bus, where I could lie down. I looked to Bill for support, and he said, "You go ahead, Fred. We will meet you there—I'd kind of like to see Istanbul."

I chimed in, "Me too!"

Fred patted his friend on the shoulder in a gesture of affection and said, "Thank you, but I am going to stay with my friends."

We got back on the bus for another two hours of jarred brains on an exceedingly bumpy road. A marked change could be seen in the people as soon as we crossed the border. Almost all of them were foot travelers. They looked friendly with smiles on their faces but quite poor. Even so, spirits picked up in the bus. An old man in front of me who had ridden in silence for three days, turned around and grinned toothlessly at me. "Istanbul," he announced proudly, pointing out the window. As we entered the large, extremely old city, he kept pointing and repeating, "Istanbul!" A Turkish lady also tugged at my sleeve and pointed out the window, saying "Istanbul." It reminded me of San Francisco in the good old days, only much bigger, older, friendlier, and warmer. We had arrived.

In my next book, I will share the full scope of my adventures, but for now, suffice to say, my memories of traveling through Hamburg, Tehran, Istanbul, and Turkey are far too various to pack into this book at this time. So, stay tuned until next time . . .

CHAPTER 40

What Italians call a big-a mist

For some inexplicable reason, I decided that Bill needed to go out on his own. He had been frustrated and restless because he did not know what he wanted to do with his life. Since I felt that I had been making all his decisions for him and that he was floundering like a ship without a rudder, I decided that it would be good for our marriage if he went out on his own for a while to figure out what he wanted to do.

One night on a whim, our neighbor talked him into training for work as an insurance broker. To become job-ready, he would have to go to Hartford, Connecticut. Looking back, if either of us had given any real thought to what that entailed, we would have realized that he was not a born salesman. In fact, he was no good at it. It was his nature to try to please others and be accommodating, so when presented with the idea, he decided to go to Hartford and give it a try.

One night while Bill was gone, Kelly and I went out for a drink at our favorite watering hole. To this day, I cannot even remember the name of the place, but it would become the setting for perhaps the biggest mistake of my life—and one, that if I think about it to this day, still brings me to tears, with a tug on my heart.

Sitting on that bar stool, Bill was far away in Hartford, and our bartender, Greg from Ohio, with his bright-blue eyes, curly brown hair, charming manner, and inviting, sexy smile was right in front of me. In a moment of immediate attraction, when he invited me to lunch, I neglected to mention that I was married and accepted his invitation. Lunch led to another and finally, an affair.

Photo 19 - Greg

Looking back, I know that was one of the craziest things I had ever done in my entire life. I have no idea why I did what I did—it was stupid. I was in love with Bill. I was not in love with Greg. Greg was a student going to UCSC having trouble paying for his tuition, so with my usual "save everybody" tendency, I said, "Why don't you marry me to get money for tuition?" I had heard somewhere that married students could get student loans more easily—and I had married one man to save him from the draft, so why not help Greg stay in school? We were married straight-away at the Santa Cruz Courthouse.

What—you ask? Wasn't I already married? Yes, I was, quite legally to Bill. Despite how I had rationalized it in my brain, that meant I had become a bigamist: married to two people at the same time. Lord, what was I thinking?

When Bill came home, I drove him up to our favorite place in the Sierras. As we sat side-by-side down on a log, I said matter-of-factly, "While you were gone, I got married."

Eyes widening, his body stiffening, he just shook his head. Curiously, right at that moment, a little red fox walked out of the woods and sat down, just looking at the two humans sitting on a log in our impossible situation. We all just paused silently, staring at each other for a few minutes.

As we drove home, I told Bill about Greg. When we got back to Santa Cruz, Bill went over to Greg's house and told him that if he ever hurt me, he would kill him. Bill was not a violent man, but I was the love of Bill's life and, nothing could have been truer than he being the love of mine.

At that point, I was inexplicably married to two men. Greg went to San Diego State and we bought a house down there. Bill and I owned a house in Santa Cruz. I spent the better part of a year traveling between both places. The sad fact is, thinking Bill needed time away from me to figure out who he was, I ruined a perfectly beautiful relationship.

That year at Christmas dinner, with Greg at one end of the table and Bill at the other, my mother kept looking back and forth at them. When she left and hugged me at the door, she said, "I don't know which one I like better." At the time, neither did I.

Greg moved in with us. The two men were so polite to each other and sensitive of each other's feelings that I never got any sex. One day Bill said I had to make up my mind which one of them I wanted. I told him, "I choose neither."

Bill packed up and moved out. Sorrowfully, this has been the nightmare I have lived for years and have regretted every day of my life. My kids cried so hard. It was the worst thing I have ever done. Bill died of cancer this year, so I never got to tell him how badly I messed up nor how he was always my one and only soulmate.

Recently I found a letter he wrote to me when we were together and as I poured over the words, I bawled like a baby:

Your eyes are so beautiful, I couldn't get away from them this weekend. Still can't, I saw them in the sunset this afternoon. What mysteries, what secrets, what lies beneath them? Where did you come from, you soul of my soul, heart in my heart, spirits united in—dare I say it—holy love. Course, it ain't that holy, cause my whizebang gets hard thinking about your material self. Still, and yet it's still pretty high. Getting higher all the time, isn't it? Where do we go from here? What course of action, what place of dwelling, to what existence are we going? I want to live with you in a place where when we wake up, all we hear are birds and animals. I don't, repeat DO NOT want to wake up to the sound of machines. Lover, woman, wife of my life, we've got to get there, time's a wastin'. I love you. I love you. I love you. I love, love, love, love, love, love . . . words are nothing, talk is nothing, everything is nothing without love. Spread it, grow it, tend it, nurture it, watch it flower and bloom. It takes me away. It takes me to you. It brings us all together. How can I write this down, you person who has touched my life? There are no words for expression, there is only the doing. I love you more than I will ever tell you with my mouth. Look for the other ways.

If only I had known then what I know now about myself and true love, I would not have been so stupid as to let it go. Such is the folly of youth.

-COP KARMA-
Let the Races Begin

In September 1972, my brother Willy, my son Beau, and yes, my little, old red-headed grandmother, aka Doris or the "Red Fox," as I now called her, were having dinner at the Aptos Hotel. The ambience there was wonderful, the food great, and the service charming. A couple of martinis and a few bottles of wine later, we decided to go to an upscale restaurant overlooking the Capitola River, the Shadowbrook, for a nightcap. The Red Fox loved the Shadowbrook.

As we headed into the parking lot, Willy in his black Porsche and me in my silver Targa, Willy said, "Race you there."

"Okay," I said, helping Doris into the passenger seat.

Beau rode with Willy, who took the freeway. I took the back road. Liking how the Porsche held the turns, I "put the pedal to the metal" and raced like I was at the Indy 500. In my rear-view mirror, I saw patrol lights flashing, but I did not slow down because I was within a mile of winning. As I approached the parking lot, my brother came in from the other side, a close second.

When he saw the black and white, he got out of his car laughing. I got out of my Porsche and ran around to the passenger door, and letting Doris out, pointed her to the elevator. "Go!" I instructed. I turned to the highway patrolman, and pointing at my aged grandmother, Doris, I said, "She had to go to the bathroom."

"Oh," he said, smiling, and got back in his car. My brother, who was doubled over laughing, looked up, startled as the black and white pulled out of the parking lot.

"Guess I won," I said, winking at him. "You're buying."

CHAPTER 41

The Santa Cruz
Costume Bank 1972

One October in the late 1960s, after searching everywhere for a Halloween costume, I became so frustrated that I was unable to find a suitable mask, hat, or costume, I decided to design my own. With no experience in sewing, but a lot of determination, alone in my basement I diligently crafted my first costume. This led to making costumes for other people, and finally to opening my costume design studio and the Santa Cruz Costume Bank.

Photo 20 – Santa Cruz Costume Bank

To promote my costume business, I persuaded a local theater company to let me design a show for free. The most fun when I had my costume rental shop was watching people put on costumes and become the characters and their fantasies. Large men wanted to be soft, cuddly Easter bunnies. Short men were drawn to swashbuckling military and pirate costumes. Women homemakers wanted to be glamorous—usually playboy bunnies.

Santa Cruz costumes had grown, and my basement was full of workers, or as Lisa called them, "your workers." Yes, I was the Queen Bee, having the time of my life, making more money than ever before, and spending it wildly.

Putting an ad in the paper for costume designer trainees, I received about seventy calls. After phone interviews, I narrowed it down to twenty and hired a great crew of ten.

Debby Erickson, a "mountain mama" who drove a green Volkswagen van that broke constantly, worked hardest when it needed repair, which was often. She had a brief affair with M (my sister martha). That was interesting, especially when M decided to break it off and Debby stood in the driveway and hollered, "But why M?"

Then there was Slats, but her real name was Rebecca. Debby hung the title of Slats on her because Rebecca was so thin that she could have fallen through the slats of a wooden foot bridge. However, her boobs would have caught her; they were perfect. Slats had two kids and a husband. Insanely jealous of him, they fought all the time at every social occasion and usually managed to inspire some do-gooder into it trying to help save their marriage. Still, after a while, the pattern was clear. They fought like cats and dogs. Then they had make up sex. But the person that got dragged into their fight did not reap the benefits. He or she was left feeling drained and frustrated. Plus, a party night was ruined. Most everyone caught on after a while. Slats was a bright young lady and later went on to be a civil engineer.

Pamela was a little pretty thing with big blue eyes and curly blond hair who looked positively cherubic. But she had the foulest mouth I have ever heard and enjoyed shocking people.

Janan was the head designer. Janice, her daughter, who eventually became the gown designer, and her sister—boy, could they make costumes!

Janice was completely immoral, loved cocaine, and would do anyone for it. She did most of the salesman and the delivery men. She would disappear into the back room, M's bedroom, and they would both come out smiling a few minutes later. Janice would have been perfect if I had ever chosen to open a whore house. She loved sex and would walk up to a man with a glint in her eye and say, "Wanna have a cheap, meaningless affair?" She loved to hang around people that drank, though she never touched a drop. She would not even eat the minestrone when I put wine in it. I fixed lunch almost every day for the entire crew until one day, I realized that they always walked out without thanking me and left me with the dishes. That was the end of free lunch.

Madeline was a strange one. She came from a wealthy family, was well educated, and spoke Russian. An eccentric, bohemian intellectual, I suspect she had Russian gypsy blood. She had moved to Santa Cruz from the East Coast and lived in her car. Completely nonconformist, she was thin, blonde, and looked aristocratic. She thought she could just live on the beach in California for free and was upset when the law told her otherwise. She would find different places to park her car. To avoid being cited, everything she owned was in her car, or so I thought. Later, I discovered that she had an entire household in storage. Meanwhile, she showered in the basement bathroom off my office. Evenings I would find her cooking in an electric frying pan in the basement. Once, I heard her tell Slats, "Let's go out to lunch and use big words." I pretended not to notice that Madeline was living in the basement. When she decided she wanted a baby, she picked out a man and had a brief affair just long enough to get pregnant, and then dumped him. She neglected to tell him that she had his baby until years later. Not wanting to be bothered with a man, she just wanted a baby.

The entire crew had a secret meeting and agreed that we would all watch over the baby. We need not have bothered. Madeline was an exceptional mother. Viva was born in the summer of '74. Madeline hardly ever let go of the child except to put her in the scrap bin while working.

Madeline was a talented designer with flair and technique and caught on to making hats right away. She became a valued employee and friend. Once she got mad at me. I do not remember why but I knew she was because when she saw me stopped at a stoplight and was in the lane facing me, she flipped me off. Later, feeling remorse, she left a six-pack of Heineken Dark at my doorstep.

A stickler for detail, my costumes were well-known for their authenticity. For example, we created Star War head pieces that were exactly like those worn by the warriors of the Galactic Empire. Staff members were required to sit through movies and sketch characters like Chewbacca, C-3PO and R2D2. These were even purchased from my store by renowned mask maker, Don Post.

Costume rental was my initial enterprise, but after visiting Hollywood with six hats, I discovered a real need there. My business blossomed into manufacturing of hats. I traveled nationwide marketing my costumes, masks, and hats. Sir Elton John even bought one of my hats.

One young evening, sitting in the Oak Room enjoying my favorite beverage, a young man approached me and introduced himself by saying he was a photographer for the Good Times weekly news. "I am doing an article on glamorous women in Santa Cruz, and I would like to photograph you." I threw back my head and laughed.

"Me? Haha, you must be kidding! Besides, I don't photograph well."

"How 'bout if I photograph you, and if you don't like it, I don't print it?"

"You're serious?"

"Yep, I am. How 'bout meeting me here tomorrow afternoon and see what comes of it."

So that is how I came to be on the front cover of the Good Times magazine, and became friends with Dan Coryo.

Photo 21 - Me as "most glamorous
women in Santa Cruz"

CHAPTER 42

Patt

One afternoon while sitting in my office with my assistant, Sherry, a tall, lanky biker pushed his Harley into my driveway. A shifty-looking character, he wore a skull bandana over his long, greasy hair, a torn black t-shirt, worn jeans, and motorcycle boots. He knocked and came in.

He announced boldly, "I'm here to apply for the job of costume designer!"

Good lord, I thought, a biker. I looked at him and asked, "What experience do you have?"

He answered, "Well, I've made puppets."

"Okay," I said. "Come with me."

He followed me into the basement workshop where several women were busy making mascots. I gave him some foam and said, "Make something for me." Then I left the workshop, went back to my office, and forgot about him.

As I was closing, he came out of the shadows and startled me. He was holding a giant rat head!

"You are hired!" I exclaimed. "You start tomorrow."

"Cool!" He said as he left.

That was how Patterson, aka "Patt," a gifted designer with natural talent, came into my life. It was not till later that I found out the reason he was pushing his Harley was because he did not have gas money and had been sleeping on a friend's couch.

A native of Santa Cruz, Patt had gone to Santa Cruz High, after which he spent four years in the Army in Korea. When he came home from the Army, he took the first job he could get, which was working in a feed store stomping on imperfect baby chicks. This . . . I could have lived without knowing. When he got his first paycheck, he started riding his Harley and eating his lunch sitting on the curb in front of a 7-11.

I had just separated from Mr. Wonderful, and friends of mine had invited me to their Super Bowl party. They told me they had also invited Mr. Wonderful. As I was discussing my options with my assistant, Patt slipped into the office and sat quietly while I thought out loud, "I think I will rent a hunk of a man and take him with me!"

Patt piped in, holding his hands a foot apart, "Yeah, and tell your ex with your fingers that your hunk is this big!" That's when I noticed the twinkle in Patt's eye. He had a keen sense of humor.

I picked up the phone and called a gym, telling the person who answered that I would pay $200 for an escort, and that he had to be good looking and muscular. I got a call back immediately and agreed to meet Joe at a bar near the gym. He was what I asked for: Six two, sweet-faced and well built. I explained that he was to be my date for the evening and that he needed to act like he was in love with me.

"Can you act?" I asked him.

"Yes ma'am! I can, and it will not be difficult."

Okay, so the stage was set. When I walked into the party with this hunk on my arm, Steve, my host, said, "You always have good looking men! Where do you get them?"

I laughed and replied, "I rent them!"

Funny thing, Mr. Wonderful was a no show. Joe kept nodding at one man after another, asking, "Is that him?"

"No," I'd say.

I was having a great time with that sweet thing, and he suggested, "I could come home with you afterwards."

I said, "No, thank you," and paid him. What was I thinking? It could have been great.

Oh well. Back to Patt, who had been working for me for several weeks when he called me at home and asked if he could come over. It was a rainy night and I lived in the Bonny Doon miles from town in the mountains. I was puzzled, but said yes.

Several hours later he appeared at my door soaking wet. I invited him in and gave him a towel and a drink. Settling down in front of the fire, Patt talked, and I pretended to listen. He was a wealth of information, none of which interested me. Boy did he like to talk.

It was growing late and still pouring rain, so I said, "It's late, why don't you spend the night?" He did, lying down under the Christmas tree. He crossed his hands across his chest and fell asleep before I could bring him a blanket and pillow.

In the morning, it was still raining so I suggested he leave his motorcycle and ride with me into town. On the ride into town Patt told me how to break down an M16 piece by piece, clean it, and put it back together. How fascinating! (I'm being facetious) Patt talked a lot about things I did not need to know. After work, I brought him home and it was still raining. While Patt talked nonstop, I fixed dinner. After dinner, he took his position under the Christmas tree—and the next day I drove us to work again, and again home. It had rained nonstop. On the fourth day, I suggested Patt take a shower. He was beginning to smell ripe.

Smiling at him, I said, "If you take a shower, you may share my bed."

"Okay," he said—and did.

On the fifth day, driving into town I said, "You are living with me."

"Yeah," he answered, with a smirk of a smile.

So began a long relationship with many adventures, travel, laughs, and tears while Patt went from bad biker to being a Klingon, ever learning the language. Then a gunslinger, and then a pirate. Now when I say he became these, he really did. He dressed, talked, and lived each character. People no longer called him Patt. This went on for years.

Photo 22 – Patterson Pirate

He was always the costume designer who could turn out a costume on demand in less than an hour, draw a rendering in minutes while he talked nonstop. His brain was on speed dial like someone who'd just taken bennies and washed them down with ten cups of coffee, though he did not do drugs and was honest as the day was long. He was just naturally wired. He also had a shifty look about him that attracted police. Once in San Diego on costume business, we stopped at a phone booth to look up an address (remember phone booths?), and I was in the car. A police car pulled up, and two cops got out of the car and began to question Patt, took his ID, and ran a make on him. He came up clean. Of course, he did. I knew that.

I got out of the car and told them, "He works for me. What is this about?"

"Well, he looked suspicious," they answered. Really!

Patt got in the car. I glared at them and said, "Good night, officers."

Another time coming back from Mexico, we got stopped by boarder control on the Mexican side. Patt was taken from the car and escorted inside. I waited for almost an hour while I watched the federales tear apart a red corvette driven by two young white boys. The federales pried the door panels off, pulled the seats out, and tore up the trunk lining. When they found nothing, they left the guys to put their car back together. Wow! Meanwhile, one of these federales came out and told me I could leave.

Objecting, I answered, "Not until my companion comes out."

"Oh, he won't, we will find something," he replied.

Not much later, Patt came out looking white as a sheet. They had strip searched him. Poor Patt. I knew they would find nothing; he was a law-abiding citizen, a veteran, didn't do drugs, and never even had a traffic ticket. He just looked shifty.

Me, on the other hand, could be carrying a kilo of weed in the trunk with fifty hits of acid in the glove compartment, driving under the influence, and the police would smile at me and tell me to have a nice day.

Patt loved dive bars, which he went to when we were on business trips for trade shows, while I got a good night's sleep so I could be on my game the next day. He would roam the city looking for low-life bars, sit there and drink cheap beer while drawing on cocktail napkins. He had ink in his veins.

Once upon a time in Mexico, we delivered five mascots to a pizza parlor in Guadalajara. There were no places to park in front, so Patt dropped me off there with the five big boxes and went to find a place to park. After a long while he did not show up, so I walked around the corner. Sure enough, there was the van with Patt outside with two Mexican cops. Storming up to them, I demanded to know what was going on. Again, the answer was he looked suspicious. In broken Spanish, I explained that he worked for me and that we were delivering merchandise to the pizza parlor. I suggested they come with me and talk to the owner. Instead, they wanted money. I gave them each twenty dollars and they pointed out a parking place behind the pizza joint. The owner paid me in cash. It was a lot. The neighborhood was not the best and I was uneasy about walking out with that much cash, so I split up the five thousand and hid most of it on different parts of my body, with a small amount in my purse. Requesting that he send the rest to my office in a money order with no problem getting out, we headed to Puerta Vallarta and the beach.

As I mentioned, Patt likes to drink. At a tiny Palapa bar on the beach, there was a sign that read:

"IF YOU EAT ONE OF OUR PEPPERS, DRINKS ARE FREE ALL NIGHT."

Patt looked at me and his eyes lit up.

"Oh Boy! Free drinks," he exclaimed.

Replying, I added, "I will do it if you do."

We asked the bartender about it, and he said, "Sí señor . . . es cierto. Yes, it's true."

Patt said, "I'll have one." The bartender turned and rang a huge bell that hung from the bar, and in a few minutes at least ten people showed up to watch. That alone should have been a warning! The bartender produced a small reddish pepper from under the bar. It looked innocent! Patt popped it into his mouth and began chewing. His face turned red, then white, then red again. His eyes popped out of his head, and he tried to talk, but nothing came out. That pepper completely took his breath away. Watching him, I decided to pay for my drinks. Patt was unable to finish the drink he had and could not drink for the rest of the night. He was completely miserable for the rest of the night. Moral to this story: if the bell rings, don't eat the pepper.

Patt wrote the following once in script and though a bit faded now, it still hangs on my office wall:

DURING THE SEQUENCE OF EVENTS THAT WE CALL LIFE, MANY SITUATIONS AND ADVENTURES PRESENT THEMSELVES BY

*LIVING LIFE AND FLOWING WITH THE
LESSONS OF LIVING, LEARNING, AND LOVING.
WE ALLOW PEOPLE TO TOUCH AND BE A PART
OF OURSELVES TO HELP MOULD AND SHAPE
THE PERSON THAT WE ARE AND THE PERSON
THAT WE CAN BECOME. YOU HAVE BEEN AN
IMPORTANT PART OF MY LIFE; A PUSH AND
PULL OF IDEAS AND CONCEPTS, JOY, SORROW
AND PAIN—ALL THE THINGS THAT MAKE LIFE
LIVING. I LOOK FORWARD TO THE FUTURE
OF OUR FRIENDSHIP AND THE CONTINUING
ADVENTURE OF LIFE.*

He is still just as positive, bright, witty, unselfish, gifted, and talented as he was when I first met him. A hero in every sense. I will always be thankful that he pushed his Harley into my life that day.

CHAPTER 43

Halloween: We all dress up

Being the only costume shop in Santa Cruz and an especially good one, Santa Cruz Costumes did a booming business at Halloween. It took all of us to run it. The week before Halloween, we opened at ten in the morning and closed at nine at night. Carmen, a large woman with jet-black hair, who joined weight watchers but drank two liters of diet soda a day, was our mainstay. Pamela, the dirty mouth kid, backed her. And Bruce, who had not yet changed his name to Kelly, and I worked it. Beau got into it, and so did the girls. It was a madhouse.

One morning before we opened, a line had even formed at the door. Unbelievable! By noon, the place was so packed that we had to put a monitor on the door to stop people from coming in. When two went out, two more were allowed in. We had no less than twenty people in the shop at one time. We got them into costumes, signed contracts, and took their money as fast as we could. I have never made so much money in all my life. The three days before Halloween, we would make $40,000 in cash.

I would sit on the floor behind the counter, bundling the huge stacks of money. But it did not come easy. We worked continuously without meals, living on trail mix and water, and not going to the bathroom.

Finally, we worked out a system. When one of us had to go, we would raise our hand like in school, and someone else would step up and take over. We were so tired at the end of the night that I would order pizza— and we would drink, eat, and laugh. Then we would lie down in the shop and fall asleep exhausted. Madeline and I would put on Cleopatra gowns as nightgowns. Our slogan was "sleep in it tonight, rent it tomorrow." Lots of strange and funny things took place in that shop.

People would get weird about their costumes. What they wore became their alter egos. One man, I think he was an attorney, reserved an expensive gown for his wife and a tux for himself and when he came to pick it up on Halloween day, he said he did not want the gown, only the tux. I told him he could not have the tux without the gown because it had been reserved for two weeks and no one else was able to rent it.

He said, "You don't understand. I want the tux, just not the gown."

And I said, "No, you don't understand. I am not renting you the tux because you were not considerate enough to call in and cancel the gown so I could have rented it. So, you don't get the tux."

Then I held up the two costumes and said to the crowd in the room, "Anybody want to rent these costumes?" Two hands went up.

"Okay, they are yours," I said. Oh, did I mention that the attorney was a rude, unpleasant person? He would have to go back to his wife and tell her he had no costume to wear because that bitch at the costume shop would not give him his costume. So, sue me?

Then I turned to the crowd and said, "Next?" Someone waved a number. "Your costume is free, my dear," I said, "because you are a nice person." The crowd was pleased.

When someone needed a costume that we did not have and it was an easy costume to make, such as a black cat, we would tell them to come back in a few hours. We would call the shop on Bixby Street, and someone would whip up a black cat.

We rented more monks and nuns than anything else. Debby Erickson could turn one out in twenty minutes, one arm might be a little longer than the other one, but we were now doing costumes while you wait. It was interesting to watch people choose their costumes. Usually, I knew what they would be when they walked in the door. I loved the ones that thought they were so clever. They would lean over the counter and whisper, "I'm going to be a pregnant nun." Somewhere there must have been an entire covey of nuns.

I loved to do drag. If I could talk a man into drag, I had fun. Once I talked a tall, thin, good-looking man who was going to emcee the Good Times Ball into a gold sequin showgirl outfit with fishnets and a giant pink bow at his crotch. He had a ball, and I laughed my ass off. It was the five-inch heels that did it when he wobbled on stage.

That year, I wore my black leather S and M costume. It had an extremely short skirt, a vest that was mostly two strips of leather held together with lacing, thigh-high boots, a choker and belt with studs, a riding crop, and a cat of nine tails at my hip. I won first place in the most perverse category, much to the embarrassment of my daughter Lisa.

Another year I was a Mermaid in gold sequin. I had sewn the tail together, so I could not walk. Men carried me around all night and handed me from one to another as a true mermaid. I wore a long wig but was topless, another embarrassment to Lisa. When I had to go to the bathroom, I would have someone carry me in, and then I would say, "Don't leave me too long. I'm fast!" It was a great lot of fun.

Halloween was a favorite time. Not only did we make lots of money, but we also had a great time. After the shop closed, we would break out the champagne, dress in costume, and go out to dinner. One year Bruce (aka Kelly) went as a maid. He was utterly hilarious with his hose bagging down around his white waitress shoes, a baggy black dress, white apron, and saggy boobs. His wig kept falling askew and he kept straightening it—but the best part was Kelly himself. Being an actor, he really got into character.

That year, the entire crew went to The Woodshed restaurant for dinner and drank enough champagne to run up a thousand-dollar bill, but I could afford it. It was Halloween.

The next year, after having a few bottles of bubbly at the shop while we dressed ourselves, we decided to go to the Holiday Inn. It was just up the street a few blocks, and the food was decent, so we all piled into cars laughing.

The last time I saw Madeline, she was wearing a witch costume with one tooth blacked out. She was the last to leave, but she never showed up. We waited and wondered and speculated about where she had gone and finally went on with our merrymaking without her. Little did we know she had been stopped a block away and spent the night in jail for driving under the influence. We laughed about it for years after, but it sure as hell was not funny for Madeline that night.

CHAPTER 44

Tommy

It was a beautiful sunny day, as was my practice, lying in the sun nude in my backyard. My phone rang. A girlish man's voice, obviously disguised asked, "What are you wearing?"

Wondering which one of my friends was pulling a joke on me, I laughed, rolled over, and said, "My birthday suit."

"Oh, isn't that nice?" he replied. "Mind if I talk to you while I make myself come?"

I laughed again, and decided it was Paul. I said, "Sure! What are you wearing?"

"Well," replied the girlish voice. "I am wearing my sister's underwear, a little pink bra with lace trim and tiny flowers, and little pink bikini panties with lace and flowers. They are kinda see-through, butter soft, and they fit me really good. Oh, Oh … I am commming!"

"Well, that's nice," I laughed. "I am happy for you."

"Oh, thank you, thank you," the man's girlish voice said, "Can I call you again sometime?"

"Sure," I said.

"Oh," he said, "I need your number."

"You have my number," I said.

"No, I do not," he said. "I dialed at random."

Going along with the gag, I rattled off my number in a sing-song voice. He thanked me again and hung up. And I laughed again. Paul was getting unusually creative in his pranks.

Rubbing more baby oil into my skin, I forgot about it until the next time. A week later, I was in my office when the same girlish voice called and said, "Hi, remember me? I am Tommy, and you were so nice to me and made me come. Can we do it again?"

Tommy then proceeded to tell me that he was again in his sister's underwear, describing it in intimate detail while telling me he was being watched from across the street by two construction workers, and he was giving them a glimpse of himself in his sister's underwear, and this was arousing him. He liked to tease while he played with himself.

Paul was getting out there! I would take this up with him when I saw him next. After a few moments, Tommy, aka Paul, came again, thanked me, and hung up. I forgot about it until next time. When Tommy called, I was busy, so I passed the phone to my secretary and ordered her to talk to him. Her eyes grew wider and wider while she listened to the description of what Tommy was wearing. She put the phone down and said, "What was that!?"

"Oh," I replied. "A sick friend of mine is having some fun."

The next day I saw Paul and confronted him, and of course, he denied it in a high girlie voice, and we both had a good laugh and he said, "You mean that you talked to some pervert on the phone and made him come?"

"Yeah," I said. "It was the least I could do for a friend. I figure it keeps him off the streets." We laughed some more, and the subject was dropped.

The calls continued. Tommy called about once a month and always described what he was wearing and I, in return, became very inventive as to what I was wearing though I never wore underwear for Tommy. I just made up what I was wearing, with the help of a Victoria's Secret catalog. It always ended the same with him announcing he had come and politely thanking me.

One day, while Paul was visiting, the phone rang, and Tommy announced himself, with "Do you have time to make me come?" I stared blankly at Paul, dumbstruck. My mouth dropped open, and I asked stupidly, "How do you do that?"

"Do what?" Paul whispered back.

"It is Tommy," I whispered, holding the phone to my ass. I had heard if you hold it to your chest, they can hear you. "I thought you were Tommy!"

"I told you I wasn't," Paul persisted, "but you didn't want to believe me."

"I thought it was a joke!" I mouthed.

Tommy was still describing his latest outfit while he got himself off or while I got him off. He thanked me and hung up.

Paul and I looked at each other. He said, "You've been talking to a pervert all this time!"

We burst into peals of laughter. "Oh well," I said, "no harm done. It is a dirty job, but someone's got to do it."

So began the time of Tommy's calls for the next five years, always polite and always in underwear. If I were too busy to talk to him, I would pawn him off on some unsuspecting employee or friend. I gave him numbers of my friends to call. Only Valeska hung up on him shouting, "Filthy pervert! You're sick!"

I guess she wasn't into delivering public service in the same way I was. On the other hand, Janice became extra creative and would time herself to see how fast she could make Tommy come.

Once Tommy called and I was having a bad day. I said, "Oh, not today, Tommy. I am having a bad day."

Tommy said, "Oh, you poor baby, tell me all about it," and I did. He was appropriately sympathetic, listening while I poured out all my woes. I thanked him for listening to me and realized what just happened. The tables were turned. Tommy was helping me by listening.

I invited Tommy to the annual Christmas party. We all speculated if we would know him if he showed up, but he never did—or at least we think he didn't.

When I moved to the Sierras, I forgot to give Tommy my phone number, so I lost him. Oddly, I miss him.

CHAPTER 45

Cheech and Chong

Because of my background as a booking agent, a friend, Victor Camacho, approached me, asking if I could get Cheech and Chong to do a benefit for a friend who was running for a political office. "Sure, I'll try," I replied. I checked their show schedule and found they were playing in San Diego the next Saturday. So, I flew to San Diego and presented myself at the stage door in my cream-colored satin dress.

"Are you on the guestlist," I was asked.

"No, but I should be."

That got me in. The show was about to start. I was ushered to stage left and given a stool to perch on by Richie (Cheech).

The show was funny but crude. I laughed while Cheech crawled around the floor, pretending he was a dog and pissing on everything. After the show, I was offered a Heineken Dark, which I love, and was allowed to broach the subject I had come for. Would they consider a benefit for Camacho? I handed the two of them flyers stating the "would-be" Senator's credentials and Cheech's only response was, "Well, he's a beaner." Tommy (Chong) was the serious one and a political junky who watched the news every day. They both agreed to meet him, and dinner was arranged.

I learned several things about Cheech and Chong on that trip. Both were from Canada and are musicians who took a left turn and became comics. They do not drink hard alcohol. They had a written contract with William Morris that had listed their necessities for each and every show:

1. A Case of Heineken Dark
2. Two bottles of Blue Nun wine
3. M&M's with all of the green ones picked out

Back in Santa Cruz, I reported to Victor that Cheech and Chong were a possibility. They would agree to do the benefit, but they wanted to meet him first. I also told him their act was pretty raunchy and did not think it was appropriate for all ages, and maybe he should reconsider.

"Oh no," he insisted, "I've heard their records, and they are funny."

And so, the fun began. Camacho and I flew to Los Angeles. I remember getting off the plane with him and being a gentleman; he offered to carry my bag. My bag happened to be a carpet bag that I had purchased in Persia. When he realized it was a carpetbag, he handed it back to me, saying he could not be photographed carrying a carpet. Hmmm, I wonder what he was reading? We met Richie and Tommy along with their beautiful blonde wives in a Chinese restaurant.

The conversation was lively but did not touch on politics at all. Then the main dish was served, a giant pouched fish with head-on and eyes glazed. Richie did the honors of serving, and Camacho got the head with the eyeballs. Tommy explained.

"As the guest of honor, Camacho gets to eat the eyeballs. It's tradition, I insist!"

Richie chipped in. "Yeah, man. It's an honor. Please, enjoy! The eyes are the best part."

Comanche was turning a lighter shade of pale. He swallowed, tugged at his collar, and forked a fisheye onto his plate. Everyone was watching him. He took a deep breath, put the eye in his mouth and swallowed it whole. Cheech and Chong laughed hysterically, and everyone at the table followed suit, including Camacho.

Richie got up from the table, slapped Camacho on the back, and said, "You're alright, man!"

Tommy raised his glass and said, "We will do the benefit for you. And you don't have to eat the other eye."

Back in Santa Cruz, I began the work of booking the Santa Cruz civic auditorium for the show and putting out promo . . . how did I get roped into this? I got a call from the Morris agency and Cheech and Chong's agency, telling me bluntly that Cheech and Chong could not do a benefit according to their contract without their consent. And they were not consenting. Oh, shit. Now what? My vision was blurring, my face flushed—signs of stress. The Morris agency are SOBs. One of the reasons I quit the music business. I gathered my thoughts and dialed Tommy. I left a message with his answering service. Twenty-four restless hours later, I got a conference call from Tommy and Richie. I told them about my call from William Morris. There was not even a pause. "Fuck him! He doesn't own us! Don't worry. We will be there,"—big sigh of relief on my part.

The day of the concert, if you can call it that, I picked up Cheech and Chong from the airport and dropped them at the best motel that Santa Cruz had to offer. The only hotel at that time was on Pacific Avenue and very old. Full of retired seniors living there permanently, I went in with them to check out their accommodations. Richie dropped down on the bed and unzipped his fly and—you guessed it— pulled it out and asked me for a blow job. Ha! I was out of there in two shakes of a lamb's tail.

I had invited them to dinner at my Victorian on Bixby Street and hired a chef to cook. Last-minute preparations were made, including fresh flowers and good linen placed on the table. They showed up on time. Heinekens were opened and poured into pilsner glasses; Blue Nun was iced on the table. I made everything as lovely as possible. Why, I have never seen such poor manners. Richie ate with his hands, burped and farted, wiped his face on my good linen tablecloth. What a class act!

Tommy ignored him and ate quietly. Time for the concert. I drove them to the civic auditorium, dropped them off, and went to park.

When I returned and walked down the hall to their dressing room, I could not help but notice the cloud of smoke billowing up from the closed door. Good Lord, every dope dealer in town was in their dressing room showcasing their wares; pot and pills were everywhere. The local police were standing guard. Camacho would shit his pants! I left and checked the audience. The front rows were filled with family, parents, and children. Mostly Hispanic. I knew this show was not PG. I left the building and went around the corner to the Oak Room and ordered a double Jack. When I returned, I was fortified. People were leaving the concert, mostly people with children, the ones that had filled the front seats earlier. Camacho, who had introduced Cheech and Chong, must be having a heart attack. Oh well, I warned him . . . needless to say, Camacho was not elected.

CHAPTER 46

Sweet Brucie and friends and how Brucie became Kelly Houston

Bruce and I were inseparable. Thicker than thieves, we worked and played together. To clarify, this is not Bruce Aidells, but another one of my dear friends, also named Bruce. He learned to make hats, and had moved upstairs into the office, where he became my assistant. He had a photographic memory. Even now, I could call him and ask him for the phone number of someone in Texas that we did business with years ago, and he could give it to me.

Photo 23 - Brucie

I bought a brand-new recreational vehicle in Watsonville that had green carpeting and green and gold upholstery. We traveled the states selling costumes. We had great fun. He drove and I fixed cocktails.

Bruce could find his way to each account without ever making a wrong turn. This was before GPS. He would announce, "We're here." Then I would take my bag, go in, and make my sales. We would be off to our next account. We could easily call on three or four accounts per day.

Nancy would travel with me for a week, then Monah would fly in, and Nancy would fly out. That way, I got to spend one-on-one time with my kids while we traveled. Bruce and I met them at an airport. They got to see the Grand Canyon and Carlsbad Caverns—awesome! We stopped at historical sites and even went several miles out of our way to see the camel driver's tomb. What the hell was a camel driver doing in Arizona?

The RV was a Sundance and had two bunk beds, an overhead bed, and a table that made into a bed so I could take the kids with me on trips. Also, there was a bathtub. When it got too hot, like in Houston, I would sit in the tub and drink champagne. We could fix meals in it, too, or we could stop for dinner if we chose. It also had a louvered door in between the kitchen and bedroom that fell off on the way home from the dealership. I should have known then that it was a bad omen. That wasn't the only problem. Many times, the engine would not start, and we would have to wait until it cooled down, maybe forty minutes, before it would start again. I called the dealer many times before we headed to the next dealership that could fix it in Colorado. But until then, we had many adventures.

Good-natured Bruce always took it in stride and made it fun, like when our huge twenty-five-foot RV stalled, blocking a 7-11 parking lot and none of the customers could get out. Bruce merely invited them in for a cold drink, while I made snacks. We had a parking lot party until we could get the damm thing started again.

We avoided RV parks and usually parked in the best sections of town on tree-shaded streets knowing no one would bother us there. The neighbors would think we were someone's family. The next morning, we would be gone.

We were able to carry many samples, and M could dropship more to our next account. Once in Texas, we were invited to the home of one of our customers for dinner, a nice Texas couple. The guy carried a gun in his boot, and she looked like a plump Liz Taylor. As we passed one of her employees in the parking lot, the employee had the hood of her car up. As she was looking under it, Liz walked right passed her.

I asked, "Shouldn't we help?"

Liz answered in her thick Texas twang, "I hate her, I wish she would die."

Bruce's eyes got bigger and rounder as we just looked at each other. Well, they took us home with them and when we walked into their nice home, instant karma. Their three dogs had shit all over their living room. How embarrassing. I almost felt sorry for her. But really, it was funny.

We ended up going out to dinner at the San Jacinto Inn, a large barn-like restaurant with the best seafood I had eaten in a long time, with huge portions. We started with an all-you-can-eat gulf shrimp served on huge silver platters and ended up with fried chicken and biscuits. Bruce could not keep his eyes off Liz. However, it wasn't her cleavage he was looking at. It was the portion she consumed. "I don't know where she put it," he exclaimed. "That women could eat a horse!"

Although our time traveling across the country was a hoot, I want to explain how Bruce became Kelly Houston. Bruce Hill had a dream. He confided in me that he had always wanted to do a cabaret show. "Well," I said, "let's do it!"

We rented a theater and brought together a cast of characters. The show was to be called "Sweet Brucie and Friends." Greg was still around, and he became co-producer. We sold advertising for the program and borrowed more money from my friend, Bob Williams, when we ran out. It was said that he made large amounts of money by dealing dope and had two bodies of guys who had tried to rip him off buried in his backyard. We avoided personal questions.

Anyway, Brucie was practicing with the band, going over his music, while Greg and I took care of the business. Donna Kruskauf, a tall, busty young lady, Jewish with kinky hair and a lot of talent, was going to do a couple of duets with Bruce. Her forte was opera, but she did jazz as well. Of course, as the costume designer, I dressed everyone. Bruce had several changes—including a pale-blue leisure suit (yeah, it was the seventies)— and a royal-blue velvet dinner jacket for his reading of "Crackers" by Mason Williams, and a white satin suit with a vest and top hat for the finale.

Unbeknownst to Bruce, I had identical outfits made for myself and my neighbor Donna, who had moved to Santa Cruz after a bad divorce. However, our vests were backless and sexy. Donna's husband had run off with a younger woman and—yadda yadda—same old heartbroken, bitter story. She had two sons, did not work, and was very naive and straight. We took her in and corrupted her. She was starting to have fun and became part of the show. She also put money into it. We all did! Anyway, there were the two dancers who improvised in front of Bruce.

After dress rehearsals and light checks, I decided we needed to have a grand opening. The show would run for two weekends, but the grand opening called for champagne and, of course, a buffet supper after the show. I hired Bruce Aidells to do the catering.

At seven years old, Nancy, my daughter, had been in an accident months before. I was in my room upstairs early on a Sunday morning. I had heard screaming and jumped and ran. She had been standing in front of the fireplace, and a spark had jumped out and caught her cotton robe on fire. She was in flames. Rolling her on the floor, I screamed for help, and got our neighbor, "Clean Jean" to drive us to the hospital. It was faster than waiting for an ambulance. Nancy had third-degree burns on her side and arm. It was horribly scary. While I held her in my lap on the way to the hospital, she looked at me with those big blue eyes and asked, "Mama, am I going to die?"

"No, sweetheart you are not going to die, not now," I had assured her. "You are going to be alright."

Her recovery was a long, hard haul. I spent my nights in the hospital on a cot in her room and watched as they bathed the burns. A very painful experience for her, she was in the hospital for six weeks. When she got out, I made her a lavender polka dot dress with three-tier ruffles that opened on the side to fit over her brace. She had a special place in the front row for Bruce's show.

Opening Night, it rained in solid sheets. There was no dodging between the drops. You could not get between the car and the door without getting sopping wet. The few people that did make it out were not happy campers when they got there. We were not happy with the weather and the poor turnout, either. Greg was uptight and in a bad mood. Bruce and I were trying to hold it together. I decided to open a champagne bottle to take the edge off, but Greg grabbed it from my hands and said no. We waited until he went out front and opened one anyway. This was a night to be remembered.

Bruce was nervous. I had never seen him nervous but there was good cause for it because a series of unfortunate events had occurred. Donna K. had decided she did not want to be in the show, and simply given notice. The band of musicians that Brucie had been rehearsing with suddenly had other things to do. Instead, I hired a trio from San Francisco and paid them a lot of traveling wages. They were professionals and could read music, however, since I was paying them so much, I decided to dress them in costumes. I put one in a white bunny suit and one in a Superman suit and the tall bassist in a ballerina outfit. It had nothing to do with the show, but neither did anything.

Valeska and her husband, Real George, were in the audience. Valeska was a Doctor's doctor, raised in the best boarding schools. She had a mouth on her like a sailor, and when she drank, which was often, she did outrageously. She was tall, thin, and beautiful—and looked like a model. All cheekbones, with long dark hair and large almond eyes, she had no breasts to speak of. She told me once that when she was a teen, she had prayed every night to for her chest to develop, and every morning she checked and found nothing. She lost faith in God. I went with her to San Francisco when she got implants, and then, she felt complete. So, of course, she flashed them. Every time we saw each other in a crowded restaurant or club, she lifted her blouse and flashed. It was kinda her way of saying hello.

Real George, her husband, owned a men's clothing store downtown. He was a big gentle giant with a droll sense of humor. One night, after a night of drinking, Valeska and Real George got into a fight on the way home. George was driving. Valeska started hitting George over the head with her handbag. There happened to be a highway patrol behind them. He pulled them over. Valeska turned her wrath on him and went to jail wearing my blue quinna gown. She looked fabulous in it. George was permitted to go home.

Several hours later, a sheriff opened the cell door to check on Valeska's image. Imagine his surprise when this striking vision in a blue evening gown put her head down and rammed him in his ample belly, knocking him to the floor, and then flung herself on him, pounding him with her fists. When he was able to untangle himself from her and secure her back in her cell the only thing he said was, "I guess you're not ready to come out yet!"

Valeska appeared in court the next morning in my evening gown and, batting her eyes, told the Judge, "I just don't what came over me, your honor." She was released. You get the picture.

Bob Williams was there because he had invested money in our show. Big Brucie, aka Aidells' sausage, was there because he had catered the affair. And Bill, my soon to be ex-husband was there because he still loved me and wanted me to succeed. A few other faithfuls also came out to support us in all that rain—about thirty people in a theatre that seated two-hundred.

The show went on. Brucie sang off-key. The dancers danced like no one was watching. With a spotlight on him, Bruce went into the audience, knelt on one knee, and sang directly to Nancy, my daughter with the laughing eyes. But, in her cast fresh out of the hospital, her eyes were anything but laughing. She cried, not softly weeping tears, but bellowing angry, hurtful tears. She did not want to be in the spotlight wearing her brace and cried uncontrollably. Poor Bruce was unnerved, to say the least.

Then Brucie did his reading of Mason Williams, "Crackers." If you have never read it, find a copy! As he sang his final song, unbeknownst to him, Donna and I came out in our white satin outfits with two banana cream pies that I had bought at Albertsons. The audience could see us coming, but not poor Bruce. As we hit him smack in the face, the pie went flying everywhere. How was I to know that in the movies they use shaving cream, not real pies? Well, these pies went into the audience, and caused such a mess that I had to pay to have the carpets cleaned in the theatre. Bruce, bless his heart, always the comic, did not think it was funny at all. Without taking a bow, he retired to his dressing room to cry.

Meanwhile, I hustled about cleaning things up so Big Brucie could set up his buffet that he had planned for one hundred people that had cost him a pretty penny. I am not too fond of carrot soup, but that evening sealed my dislike of it. Of course, I opened a bottle of champagne. Greg was too mad to even speak to me, and with the champagne bottle and glass in hand, I climbed the stairs to say hello to Valeska.

Low and behold, who was standing next to her but Donna Kruskauf. She was too high and mighty to be in the show that she thought would be a flop but not too proud to come and witness the train wreck. Valeska knew I was steaming angry, so she reached over and took George's cigar from him and put it into Donna's drink. But that was not enough. Valeska took my champagne from me and poured it down Donna's ample cleavage.

You gotta love Valeska! It was better than anything I could have said or done.

The show closed after one night. Bill went home and slept with Donna! Greg slept on the couch, and Nancy and I cried ourselves to sleep. Brucie, I am sure, was doing the same thing while the rain pounded its wrath on all of us.

A week later I saw my dear friend again. Brucie showed up on my doorstep with flowers and a wistful grin. He said, "I've decided to change my name to Kelly Houston." I thought it was a good idea.

CHAPTER 47

Greg and Ohio

Greg left for Ohio, Bill moved to the mountains and was strangely enough living in a house we had considered buying before we went to Persia. It was a great house with a massive stone fireplace, and acres of gardening space. He was rooming there with another woodsy guy.

Greg's plan was to find a job, buy a house, and then send for me. I worked Halloween alone that year. Well, not alone. Kelly was with Carmen and me, and a new employee Sylvia—a hippie chick with long brown hair. We had been so busy the year before that I decided to open another location and rented a building at the other end of Ocean Street. That way, people had a choice to rent costumes at Santa Cruz Costume Bank or rent from Fantasy Costumes if they didn't like us. We lowered the prices at the new store and sent most of the junk there. Not that any of our stuff was junk, but we kept the high-priced gowns and novelty costumes at Santa Cruz Costume Bank. Carmen operated the new store, and in the end, she made more money. Lord, she was good.

After another successful season, I flew to Ohio. Greg picked me up at the airport and gave me a peck on the cheek. "We have to hurry," he said.

"Hurry? Why?" I asked.

"I bought a house, and it's closing today, and I need you to sign."

Taking me for a quick tour of the older stately two-story house with a magnificent garden of old shade trees and beautifully landscaped, it had four bedrooms and a basement the width and length of the house. "This," Greg declared, "will be my workshop." He looked at his watch and said, "Gotta go." He took me to the realtor's office.

Buying a home in Ohio is different than in California. Ten people were sitting around a long rectangular desk. It was more like judge and jury than a title company, and realtor Greg, of course, had used Santa Cruz costumes as a credit reference. It was more like judge and jury than a realtor company, and Greg, of course, had used Santa Cruz Costumes as a credit reference. After all, he was married to me, and I was doing quite well in business. Questions were asked, papers were passed around to be signed, and the next thing, hands were being shaken, and we were homeowners.

Greg took me back to his parent's house to get some rest. His mother disliked me and made no pretenses about it. She had not liked me ever since she had picked up a book in the San Diego home signed to Bill from me, "To my friend and lover, may we always be."

I took a nap in their guest room until Greg woke me for dinner. We were going out. His parents had left town. How convenient! Greg took me to a little candle-lit French restaurant. He ordered fine wine, the staff seemed to know him, and he was familiar with the menu. He ordered for me.

I said, "How charming, have you been here before?"

He had smiled and said, "I thought you would like it."

I repeated, "Have you been here before?"

As he forked a mouthful of coq au vin, he said, "There's something I need to tell you."

Interrupting him as I sipped my glass of wine, I said, "You brought someone else here?"

"Yes," he said. "That's what I'm trying to tell you. I want a divorce."

With stunned realization, it did not take me long to realize why he had brought me to Ohio. He used me to buy a house and now he was with another woman. I stood up and hollered, "You fucker!" and like a magician, much to the astonishment of the staff and customers, ripped the tablecloth out from under all the lovely china, dumping it in his lap. Then I walked out, took a cab to his parent's house, packed my stuff, and was on the next flight back to California.

Though I was hurt, I was never really in love with Greg—just infatuated. I had thrown away the best relationship I ever had and pushed my one true love and soulmate out the door for Greg.

One afternoon, Bill made an appearance in my kitchen. Looking sheepish, he said, staring me in the eye, "I'm on my honeymoon."

I replied, "When's the baby due?"

Shuffling his feet slightly, he said, "Sometime in September."

Apparently heartbroken, he had taken solace in another woman's arms and she had used the oldest trick in the book and gotten herself pregnant. Bill being the honorable nobleman, married her. After two torturous years of craziness, now the door was closed.

After five beautiful years in the truest sense, Bill and I were over. Yet, he stayed in my life for another couple of years. At Christmas, he showed up with a pair of emerald earrings for me. He stayed in touch with my kids, who all adored him, especially Lisa, who never forgave me for letting him go.

★★★

Throwing myself into my business with a passion, it was time to put myself in order. I worked starting at six in the morning and continued until dinner time. I sold costumes and ordered supplies overseeing the costume, and cooked breakfast for the kids. Dinner had always been a family time, and everyone sat down together in the kitchen at the beautiful, old spool top round table with the glass top that George had made. As beautiful as it was, though, it still had a flaw. The table sloped on one edge. Anything placed there would slide into the person's lap or onto the floor. Family members knew about it, but it was fun to put guests there. Most of the time, dinner was fun. We played games at dinner like "Telephone." I am still amazed at how a sentence can get scrambled going around a table with half a dozen people.

Another thing we did was play "Miss Manners." The person with the best manners did not have to help with the dishes. Nancy was good at this. Nancy also had emotional problems, and if anyone said anything to her, she would cry. Then it got to the point if anyone looked at her, her big blue eyes would well up, her mouth would open, and a wail would come out. It wasn't a sniffle or a sob. It sounded more like a siren. We took turns talking to her and comforting her, but it didn't help. After a while, it just became an annoying ritual.

Beau was at the end of his rope. He turned to me during dinner one night and lifting his glass, said, "Can I throw water in her face?"

Looking around the table, I saw that everyone agreed. We had all had it. I nodded, and he doused her. Looking back, it was the wrong thing to do. But I was a young mother, and I made some poor decisions.

After I came back from Ohio, following the breakup with Greg, I had a fling with a young man—a very young one. Seventeen to be exact. He was Monah's friend, Jim. He made eyes at me, and I thought, What the hell? He was cute and sexy. He became a regular at the house.

One night his father called me and accused me of allowing him to sleep with my daughter. I told him I could assure him that he was not, but I did not tell him his son was sleeping with me!

Jim and I had a lot of fun together. I introduced him to fine wine and bought him suitable clothes so he could escort me to dinner. We skied together; he was a much better skier then I was. We made what we called "snowshoes," which was Wild Turkey and banana liquor poured over snow in silver goblets and drank them in the car.

On returning from a business trip to New York City later that year, I felt like I had the flu or some bug, so I went to a doctor. When he examined me, he told me I was pregnant.

"What?" I said, astonished. "I can't be!"

"Who do you think you are?" he retorted. "The Virgin Mary?"

"No, that's impossible!" I replied, "My doctor said I could not have any more children."

"Well, he's wrong," the doctor told me.

This was a lot to take in. What the hell was I going to do? I didn't believe in abortion. I had to think this through! I chose to keep the pregnancy and the result of my decision was my daughter, Chinarose.

I told Jim, my young sweetheart, about the pregnancy and he was thrilled. "I'll get a job and pay for the delivery," he willingly offered. However, he did not have to pay for it because my darling Doctor Gray who had told me I could not get pregnant delivered her for free. However, I had to fly to Los Angeles, where he was now practicing, and stay with my old neighbor Paul, which did not make his wife happy. She was cordial when he was around and hateful when he left, making my stay uncomfortable. I hid my pregnancy from Beau by sitting down every time he came over either behind my desk or in my big chair with a pillow on my lap. When he finally found out, he roared away leaving skid marks on the street, and did not speak to me for two years! The girls, however, had no problem with it and easily went about their play.

Jim was so proud and loving. He was the best father, ever. I was embarrassed and a little afraid of his parents and the law. His parents did not find out until years later. Our secret was kept. I should have married him. He turned out to be a responsible and loving father and always saw that our girl had what she needed. He still does. We remain friends. Chinarose is beautiful and well balanced, like her father.

★★★

By the end of the 1970s in Santa Cruz, I had met more than a few interesting people, some mentioned and some not: Rambling Jack Elliott, Cheech and Chong, Lacy J. Dalton, Kelly Houston, Peter Beagle, Charles Patterson, and Paul Bartko. Each carried their own stories, large enough to fill another book. Santa Cruz County during that time attracted a host of creative, even edgy personalities. I guess you could say I was one of them.

CHAPTER 48

Mr. Wonderful

Everything was going well; I was at the height of my career. The costume shop was functioning well under the management of Carmen. The studio was pumping out costume packages that I sold for $1,200 each, along with my services as a consultant. Setting up costume shops, I did two consultant jobs in Hawaii. I was getting $200 an hour with a minimum of sixteen hours. Financially I was on top.

After twenty years of renovation, the Victorian on Bixby Street was also finished and was beautiful. My weight was down to a slim 110 pounds, and my clothes, which were new, fit me well. I had it all!

Enter Mr. Wonderful, my new insurance agent. A surfer too, he looked like a blonde Tom Selleck, with wavy blonde hair, twinkling blue eyes, dimples, and perfect white teeth. He worked out and had great arms and a tight ass. He was funny, witty, and obviously smitten with me. He loved the motor home—who wouldn't? He asked if we could take it to the beach to watch the sunset that evening and brought a bottle of wine. So began our courtship. We dated; he kept me amused. I was not in love or lust, but at the time, I thought that was a good thing. He introduced me to his sister, who was not as charming as he was, but nice. He announced to her in front of me how much he liked me imitating Betty Boop. I liked her! We dined, went to the beach, danced, and laughed. Then one day, flowers arrived in the morning, and more flowers an hour later.

Photo 24 - Mr. Wonderful

During lunch at the Cooper House, a barrette with flowers for my hair were delivered to the table. After lunch, flowers were delivered to the shop. Carmen told me to hold out for the long-stemmed roses. They arrived with dinner at the Santa Cruz Hotel, where Jim got down on his knee and asked for my hand in marriage. I was flattered because it was romantic, and I said that I would think about it. We had a serious discussion about marriage: Jim said he was old-fashioned and did not want to have sex before marriage. We did not need to have children, he said mine were enough, but that he would like to move out of the Victorian where I had slept with other men and start life anew, in a new house. I considered all this. I had married for love before. Where did that get me? Maybe a planned marriage with someone who adored me would work better.

He had a job and was buying into the company as a partner. He was funny and cute—maybe this could work. I said yes. He apologized for not buying me a ring because he was buying into the company but promised a ring worthy of me later. We flew to Hawaii to be married, taking two-year-old Chinarose with us. On the way to the airport, she reached up and tore the garnet necklace from my throat that Jim had given to me. It was on a small gold chain. I searched in the car, but it was never found. I should have taken this as an omen.

In Oahu, we met with Tamar at the Illakai, an expensive hotel on the beach at Waikiki, and she took us upstairs to the minister who would marry us. Chinarose cried through the entire ceremony, but not only cried, she hollered loud. She was opposed to this union. This is one of those times I should have stopped what I was doing, turned around, and walked out, but it would take me years to learn this fact.

Now that I was married, there were a few rules to be followed explained to me by Mr. Wonderful on the flight home. I was not to go into bars without him. This provoked a problem because I took my entire staff to happy hour every Friday. Well, if he joined us, that would be okay. I was not to spend a night away from home without him. This was another problem. I had a two-day consultant job in Washington State coming up.

Well, I have always been a man-pleaser. I call it my "Geisha training." Keeping my man happy is a job I do well. When I leave them, I want them to want me back. Silly ego trip, maybe? When the time came, I flew to Seattle, consulted until my voice was hoarse, and flew back to San Francisco. I drove to Santa Cruz, slept in my bed for four hours, drove back to San Francisco, and was in Seattle at nine on the job the next morning—all to appease Mr. Wonderful. Crazy, huh?

Mr. Wonderful and I house hunted in the hills of Bonny Doon and found an affordable house where I could keep horses. It was dark and dank, and Lisa didn't like it. In fact, she hated it. So, we continued to hunt.

On the way home one day, we passed a sunny pasture on the side of a hill with a long, low, wood frame house partly surrounded by redwoods with a sunny deck. "Stop!" I shouted, "There's a 'for sale' sign. For sale by owner!" We backed up and pulled into the gravel driveway lined with Myer lemon trees and a fenced garden on the right. It was heaven! I knocked on the door, and an elderly German lady answered.

"I'm interested in your house," I said excitedly.

"Come in. Come in," she said, as she peered over my shoulder at the man in the car. "Invite your husband in, too." I turned around and waved him in.

The entrance had a green shag carpet. I would get rid of that. The dining room faced a sunny deck, and the living room had a huge stone fireplace. The back wall was floor-to-ceiling glass with a redwood forest view. Sun filtered through the trees. I loved it.

Her husband came in, wiping his hands. He had been gardening, and we proceeded to talk about gardening. My mind was spinning. Could I afford this place? I would have to sell my Bixby Street home. Or not, maybe I could cut a deal. I did! Not until the old couple came to visit us on Bixby Street to see how we lived. There was a flurry of house cleaning, and apparently, we passed because they agreed to sell their home to us for $225,000. Twenty-five down. Jim borrowed twelve from his father, and I put up the rest.

Here was the kicker, though. We had balloon payments of $10,000 every six months. I was going to have to sell a lot of costumes. This was my dream house. I had a garden and a deck where I could sunbathe nude in private. At the top of the property, I had two acres for my horse. It was also only thirty minutes from town. We bought the house and moved in.

That was the good part. Now, I will tell you about the bad part. A year later, my friends told me they saw it coming.

"Why, didn't you say anything to me?" I asked.

"You would not have listened," they answered.

Okay, here we go. Jim did not want to have sex before we were married because I suspect he knew that I would not have married him if we did. He had the smallest, tiniest, ugliest pee-pee I have ever seen. Even he knew it as he apologized when it was unveiled. Of course, I said it was nothing, but I did agreed with him. Wanting to appease him, I said it was not important, when in fact, it was. The fact that he did not know how to use it didn't help either.

Jim began to ask me for things. His nickname for me was "Brinks," and it took me a while to figure it out. Duh! I had all the money.

"Brinks, will you buy me some new work shirts?" he would say. "No, not those. The expensive ones and some cuff links, and a surfboard and a new car."

I drew the line at the new car. He pouted. He argued that I had a new car, so he should have one. Ultimately, his father bought him a new car.

When I first met Jim, he lived in a rented apartment with a bed, an alarm clock, and a microwave. Now my furniture was not good enough. We shopped for a brass bed. It had to be a real brass bed, not a replicate. We found one in San Francisco for $3,000. Then there were trimmings: a brass ship's mirror, brass candle holders, a gentleman's wooden valet to hang his jacket on. We began to dislike each other, though we did not fight. We just lived with an angry silence and began to drink. At home, when we drove home from work in town, I still had the costume shop and the Bixby street house where I had kept my office and sweatshop. He went to his office, and I would pick him up at the end of the day. He left his car at his office, "no use burning up both of our wheels," he would say. He would drive and I would crane my neck looking out the window to avoid conversation with him. At home, I would make martinis. He would sit in a recliner in front of the television while I served him his dinner. After two or four martinis, he would fall asleep there, and I would go to bed alone.

When we stayed in town on a Friday night and had dinner and drinks, he would drink too much and become very funny and giggle a lot. This was tolerable but what he did for fun was not. He would stop the car and sneak onto people's porches and steal plants, kids' toys, and shoes. Giggling and snickering, he would then get into the car, drive away and then put them on someone else's porch. His humor with me had changed; he had become sullen and moody.

He was also the most paranoid person I have ever met. I was growing some beautiful pot in the hothouse. It was six feet tall and bushy and almost ready to harvest. When Mr. wonderful saw a news report on television about a pot bust, he drove home from work in the middle of the day and pulled up my plants and threw them over the fence in the woods.

On a surf trip to Mexico in the motor home with my daughters Nancy and Chinarose, and a surf buddy of Jim's, coming across the border we did an okay check; who has what? Are we clean? I had a tab of acid and a little pot in a baggie. I put it in the bathing suit Nancy was wearing. At the border check with Mr. Wonderful at the wheel, a Federales officer stepped up to the driver's window and asked if we had anything illegal. Jim shook his head no. The officer looked him in the eye and said, "I think you do, and I am coming in."

The blood drained out of Jim's face. He turned white as a ghost. I opened the door, and Jim's briefcase was on the floor in front of the door. Without coming in, he opened it. The case contained a razor, a bar of soap and rolling papers, and enough shake to get us busted. The officer looked up at me and said, "What do we have here?"

I shrugged and replied, "Looks like debris to me."

Our relationship was not working. We did not like each other. He had married me solely for my money and he had a plan.

One morning, he stood in the kitchen door, briefcase in hand, and announced, "I hate you and your kids. I'm leaving. I don't want anything." He left. Good riddance. However, two weeks later while I was giving Monah away at her wedding, he backed a U-Haul up to the door and took everything of value, including the brass bed. What really pissed me off, though, is he took the safe he had given to me for my birthday containing a ten-thousand-dollar bill and an amethyst ring Bill had given me. The only thing in the safe that was truly his was a set of false teeth he found in the garden and an ash tray he stole from the desk of our realtor. Ultimately, I did get my things back, but his lawyer was better than mine. Jim had kept a record of the money I spent on him, proving I had been supporting him, so he got alimony and half the house, which meant I had to sell the house and give him half the money. Really! I was beside myself with anger.

On November 25, 1981, I wrote a letter to the legal office of Comstock, Yonts, Coyle, and Black in Santa Cruz, California, and noted that "I felt there was no need to retain an attorney against someone I promised to love and honor." However, I did detail that some personal items were taken from me by Mr. Jim Novak, and that I would appreciate it if he would return them, through their office. These items were two small antique chairs, a *Sunset Gardening* book, which was a present from a dear friend, a safe, which was a Christmas present from Jim, and the contents of that safe, which included the gold amethyst ring that Bill had given me, a silver and turquoise beret, a small blue carved box containing several unset stones; one polished bone ring; and one US Treasury Bill Certificate valued at $10,000.

Two weeks later, I found his car in town and figured he would have to drive it at least until he got a new paint job. With a can of red spray paint, I sprayed, "the bigger the mustache, the smaller the wiener" on it. However, my anger was all-consuming, so this was not enough. I cut a chicken's head off and threw it in his car. Do you know how much blood a chicken can spray?

Afterwards, I met friends for cocktails at a local bar, Lulu Carpenters. After a couple of drinks, I excused myself and walked down the street to a sporting goods shop, where I bought a gun. At the checkout desk, the clerk gave me a form to fill out with questions. Have you ever been arrested? Are you a felon? Are you on parole? Do you have anger issues? Have you ever been in a mental hospital? I answered yes to all of them, and the clerk took my money, asked if I wanted a bag, and told me to have a nice day. I walked out with the shotgun and returned to Lulu Carpenters to join my friends.

"Do you want to talk," asked John. "No," I replied, "I'm fine." Resting the weapon on the table, I ordered another drink.

Santa Cruz was not big enough for the both of us. If I had stayed longer, I might have killed the son-of-a-bitch. I put my dream house on the market and began searching for another house in the Sierra Nevada mountains—and a new life began.

To be continued . . .

###

Printed in the United States
by Baker & Taylor Publisher Services